Britain's second Labour government, 1929–31: a reappraisal

Britain's second Labour government, 1929–31: a reappraisal

Edited by
John Shepherd, Jonathan Davis and Chris Wrigley

Manchester University Press
Manchester and New York
distributed in the United States exclusively by Palgrave Macmillan

Copyright © Manchester University Press 2011

While copyright in the volume as a whole is vested in Manchester University Press, copyright in individual chapters belongs to their respective authors, and no chapter may be reproduced wholly or in part without the express permission in writing of both author and publisher.

Published by Manchester University Press
Oxford Road, Manchester M13 9NR, UK
and Room 400, 175 Fifth Avenue, New York, NY 10010, USA
www.manchesteruniversitypress.co.uk

Distributed in the United States exclusively by
Palgrave Macmillan, 175 Fifth Avenue, New York,
NY 10010, USA

Distributed in Canada exclusively by
UBC Press, University of British Columbia, 2029 West Mall,
Vancouver, BC, Canada V6T 1Z2

British Library Cataloguing-in-Publication Data
A catalogue record for this book is available from the British Library

Library of Congress Cataloging-in-Publication Data applied for

ISBN 978 07190 8614 4 *hardback*

First published 2011

The publisher has no responsibility for the persistence or accuracy of URLs for any external or third-party internet websites referred to in this book, and does not guarantee that any content on such websites is, or will remain, accurate or appropriate.

Typeset in Garamond by R. J. Footring Ltd, Derby
Printed and bound by
CPI Group (UK) Ltd, Croydon, CR0 4YY

*This book is dedicated to the memory of
Professor Duncan Tanner (1958–2010)*

Contents

List of tables								*page* ix
List of contributors							x
Acknowledgements							xiv
List of abbreviations							xv

1 Britain's second Labour government, 1929–31: an introduction			1
   John Shepherd and Jonathan Davis

2 The 1929 general election and the second Labour government			16
   Andrew Thorpe

3 Labour dealing with labour: aspects of economic policy			37
   Chris Wrigley

4 Why was there no Keynesian revolution under the second Labour government? A reassessment of Sir Oswald Mosley's alternative economic agenda in 1930–31			55
   Daniel Ritschel

5 A 'reef of granite' or 'damp cement': conflicting loyalties inside the Parliamentary Labour Party, June 1929–September 1931			85
   Robert Taylor

6 The Independent Labour Party and the second Labour government *c.* 1929–31: the move towards revolutionary change			100
   Keith Laybourn

7	The second Labour government and the consumer *Nicole Robertson*	117
8	Making farming pay: agricultural crisis and the politics of the national interest, 1930–31 *Clare Griffiths*	133
9	Labour and the Kremlin *Jonathan Davis*	150
10	'Bolshevism run mad': Labour and socialism *John Callaghan*	170
11	The right looks left? The young Tory response to MacDonald's second Labour government *Richard Carr*	185
12	Remembering 1931: an invention of tradition *David Howell*	203
13	Conclusion *Chris Wrigley*	220

Index 225

Tables

1	Results of the 1929 general election	24
2	Parties returned by the 50 most middle-class constituencies (1931 census) at general elections, 1918–45	26
3	Parties returned by the 100 most middle-class constituencies (1931 census) at general elections, 1918–45	26
4	Parties returned by the 50 most agricultural constituencies (1931 census) at general elections, 1918–45	28
5	Parties returned by the 100 most agricultural constituencies (1931 census) at general elections, 1918–45	28
6	Parties returned by the 150 most agricultural constituencies (1931 census) at general elections, 1918–45	28
7	Parties returned by the 50 least middle-class constituencies (1931 census) at general elections, 1918–45	29
8	Parties returned by the 100 least middle-class constituencies (1931 census) at general elections, 1918–45	29
9	Parties returned by the 50 constituencies with the most mining (1931 census) at general elections, 1918–45	29

Contributors

John Callaghan is Professor of Politics and Contemporary History at the University of Salford. He has published on socialist, communist and social democratic history, ideology and politics. His work has also focused on aspects of twentieth-century history, such as the Cold War and British and US foreign policy. His current research is concerned with ideology and foreign policy, with a longer-term focus on anti-communism. His recent publications include: *In Search of Social Democracy*, jointly edited with Ben Jackson, Martin McIvor and Nina Fishman (Manchester University Press, 2009); 'Labour's turn to socialism in 1931', *Journal of Political Ideologies*, 14:2 (2009), pp. 115–32; and *The Labour Party and Foreign Policy: A History* (Routledge, 2007). He is General Editor of the Manchester University Press series 'Critical Labour Movement Studies'.

Richard Carr is a Postdoctoral Lecturing Fellow in Modern British Diplomatic History at the University of East Anglia (UEA). Having secured a first-class degree from UEA, followed by an MPhil at Churchill College, Cambridge, he returned to East Anglia to complete his PhD in 2010. He has published on various aspects of British inter-war politics – most recently 'Veterans of the First World War and Conservative anti-appeasement', *Twentieth Century British History*, 22:1 (2011), pp. 28–51 – with a particular focus on ex-servicemen who became MPs after 1918. Of late, he has been awarded a Winston Churchill Memorial Trust grant to undertake a By-Fellowship at the Churchill Archives Centre, Cambridge, which focuses on party political reactions to economic slumps across the twentieth century, and pro-European discourse in Britain between the wars.

List of contributors

Jonathan Davis is Principal Lecturer in Russian and Modern History and Co-Director of the Labour History Research Unit at Anglia Ruskin University. His research focuses on Anglo-Russian relations, especially the influence the Soviet Union had on the British Labour Party and its ideology in the inter-war years. He has published a number of journal articles on Russian history and is a member of the Study Group on the Russian Revolution. Recent publications include (jointly edited with Paul Corthorn) *The British Labour Party and the Wider World: Domestic Politics, Internationalism and Foreign Policy* (Tauris, 2008), which featured his essay 'Labour's political thought: the Soviet influence in the interwar years', and *Stalin: From Grey Blur to Great Terror* (Philip Allan, 2008).

Clare Griffiths is Senior Lecturer in Modern History at the University of Sheffield. Much of her research has explored the rural and agricultural history of Britain in the twentieth century, with particular interest in the intersection with political ideas and organisation. Her publications include *Labour and the Countryside: The Politics of Rural Britain 1918–1939* (Oxford University Press, 2007) and (as co-editor) *Classes, Cultures and Politics: Essays on British History for Ross McKibbin* (Oxford University Press, 2011). She was guest curator for the exhibition 'Farming for the New Britain: Images of Farmers in War and Peace', at the Museum of English Rural Life in 2010.

David Howell is Professor of Politics at the University of York. His research interests are in the fields of British political history, especially the labour movement, comparative labour studies, and politics and literature. Since 1988 he has been the Editor of the *Dictionary of Labour Biography*, as well as Advisory Editor to the *Dictionary of National Biography*. His recent publications include *Attlee* (Haus Publishing, 2006) and *MacDonald's Party: Labour Identities and Crisis 1922–1931* (Oxford University Press, 2002).

Keith Laybourn is Professor of History at the University of Huddersfield. He has written over 45 books and 76 articles. His recent publications include: *Unemployment and Employment Policies Concerning Women, 1900–1951* (Edwin Mellen Press, 2002); *Marxism in Britain: Dissent, Decline and Re-emergence 1945–c.2000* (Routledge, 2006); *Britain's First Labour Government* (Palgrave, 2006) (jointly written with John Shepherd); and *Working-Class Gambling in Britain c. 1906–1960s: The Stages of the Political Debate* (Edwin Mellen Press, 2007). His new book (jointly written with David Taylor) is *Policing in England and Wales 1918–1939: The Fed, the Flying Squad and Forensics* (Palgrave Macmillan, 2011).

Daniel Ritschel is Associate Professor of History at the University of Maryland, Baltimore County (UMBC). His main research interest is in the relationship between politics and economic policy in inter-war Britain. He has published on a variety of subjects related to this field, including *The Politics of Planning: The Debate on Economic Planning in Britain in the 1930s* (Oxford University Press, 1997). He has also written on business and Conservative industrial policies between the wars, corporatist thought in inter-war political culture, the ideological origins of British fascism, and the making of the Keynesian consensus during the Second World War. He is currently writing a study of radical economic ideas in inter-war Britain.

Nicole Robertson is Lecturer in History at the University of Northumbria. She studied for her PhD at the University of Nottingham and was awarded the Economic History Society's R. H. Tawney Fellowship 2006–7. Her recent publications include *The Co-operative Movement and Communities in Britain, 1914–60: Minding Their Own Business* (Ashgate, 2010) and *Consumerism and the Co-operative Movement in Modern British History: Taking Stock* (Manchester University Press, 2009) (jointly edited with Lawrence Black). She has also published on the relationship between the Co-operative Party and the Labour Party in M. Worley (ed.), *The Foundations of the British Labour Party: Identities, Cultures and Perspectives, 1900–39* (Ashgate, 2009). Her research interests include the co-operative movement in Britain, retailing, consumption and consumer protection, and the labour movement.

John Shepherd is Visiting Professor at the University of Huddersfield and formerly Senior Research Associate and Co-Director of the Labour History Research Unit at Anglia Ruskin University. He is currently completing *James Callaghan's Labour Government and the British 'Winter of Discontent', 1978–79* for Manchester University Press. His recent publications include *George Lansbury: At the Heart of Old Labour* (Oxford University Press, 2004); *Britain's First Labour Government* (Palgrave, 2006) (jointly written with Professor Keith Laybourn); and *1920s Britain* (Shire Publishing, 2010) (jointly written with Dr Janet Shepherd). His essay 'A gentleman at the Foreign Office: influences shaping Ramsay MacDonald's internationalism in 1924' was published in Paul Corthorn and Jon Davis (eds), *The British Labour Party and the Wider World: Domestic Politics, Internationalism and Foreign Policy* (Tauris, 2008).

Robert Taylor is Associate Fellow at the Industrial Relations Unit, University of Warwick, and an associate member of Nuffield College, Oxford. He is completing a history of the Parliamentary Labour Party and starting

List of contributors xiii

work on a biography of Walter Citrine and the making of twentieth-century trade unionism. Former labour editor of the *Observer* and later the *Financial Times*, he is the author of nine books and many published essays on the history of industrial relations and labour markets. His books include: *The Fifth Estate: Britain's Unions in the Modern World* (Macmillan, 1978 and 1980); *The Trade Union Question in British Politics: Government and Unions since 1945* (Blackwell, 1993); and *The TUC: From the General Strike to New Unionism* (Palgrave, 2000).

Andrew Thorpe is Professor of Modern British History at the University of Exeter. His research centres on twentieth-century British political history, the history of party and policy making, and international communism in the era of the Communist International. He has worked extensively on the history of the Labour Party and also on Communist Party history. His latest book, *Parties at War: Political Organization in Second World War Britain* (Oxford University Press, 2009), analyses the organisation of all the major parties in Britain during wartime. Currently, he is researching a project on the Labour leader, trade unionist and statesman Arthur Henderson (1863–1935). Other publications include *A History of the British Labour Party* (3rd edition, Palgrave, 2008) and *The British Communist Party and the Communist International, 1919–1943* (Manchester University Press, 2000).

Chris Wrigley is Professor of Modern British History at the University of Nottingham. His many books include: *David Lloyd George and the British Labour Movement* (Harvester Press, 1976); *Arthur Henderson* (University of Wales Press, 1990); *Lloyd George and the Challenge of Labour* (Harvester-Wheatsheaf, 1990); *Lloyd George* (Blackwell, 1992); *British Trade Unions since 1933* (Cambridge University Press, 2002); *A. J. P. Taylor: Radical Historian of Europe* (Tauris, 2006); and *Churchill* (Haus, 2006). His edited publications include: *On the Move: Essays in Labour and Transport History Presented to Philip Bagwell* (Hambledon Press, 1991) (jointly edited with John Shepherd); *A History of British Industrial Relations* (Harvester Press, 2 vols, 1982, 1986, Edward Elgar, 1996); *Warfare, Diplomacy and Politics: Essays in Honour of A. J. P. Taylor* (Hamish Hamilton, 1986); *Challenges of Labour: Central and Western Europe 1917–20* (Routledge, 1993); *The Emergence of European Trade Unionism* (Ashgate, 2004); and *A Companion to Early Twentieth Century Britain* (Blackwell, 2003). He was also editor of Ashgate's Labour History series of books (19 published 1998–2005).He was President of the Historical Association, 1996–99. He is currently researching and writing the official history of the coal industry 1982–2002.

Acknowledgements

The editors would like to acknowledge the invaluable help of the following people at Anglia Ruskin University: Helen Jones, Sarah Jones, Holly Clover, Dr Rohan McWilliam, Dr Alison Ainley and Professor Derrik Ferney. We would particularly like to thank our commissioning editor, Tony Mason at Manchester University Press, for his expert guidance and generous support. Also our thanks go to his deputy editors, Jenny Howard (now at Liverpool University Press) and Sarah Hunt, and to Ralph Footring for his valuable assistance with the copy-editing. We would also like to acknowledge the help of Nina and Dr Sharon Davis, Dr Janet Shepherd and Professor Maggie Walsh.

Jonathan Davis would also like to thank Anglia Ruskin University for generously funding a sabbatical which allowed him to work on this book.

This edited volume is the result of a major history conference held at Anglia Ruskin University in May 2009. We would like to thank all who participated and attended the conference, and who have contributed to this collection.

Abbreviations

Comintern	Communist International
GDP	gross domestic product
HP	hire purchase
ILP	Independent Labour Party
LPP	Liberal Parliamentary Party
LRC	Labour Representation Committee
Narkomindel	People's Commissariat for Foreign Affairs
NEC	National Executive Committee
NEP	New Economic Policy
NFU	National Farmers' Union
NUGMW	National Union of General and Municipal Workers
PLP	Parliamentary Labour Party
PRO	Public Record Office
SSIP	Society for Socialist Inquiry and Propaganda
TGWU	Transport and General Workers' Union
TNA	The National Archives
TUC	Trades Union Congress
UDC	Union of Democratic Control
USSR	Union of Soviet Socialist Republics

1

Britain's second Labour government, 1929–31: an introduction

JOHN SHEPHERD and JONATHAN DAVIS

On 10 June 1929, the Prime Minister, Ramsay MacDonald, brought members of his second Labour Cabinet onto the terrace of 10 Downing Street before their first Cabinet meeting.[1] To capture the occasion, there was a multiplicity of cameras among the rhododendrons in the garden and two film-production vans parked outside. No one else spoke as MacDonald presented his colleagues in turn to the British nation. Among the gathering were leading members of MacDonald's 1924 administration – Philip Snowden, J. R. Clynes, Arthur Henderson and J. H. Thomas – accompanied by Margaret Bondfield, the first woman Cabinet minister, and George Lansbury, the only representative of the left.[2] Thomas and Lansbury were introduced as the government team (with fellow ministers Sir Oswald Mosley and Tom Johnston) tasked with tackling unemployment in Britain. However, as a portent of the times, this notable occurrence in Whitehall – the first 'talkie' film to feature a British Cabinet – was not the work of a British company. Instead, it was an American agency, using German equipment, which had responded to the British government's invitation to record the event.[3]

---

1 *Manchester Guardian*, 11 June 1929. See also John Shepherd, *George Lansbury: At the Heart of Old Labour* (Oxford: Oxford University Press, 2004), p. 253.
2 Susan Lawrence, MP for East Ham North, who had held a junior post in the 1924 Labour government, became Parliamentary Secretary to the Ministry of Health in the 1929–31 Labour administration.
3 R. G. Leigh to Sir Robert Vansittart, 20 June 1929, James Ramsay MacDonald Papers, The National Archives/Public Record Office, TNA/PRO, 30/69/247.

At the end of the long-awaited 1929 general election, the *Daily Herald*, Labour's only daily newspaper, had carried triumphant banner headlines: LABOUR ON TOP! THE STRONGEST PARTY. ELECTORS GIVE BALDWIN'S GOVERNMENT EMPHATIC NOTICE TO QUIT.[4] Labour had emerged, albeit without an overall majority, as the leading party in the new Parliament, with 287 MPs (37.1 per cent of the total vote). Following the difficulties of the 1920s recession, the new Labour administration had taken office in June 1929 with great optimism owing to signs of declining unemployment and improvements in the British economy.

However, in 1965 A. J. P Taylor's verdict on the hapless minority administration in the final volume of the *Oxford History of England* concluded that 'Lansbury's Lido' on the Hyde Park Serpentine was its only memorable achievement – an epitaph that largely stuck.[5] After only two years, MacDonald's second administration had collapsed in a global financial crisis following the Wall Street Crash of October 1929. Moreover, MacDonald's highly controversial decision to head a National Government with former Conservative and Liberal opponents was followed a few weeks later by his decision to call the 1931 general election. In the greatest electoral landslide in twentieth-century politics, Labour suffered its worst defeat by far. The National Government secured 67 per cent of the poll and a gargantuan total of 554 out 615 seats, compared with a rump of only forty-six Labour MPs at Westminster. According to his critics, MacDonald's actions had opened the way to the locust years of the National Governments, which lasted until May 1940. In popular parlance, it was the notorious 'Devil's Decade', indelibly identified, particularly in British industrial heartlands, with mass unemployment, the hated means test, hunger marches and the appeasement of fascism in international relations. As result, Britain's second Labour government, of 1929–31, has often been written off as a sizeable reverse in an otherwise relentless 'forward march of Labour', from the party's foundation conference in 1900 to Clement Attlee's majority Labour governments of 1945–51.[6]

In the post-First World War years, the rise of Labour had seemed inexorable and of a truly exceptional nature – at least to many contemporaries. In February 1900, during the Boer War, only nine spectators at the Memorial Hall in London had watched the uneasy alliance of trade union representatives and socialist representatives establish the

---

4 *Daily Herald*, 1 June 1929.
5 A. J. P. Taylor, *English History 1914–1945* (Oxford: Oxford University Press, 1965), pp. 271–2.
6 For an example of this view of Labour history, see Francis Williams, *Fifty Years' March: The Rise of the Labour Party* (London: Odhams Press, 1949), pp. 332–4.

An introduction 3

Labour Representation Committee (LRC). In 1917–18 Arthur Henderson and Sidney Webb's modernisation of the party organisation, including the introduction of individual membership, opened up the prospect of Labour moving on from being a parliamentary pressure group to a party of government. During the 1922 and 1923 general elections Labour outdistanced the Liberals to become the official opposition at Westminster. A confident Sidney Webb predicted in his presidential address at the annual party conference that 'a continuation of the rising curve of Labour votes' would deliver a majority Labour administration around 1926.[7]

In post-war politics, Labour appeared to benefit from the extension of the parliamentary franchise in 1918 to all adult men and most women over thirty, as well as the legacy of wartime working-class solidarity. Impressive municipal victories were recorded in East London, Sheffield and elsewhere. New women's sections were important in developing local Labour parties and in shaping policy, especially welfare, education, birth control, peace and disarmament. Yet, despite Labour's support in mining areas, the party's electoral progress in national politics was incremental and patchy. Before 1945 Labour formed only two minority governments. A significant proportion of working-class voters did not vote Labour. However, after the 1926 General Strike, an improved party organisation, more election agents and the defection of working-class voters from the Liberals assisted Labour's advance – particularly in the South-East and the Midlands – to a second spell in government in 1929.[8]

In the 1920s, Ramsay MacDonald remained Labour's most captivating platform speaker and an iconic leader, with his natural gifts of an imposing presence, handsome visage and socialist oratory, delivered with an arresting Highlands accent. His principled opposition to the First World War, as a founding member of the Union of Democratic Control, enhanced his moral reputation and standing within party circles and was a significant influence in the defection of key Liberal and Conservative politicians to Labour in the 1920s.[9] MacDonald was arguably Labour's major political

---

7 Labour Party, *Report of the 23rd Annual Conference* (London, 1923).
8 D. Tanner, 'Class voting and radical politics: the Liberal and Labour parties, 1910–31', in J. Lawrence and M. Taylor (eds), *Party, State and Society: Electoral Behaviour in Britain since 1820* (London: Scholar Press, 1997), pp. 120–2; D. Tanner, 'The politics of the labour movement, 1900–1939', in Chris Wrigley (ed.), *A Companion to Early Twentieth-Century Britain* (Chichester: Wiley-Blackwell, 2009), pp. 41–7; D. Tanner, 'Labour and its membership', in Duncan Tanner, Pat Thane and Nick Tiratsoo (eds), *Labour's First Century* (Cambridge: Cambridge University Press, 2000), pp. 248–80.
9 John Shepherd, 'The flight from the Liberal Party: Liberals who joined Labour, 1914–1931', *Journal of Liberal History*, 67 (summer 2010), pp. 24–35.

thinker and political strategist. In 13 books on social and political theory published between 1903 and 1921 he outlined an evolutionary and non-Marxist pathway to British socialism that underpinned his gradualist politics in the 1920s.[10] In 1929 Egon Wertheimer, the influential London correspondent of the German newspaper *Vorwarts*, in his acclaimed first book declared MacDonald 'the outstanding figure in European socialism'.[11]

With Keir Hardie and Arthur Henderson, MacDonald can be considered one of the three principal architects of the British Labour Party. He had become party secretary in 1900 at Labour's foundation conference in London, an early indication of his political talents. With his wife Margaret, until her early tragic death in 1911, he shared interests in socialist and international politics and visited South Africa, India, the USA, Canada, Australia and New Zealand to investigate political and social conditions at first hand. Their family home at 3, Lincoln's Inn Fields, doubled as the fledging Labour Party's central office, to the door of which political figures from Britain and abroad beat a path, during Labour's formative years.

In 1922 Ramsay MacDonald was elected to the newly designated post of leader of the Labour Party and in 1924 became Labour's first Prime Minister. Britain's first Labour government survived for only 287 days, until brought down over the 'Campbell case'. However, the administration is remembered particularly for John Wheatley's Housing Act and MacDonald's successful international diplomacy. Moreover, the Labour leader's ministry had answered Churchill's devastating taunt that Labour was 'quite unfitted for the responsibility of government'. The administration proved a significant staging post on the way to the Labour government of 1929–31.[12]

The 1929 general election, the first one under universal suffrage in Britain, produced a 'hung parliament' and a second Labour minority government. For its supporters, Labour's 287 MPs (and 37.1 per cent of the popular vote) represented a dramatic advance of 136 parliamentary seats on 1924, but the Conservatives, with 260 MPs, had had a slightly greater share of the vote, at 38.1 per cent. A brief Liberal revival had resulted in 59 MPs and 23.5 per cent of the votes polled. MacDonald's strategy of moderation and gradualness was reflected in his Labour policy document

---

10 MacDonald's writings included *Socialism and Society* (London: Independent Labour Party, 1909), *Socialism and Government* (London: Independent Labour Party, 1909), *The Awakening of India* (London: Hodder and Stoughton, 1910), *A Policy for the Labour Party* (London: L. Parsons, 1920) and *Socialism: Critical and Constructive* (London: Cassell, second edition, 1924).
11 Egon Wertheimer, *Portrait of the Labour Party* (London: G. P. Putnam's Sons, 1929).
12 For a recent study of the 1924 Labour administration, see John Shepherd and Keith Laybourn, *Britain's First Labour Government* (Basingstoke: Palgrave, 2006).

Labour and the Nation (1928) – written largely with R. H. Tawney – and demonstrated MacDonald's hold over his party.

In 1929 Labour's major figures again dominated the main Cabinet appointments. Arthur Henderson won his battle with MacDonald over the Foreign Office, despite the premier's preference for J. H. Thomas. The financially rigid and cost-conscious Philip Snowden was Chancellor of the Exchequer once more. J. R. Clynes took the Home Office and Thomas reluctantly became Lord Privy Seal, with a specific portfolio for dealing with unemployment. In 1929 MacDonald could at last choose Lord Sankey as Lord Chancellor. Also promoted to the Cabinet was Arthur Greenwood, who returned to the Ministry of Health. In addition, former Liberals held significant Cabinet posts. A junior minister in 1924, with expertise in defence and foreign affairs, A. V. Alexander became First Lord of the Admiralty. His selection also reflected his standing as the leading MP in the Co-operative Party, which had allied to Labour in 1927. Charles Trevelyan had a second spell as Minister for Education. Another former Liberal (who had crossed over to Labour only in 1927), William Wedgwood Benn, became Secretary of State for India. In 1930 the promotion of the experienced Christopher Addison brought much-needed expertise in agriculture. His Agricultural Marketing Act was probably the administration's most effective piece of legislation in response to the world economic crisis. However, himself at the age of 62, MacDonald had recruited an older set of ministers than the departing and elderly Tory Cabinet; William Graham at the Board of Trade was his youngest Labour Cabinet appointment, at 42.[13]

In home affairs, the minority administration made unemployment benefit easier to claim for men, though not for married women, and the 1930 Housing Act included an important new provision for slum clearance by local authorities. In international affairs, MacDonald's visit to New York in October 1929, when he was welcomed with a ticker-tape parade, prepared the way for the Five-Power Naval Conference held in London in January 1930. The second Labour government also restored diplomatic and commercial relations with the Soviet Union and signed the short-lived Young Plan, which modified the system of international reparations. With Henderson at the Foreign Office, despite tensions with MacDonald, British foreign policy was based on support for the League of Nations in terms of disarmament, the peaceful settlement of international grievances and collective security. In the British Empire the government

---

13 Andrew Thorpe, *A History of the British Labour Party* (Basingstoke: Macmillan, 1997), p. 68.

faced Gandhi's civil disobedience campaign in India and a worsening situation between Arabs and Jews in the mandated territory of Palestine.[14]

At Westminster MacDonald's minority government soon ran into difficulties. As in 1924, there was no formal parliamentary pact between the Labour government and its Liberal supporters. Liberal assistance for Labour's legislative programme was largely dependent on the Liberals' reluctance to fight another early parliamentary election and on the possibility of securing electoral reform from a Labour government. However, Labour had an arduous time over its major Coal Mines Act (passed by only eight votes), its attempt to repeal the 1927 Trades Disputes Act and its three education bills that eventually brought Trevelyan's resignation from the Cabinet in March 1931.[15]

In particular, the second Labour government was beset by the intractable problem of mounting unemployment, mainly the result of declining world trade and falling commodity prices after the Wall Street Crash. Britain faced 'an economic blizzard', as MacDonald notably put it. The registered workless, who numbered 1.1 million in June 1929, as Labour assumed power, increased to 2.5 million in December 1930. The second Labour government, particularly Thomas and Snowden, had few new ideas. MacDonald was more innovative than has traditionally been acknowledged, in setting up the Economic Advisory Council (with J. M. Keynes, G. D. H. Cole and other economists) and the Macmillan Committee to explore new economic thinking.[16] However, in the interwar years, the dominant and powerful orthodoxy, as represented by the Treasury, Bank of England, City interests and Tory opposition, was conventional balanced budgets and cuts in social welfare, as seen previously in 1921, in the wielding of the infamous 'Geddes Axe'.

As the world economic depression deepened, the charismatic Chancellor of the Duchy of Lancaster, Sir Oswald Mosley, produced in the spring of 1930 a manifesto of quasi-Keynesian proposals, comprising government financing of improved communications infrastructure, an extensive public

---

14 Neil Riddell, *Labour in Crisis: The Second Labour Government, 1929–1931* (Manchester: Manchester University Press, 1999), p. 203; Rhiannon Vickers, *The Evolution of Labour's Foreign Policy 1900–1951* (Manchester: Manchester University Press, 2003), pp. 92–8; Henry R. Winkler, *British Labour Seeks a Foreign Policy, 1900–1940* (New Brunswick: Transaction Publishers), pp. 81–92.

15 For MacDonald's bitter reaction to Trevelyan's resignation, see MacDonald to Trevelyan, 2 March 1931, Ramsay MacDonald Papers, John Rylands University Library, Manchester, RMD/1/1/14/83.

16 Kenneth O. Morgan, *Labour People: Leaders and Lieutenants, Hardie to Kinnock* (Oxford: Oxford University Press, 1987), pp. 46–7.

works programme and long-term economic reconstruction, to tackle unemployment. However, the 'Mosley Memorandum' was rejected by a Labour Cabinet wedded to a financial orthodoxy, and this brought Mosley's resignation in May 1930. At the 1930 party conference, Mosley narrowly lost the vote on his memorandum after a rousing condemnation of the government's lacklustre record.[17]

On 31 May 1931 the Credit Anstalt, Austria's largest bank, failed and brought about the bankruptcy of the German Danat bank and a serious international financial crisis that eventually toppled Britain's second Labour government. Contemporary financial orthodoxy decreed that Britain remain on the international gold standard, based on maintaining a balanced budget. On 30 July 1931 the report of the May Committee, established in February 1931 under the chairmanship of the chief of the Prudential Insurance Company, Sir George May, to examine ways of reducing national expenditure, was published and triggered a sterling crisis. The May report predicted a deficit of £120 million by July 1932 and recommended increased taxation and financial cuts of £96 million.

From 19 to 24 August 1931 the financial crisis centred on London as the government sought loans from American and French bankers to restore international confidence. The Trades Union Congress (TUC) and Labour movement in general rejected the bankers' view of the crisis. However, on 23 August 1931, the split within the MacDonald Cabinet, eleven votes to nine, over the proposal to reduce unemployment insurance by 10 per cent brought the end of the second Labour government.[18] The next morning MacDonald returned to announce to his speechless former ministers that he had accepted the appeal of King George V to form a National Government to steer Britain through the crisis.[19] Six weeks later, however, after passing the emergency legislation, in the face of TUC resistance and the Labour parliamentary opposition led by Henderson, the National Government – with Ramsay MacDonald at its helm – won a landslide victory in the October 1931 general election.

The second Labour government has received an exceptionally bad press since its demise in 1931. Critics on the left and right have debated Labour's

---

17 See Daniel Ritschel, chapter 4, in the present volume.
18 For the confusion over the exact number of ministers who voted for and against the proposal to reduce unemployment benefits by 10 per cent, see Reginald Bassett, *Nineteen Thirty-One* (Aldershot: Gower, second edition, with a new introduction by David Marquand, 1986), pp. 138–43.
19 On the Cabinet crisis, see V. Bogdanor, '1931 revisited: the constitutional aspects', *Twentieth Century British History*, 2:1 (1991), pp. 1–25; P. Williamson, '1931 revisited: the political realities', *Twentieth Century British History*, 2:3 (1991), pp. 328–38; V. Bogdanor, '1931 revisited: reply to P. Williamson', *Twentieth Century British History*, 2:3 (1991), pp. 330–43.

fitness to govern and have highlighted the leadership's betrayal of its own supporters. In terms of past historiography, MacDonald's government was largely seen through the prism of 1931 and most authors were concerned with the reputation of Ramsay MacDonald himself.

Odium was heaped on the Labour leader for breaking with his colleagues of thirty years to form the National Government. The 'myth of betrayal' by MacDonald, Snowden and Thomas dominated politicians' memoirs and Labour history for three decades.[20] There were bitter recriminations between those who joined MacDonald in the National Government and their former Labour colleagues. The Labour MP Mary (Molly) Agnes Hamilton, an admirer and close friend of MacDonald, had earlier published the eulogistic biography *The Man of Tomorrow* (1923) under a *nom de plume* of 'Iconoclast'. However, even before 1931, 'Iconoclast' herself had become increasingly disillusioned with the Labour leader.

George Lansbury, appointed by MacDonald as First Commissioner of Works in 1929 and one of his successors as party leader in the 1930s, was extremely censorious about MacDonald. In 1932, after leading a small trade union delegation to the Prime Minister's distant Lossiemouth home to plead for the release of imprisoned hunger marchers, he confided to Stafford Cripps: 'I came away terribly distressed that a man with his mentality should have led us all for so many years. He could never have believed in civil liberty or socialism. His whole mind is one web of tortuous conservatism.' Determined that the inside story of the second Labour government should eventually be told, Lansbury had kept his own memorandum on the Cabinet crisis, which he handed over to his son-in-law and future biographer, Raymond Postgate.[21]

Following MacDonald's death in November 1937, Harold Laski, the Marxist intellectual – a fervent admirer of the Labour leader until 1931 – was perplexed by the conundrum of MacDonald's final six reactionary years and later, with Sidney Webb (Lord Passfield), believed that MacDonald had plotted his government's downfall.[22] Clement Attlee roundly condemned his former chief's decision in 1931 to accept George V's appeal to head the National Government as an outright act of betrayal based on personal vanity. 'I think that he had had the idea [to form a National Government] for sometime at the back of his mind and that his plans were laid several months before the actual breach with the Party.'[23]

---

20 See, for example, G. D. H. Cole, *A History of the Labour Party from 1914* (London: Routledge and Kegan Paul, 1948), pp. 253–8.
21 Shepherd, *George Lansbury*, pp. 276–7, p. 298.
22 *Daily Herald*, 11 November 1937.
23 C. R. Attlee, *The Labour Party in Perspective* (London: Victor Gollancz, 1937), p. 57.

An introduction 9

In 1938 Lachlan MacNeill Weir, MacDonald's former Parliamentary Private Secretary, published *The Tragedy of Ramsay MacDonald*, which demonised his former chief in terms of careerism, class betrayal and treachery.[24] It was soon followed by Howard Spring's celebrated novel *Fame Is the Spur*, a tract for the times about the rise of the Labour movement, power and class betrayal.[25] For many years 1931 had remained the litmus test Labour politicians used to demonstrate their party loyalty, to avoid being seen as 'another Ramsay MacDonald'. During the financial crisis in 1976, when Britain had to call on the services of the International Monetary Fund, Tony Benn famously circulated the Cabinet minutes of August 1931 to remind his colleagues of the historical precedent of savage expenditure cuts. With the formation of Britain's first majority Labour government in 1945 under Clement Attlee, Labour appeared to be starting totally anew from the taint of 'MacDonaldism'.

Reginald Bassett's scholarly study of the 1931 crisis, published in 1958, contained a different and more favourable interpretation of the Labour government of 1929–31. David Marquand, Ramsay MacDonald's biographer, claimed Bassett's book was 'a landmark in the historiography of inter-war Britain'. 'In everything that matters, Bassett's account stands', he added. Bassett, who had joined MacDonald's National Labour Party in the early 1930s, without access to private papers and interviews with surviving politicians, confronted the viewpoint of those on the left who blamed MacDonald and a 'bankers' ramp' for destroying the second Labour government.[26]

In 1977 David Marquand published his long-awaited revisionist study of Ramsay MacDonald – based on the extensive MacDonald collection of diaries and papers now available at The National Archives – with six chapters devoted to the Labour leader's 'Second Innings'.[27] These provided a comprehensive defence of MacDonald's decision to place the national interest before that of party in 1931. This monumental study also acknowledged MacDonald's outstanding intellectual contribution to the development of British socialism and his central role as the strategist of the Labour alliance in his party's evolution to office and power.

Since then, other biographies have appeared, including Austen Morgan's study, in the Manchester University Press 'Lives of the Left'

---

24 Lachlan MacNeill Weir, *The Tragedy of Ramsay MacDonald* (London: Secker and Warburg, 1938).
25 Howard Spring, *Fame Is the Spur* (London: Collins, 1940).
26 Bassett, *Nineteen Thirty-One*.
27 David Marquand, *Ramsay MacDonald* (London: Jonathan Cape, 1977), pp. 488–670.

series, which provides more critical perspectives on MacDonald's career, and particularly the formation the National Government in August 1931. Kevin Morgan's 2006 biography in the Haus Publishing series 'The 20 Prime Ministers of the Twentieth Century' has many stimulating insights into the shaping of MacDonald's character, his importance as a career politician and his two Labour premierships in the 1920s.[28]

Also, MacDonald's Labour leadership has been reappraised in a number of contributions to scholarly monographs and biographical dictionaries, including an important reassessment by Duncan Tanner.[29] Particularly valuable is Chris Wrigley's illuminating and scholarly chapter on MacDonald as the 'saint and sinner' in Labour's past in a recent edited single-volume collection on Labour leaders.[30] In addition, in a persuasive entry for a new edition of the *Oxford Dictionary of National Biography* in 2005, David Marquand updated his 1970s assessment of Ramsay MacDonald to argue that, in a post-Keynesian world of global capitalism and powerful currency markets, the Labour leader's action in 1931 and his strategy of gradualist politics in the 1920s made him 'the unacknowledged precursor of the Blairs, the Schroeders and the Clintons of the 1990s and 2000s'.[31]

A number of lives of prominent Labour politicians who held office in the Labour government of 1929–31 have appeared in recent years. Among these new works are two important biographies of Arthur Henderson by Fred Leventhal and Chris Wrigley and also John Shepherd's full-length study of the Christian pacifist and Labour leader George Lansbury, which updates Raymond Postgate's earlier life of the socialist politician.[32] Philip Snowden, MacDonald's flinty Chancellor of the Exchequer in the 1924 and 1929–31 governments, published a weighty and controversial two-volume memoir after his defection from Labour, which should be read in conjunction with Colin Cross's life of Snowden and, in particular, Keith Laybourn's significant and more recent biography.[33]

---

28 Austen Morgan, *J. Ramsay MacDonald* (Manchester: Manchester University Press, 1987); Kevin Morgan, *Ramsay MacDonald* (London: Haus, 2006).
29 Duncan Tanner, 'Ramsay MacDonald,' in R. Eccleshall and G. Walker (eds), *Biographical Dictionary of British Prime Ministers* (London: Routledge, 1998), pp. 281–8.
30 Chris Wrigley, 'James Ramsay MacDonald 1922–31', in Kevin Jefferys (ed.), *Leading Labour: From Keir Hardie to Tony Blair* (London: Tauris, 1999), pp. 19–40.
31 See John Shepherd, 'The Lad from Lossiemouth', *History Today*, November 2007, p. 31.
32 Fred Leventhal, *Arthur Henderson* (Manchester: Manchester University Press, 1989); Chris Wrigley, *Arthur Henderson* (Cardiff: University of Wales Press, 1990); Shepherd, *George Lansbury*; Raymond Postgate, *The Life of George Lansbury* (London: Longmans, Green and Co., 1951).
33 Philip, Viscount Snowden, *An Autobiography* (2 vols, London: Ivor Nicholson and

An introduction 11

For many years, Robert Skidelsky's study of the second Labour government was the only single-volume on MacDonald's 1929–31 administration. Written in the age of Keynesian economics, his account of the 1931 crisis attributed the downfall of the government to its failure to tackle the major economic problem of unemployment that beset the administration from 1929 as much as the final events of August 1931. However, a radical solution such as Keynesian interventionism, combining deficit financing and large-scale programmes of government-subsidised public works, was not on Labour's socialist agenda. As Skidelsky put it over forty years ago: 'Socialism explained the past and promised the future: it had nothing constructive to offer the present'.[34] His thesis subsequently received a forthright challenge from Ross McKibbin in his *Past and Present* article on Labour's unemployment policy during 1929–31. Keynesian-style solutions had at best only partial success when adopted by other governments abroad, such as in the United States and Australia in the later 1930s.[35] More recently, in a major essay, Duncan Tanner has provided a magisterial review of politics and economic policy during the second Labour government.[36]

In 1999 Neil Riddell published a history of MacDonald's second administration. Based on his PhD, Riddell's thoroughly researched study for the most part eschewed the world of conventional high politics to analyse the fortunes of the 1929–31 administration in relation to the broader labour movement, with a meticulous investigation of local constituency party records and the archives of the co-operative and trade union movements.[37]

Fresh perspectives on this period have recently been brought in two important accounts that enable us to place the difficulties confronting the second Labour government, and the 1931 crisis in particular, in a broader context. Philip Williamson's study is a commanding analysis of the transformation of British politics and policy during 1926–31 and of

---

Watson, 1934); Colin Cross, *Philip Snowden* (London: Barrie and Rockliff, 1966); Keith Laybourn, *Philip Snowden: A Biography 1864–1937* (London: Temple Smith, 1988).

34 Robert Skidelsky, *Politicians and the Slump: The Labour Government of 1929–1931* (London: Macmillan, 1967), p. 395.

35 R. I. McKibbin, 'The economic policy of the second Labour government, 1929–1931', reprinted in the author's *The Ideologies of Class: Social Relations in Britain, 1880–1950* (Oxford: Oxford University Press, 1990), pp. 197–227.

36 Duncan Tanner, 'Political leadership, intellectual debate and economic policy during the second Labour government, 1929–31', in E. H. Green and D. M. Tanner (eds), *The Strange Survival of Liberal England: Political Leaders, Moral Values and the Reception of Economic Debate* (Cambridge: Cambridge University Press, 2007), pp. 113–50.

37 Riddell, *Labour in Crisis*.

the 1931 crisis in terms of the tensions arising from three-party politics, economic recession and imperial problems. David Howell's erudite account of Labour's history in the 1920s is an impressive and detailed study of constituent identities within the party and how these complexities contributed to the crisis that engulfed the Labour government in 1931.[38]

In 2005 Matthew Worley provided an important edited collection on local Labour parties in the inter-war years from London to the Labour heartlands and beyond. This grassroots study of local Labour communities adds a valuable and previously neglected dimension to our understanding of party life, constituency politics and its relationship to formal politics at Westminster.[39] This can be read in conjunction with Worley's recent history of the British Labour Party in the inter-war years, which includes a scholarly and thoughtful chapter on the second Labour government.[40]

There are also two major books by Andrew Thorpe that throw important light on Britain's second Labour government. His study of the 1931 general election is a significant and wide-ranging account of the election in which Labour suffered its most calamitous defeat. Thorpe's authoritative study of the history of the Labour Party remains the best single-volume account.[41] Martin Pugh's recent important work on Labour's past provides thought-provoking analysis, particularly on the failings of the party's leaders.[42]

This brief narrative of Labour's second period in office, and its historiography, highlights the various issues that have helped define how the second Labour government has often been seen and written about. Traditionally, this was a government which went down in history as being betrayed by its leadership and for being a party in crisis, unable to keep up with, let alone shape, events. While much has been said in these terms, it begs the question of what a minority government faced by global crisis did achieve in Britain and abroad during these difficult times.

---

38 Philip Williamson, *National Crisis and National Government: British Politics, the Economy and Empire, 1926–1932* (Cambridge: Cambridge University Press, 1992); David Howell, *MacDonald's Party: Labour Identities and Crisis 1922–1931* (Oxford: Oxford University Press, 2002).
39 Matthew Worley, *Labour's Grassroots: Essays on the Activities of Local Labour Party and Members, 1918–1945* (Aldershot: Ashgate, 2005).
40 Matthew Worley, *Inside the Gate: A History of the British Labour Party Between the Wars* (London: Tauris, 2005), pp. 121–68.
41 Andrew Thorpe, *A History of the British Labour Party* (London: Macmillan, 1997) and *The British General Election of 1931* (Oxford: Clarendon Press, 1991).
42 Martin Pugh, *Speak For Britain! A New History of the Labour Party* (London: The Bodley Head, 2010).

An introduction

The genesis for this edited collection can be found in a wide range of papers presented and discussed at a major history conference, organised by the Labour History Research Unit at Anglia Ruskin University, Cambridge, specifically to mark the eightieth anniversary of Britain's second Labour government. At the time, the modern context for a re-appraisal of the second Labour government seemed particularly timely. As one conference participant put it:

> A dour Scottish Prime Minister. A moderate Labour government that had taken power after years in the wilderness by distancing itself from the trade unions. A world economic crisis that challenged the economic orthodoxy endorsed by that government. This is not the current crisis [confronting Gordon Brown's Labour government in 2009], it is the description of the Labour government that took power exactly 80 years ago in 1929, just after the Wall Street Crash which ushered in the Great Depression.

That was the verdict of Steve Schifferes (then a BBC economics reporter), Marjorie Deane Professor of Financial Journalism at the City University. The Cambridge conference attracted considerable interest and support, as a re-evaluation of the second Labour government seemed academically very desirable. By the time the event took place, as Professor Schifferes shrewdly observed, it also seemed timely. While the conference did not attempt to be comparative, on 1929–31 and 2008–9 (with the later situation still unravelling), there were some similarities. Also, this occasion brought together leading Labour historians and younger scholars in this field to discuss an impressive wave of new research in Labour history. It reviewed the record of Ramsay MacDonald's second minority administration – the first Labour government to face a world economic crisis – and the lessons it might hold for today. However, neither the conference nor this collection was or is an exercise in comparing 1929–31 with Gordon Brown's last years in office.

In this edited volume, the contributors offer a number of thought-provoking chapters on the government of 1929–31, as well as analyses of the significant developments in the inter-war history of the Labour Party. While the standard assumption is that Labour achieved little, and failed at much, between 1929 and 1931, it was clear from the conference papers that there were certain aspects of MacDonald's minority administration that brought about real change, and that at times Labour was clearly successful in achieving its aims. Some chapters in this volume therefore view certain aspects of MacDonald's government in a positive light, although they also highlight how success often brought with it other problems. Other chapters throw fresh light on important subjects such as the 1929 general election, the economic debates, internal party dynamics, the Conservative Party's response to Labour's victory and the invention of the '1931 tradition'.

In chapter 2, Andrew Thorpe offers an important reappraisal of Labour's victory in 1929 and places it within the wider context of British political history. This was both the first election fought on adult universal suffrage and the first one in which Labour became the leading party (but without an overall majority). He highlights how the intricacies of the election helped bring Labour to power, arguing that it was a specific set of circumstances that aided Labour's victory. The next two chapters assess one of the most important aspects of this government's rule: economics. Chris Wrigley critically assesses the trade unions' response to the party's continued belief in free trade and Snowden's orthodox economics, and argues that leading Labour figures such as Ernest Bevin espoused radically different ideas, including planning and nationalisation. Daniel Ritschel's chapter reviews Oswald Mosley's economic ideas as he challenges the long-held view that Mosley followed a strictly Keynesian path, and instead finds that Mosley does not fit easily into any specific economic tradition.

Next, different groups within the Labour Party are examined. Robert Taylor's chapter analyses the composition of the Parliamentary Labour Party (PLP) and its relations with Ramsay MacDonald during his minority government of 1929–31 as unemployment increased. Taylor reveals the tensions within the PLP, divided over supporting the party in office and its rank and file in the constituencies. Keith Laybourn then revisits the important question of the Independent Labour Party's disaffiliation in 1932. He argues that questions over the party's socialist intent before and during the second Labour government contributed greatly to the split.

The following two chapters examine under-researched areas of the second Labour government. Nicole Robertson's chapter challenges the assumption that Labour was interested in workers only as producers, and she argues that the Labour government had some success in its desire to protect consumers, although further attempts were halted by the 1931 crisis. Clare Griffiths offers an illuminating chapter on Labour and farming, focusing on the difficulties that the party had in dealing with the agricultural crisis between 1930 and 1931.

The next two chapters deal, in different ways, with foreign policy and socialism. Jonathan Davis explores the Labour government's relationship with the Soviet Union. He argues that Labour's pragmatism where the USSR was concerned did bring success, but that this came at a price. John Callaghan assesses Labour's socialism in relation to the apparent achievements brought about by Soviet socialism at a time of international economic crisis, and finds much – long-lasting – support in Labour's ranks for the Soviet way of doing things.

In an enterprising account of opposition politics, Richard Carr offers an important assessment of how the Conservative Party responded to the Labour government. His argument focuses on how the economic ideas of 'young' Conservatives like Harold Macmillan ran counter to traditional Tory non-interventionist views, as they began to see a greater role for the state in economics.

The 1931 crisis naturally brings the book to an end, as David Howell explores how the 'tradition' of 1931 was created. He skilfully interweaves early stories of treachery and crisis with later myths and facts, all of which contributed, over time, to the construction of what he calls a 'usable' past. It is certainly true that what happened in 1931 played a significant part in Labour's history at various times, and the eightieth anniversary of the second Labour government was a timely reminder of this.

2

The 1929 general election and the second Labour government

ANDREW THORPE

The British general election of May 1929 was the first to be fought on universal adult suffrage. It was also the first at which the Labour Party emerged in Parliament as the largest single party. Although Labour did not have an overall majority – as the party's advocates had it then, and have had it ever since, it was 'in office but not in power' – the result was seen at the time as a great moment in the party's history. For Herbert Morrison, presiding as chairman at that autumn's party conference, Labour was 'the miracle of politics', its progress since its formation in 1900 'the outstanding romance of public affairs'.[1] There was to be, of course, cruel irony in such outpourings. The government that resulted from the election has generally been seen as a failure, which ended in the ignominious circumstances of the formation of the National Government in August 1931 and which was followed by Labour's heavy electoral defeat that October. When, at that election, a Conservative candidate suggested that 'Never was there such a striking contrast between promise and performance', he appeared to be speaking for most electors, whether of left or right.[2]

That said, there has been relatively little historical analysis of the 1929 election. Reviewing my book on the 1931 general election in the journal *Parliamentary History* in the early 1990s, Stuart Ball said it 'may succeed in single-handedly reviving a genre which seemed to have had its day by

---

1 Labour Party, *Report of the 29th Annual Conference* (London, 1929), p. 150.
2 J. C. M. Guy, Unionist and National Government candidate, election address in central Edinburgh, 1931 general election, Conservative Party Archive, Bodleian Library, Oxford.

the late 1970s'.[3] But the prediction was to prove as uncharacteristically erroneous as it was characteristically generous. No monograph study of an inter-war election has followed. There is, of course, good work on such elections, but much of it comes from the 1970s. In the early 1990s, John Turner offered important coverage of the 1918 poll in his book on politics in the Great War.[4] More recently, Jon Lawrence has opened up new areas of research with his important work on electioneering.[5] Regional and local studies add colour and even – occasionally – enlightenment.[6] Specifically on 1929, the best published work is that of Philip Williamson, although David Howell has also offered important insights into how Labour came to approach the election in the way that it did.[7] But the fullest study devoted to the election remains E. A. Rowe's 1959 Oxford BLitt thesis.[8]

Yet it is from complexity that we often get our best and most striking insights. Something is wrong if we do not have solid treatments of electoral politics over significant periods of time. An understanding of the 1929 election does not just offer a clearer view of the electoral politics of Britain in the 1920s. It also demonstrates the precarious nature of the second Labour government's position. It shows, furthermore, the immense reserve strength of the Conservative Party in inter-war Britain. Whatever else had been established at the end of Chris Cook's 'Age of Alignment',

---

3   Stuart Ball, 'The National Government, 1931: crisis and controversy', *Parliamentary History*, 12:2 (1993), pp. 184–200, at p. 193.
4   John Turner, *British Politics and the Great War: Coalition and Conflict, 1915–1918* (New Haven: Yale University Press, 1992), pp. 390–436.
5   Jon Lawrence, 'The transformation of British public politics after the First World War', *Past and Present*, 190 (2006), 186–216; Jon Lawrence, *Electing Our Masters: The Hustings in British Politics from Hogarth to Blair* (Oxford: Oxford University Press, 2009), especially pp. 96–129.
6   Duncan Tanner, 'The pattern of Labour politics, 1918–1939', in Duncan Tanner, Chris Williams and Deian Hopkin (eds), *The Labour Party in Wales, 1900–2000* (Cardiff: University of Wales Press, 2000), pp. 113–39; Michael Savage, *The Dynamics of Working-Class Politics: The Labour Movement in Preston, 1880–1940* (Cambridge: Cambridge University Press, 1987), p. 180; Trevor Griffiths, *The Lancashire Working Classes, c. 1880–1930* (Oxford: Oxford University Press, 2001), pp. 305–11.
7   Philip Williamson, '"Safety First": Baldwin, the Conservative Party and the 1929 general election', *Historical Journal*, 25:2 (1982), pp. 385–409; Philip Williamson, *National Crisis and National Government: British Politics, the Economy and Empire, 1926–1932* (Cambridge: Cambridge University Press, 1992), especially pp. 54–6; David Howell, *MacDonald's Party: Labour Identities and Crisis 1922–1931* (Oxford: Oxford University Press, 2002).
8   E. A. Rowe, *The British General Election of 1929* (BLitt thesis, University of Oxford, 1959). See also the excellent recent analysis by David Redvaldsen, '"Today is the dawn": the Labour Party and the 1929 general election', *Parliamentary History*, 29:3 (2010), pp. 395–415.

it was not a two-party system wherein Labour and the Conservatives competed on more or less equal terms.[9] Rather, 1929 was just about the best possible outcome that Labour could have achieved in the inter-war period, and it was a success based on a series of contingencies that could not have been repeated next time. In that sense, the 1929 election, while ushering in the second Labour government, represented an over-extension of its strength which left it very vulnerable to future developments.

Ben Pimlott referred once to the 'electoral anarchy' of Britain in the 1920s.[10] However, by the end of 1924 it appeared that much of that disorder had been laid to rest. As Maurice Cowling showed in the 1970s, the events of 1920–24 had determined that there would be no resurrection of the Lloyd George coalition.[11] The results of the October 1924 general election cemented developments further. The Conservatives, who won a landslide victory with 412 of the 615 seats, were confirmed as the leading party in British politics. The Liberals, down from 158 seats in December 1923 to only 40 ten months later, looked to be effectively finished as a major political force. So this left Labour, though defeated, as the only realistic alternative government to the Conservatives. In a sense, none of this would change before 1945: even in 1929, the Conservatives' primacy could be claimed through the fact that they took more votes than Labour (even while winning fewer seats), while the Liberal revival of the late 1920s would ultimately prove ephemeral.

However, the Conservative government of 1924–29 was not as successful as its leader, Stanley Baldwin, had hoped. Like all twentieth-century Prime Ministers, Baldwin struggled to keep the balance between the broad appeal that would get him re-elected and the more specific partisan appeal that would sustain him as leader of his party. The Conservatives had strong bonds uniting them: the Church, the Empire, the land, a close identification with patriotism that included economic nationalism (and specifically protectionism), and a commitment to strong armed forces. All of these, however, had potential to alienate large numbers of former Liberal voters who were now looking for a home, and what later generations would call 'floating voters' more generally. The problem was that in the period between 1924 and 1929 the Conservatives tended to find their partisan nature repeatedly exposed, for example over the General Strike,

---

9 Chris Cook, *The Age of Alignment: Electoral Politics in Britain, 1922–1929* (London: Macmillan, 1975).

10 Ben Pimlott (ed.), *The Political Diary of Hugh Dalton, 1918–40, 1945–60* (London: Jonathan Cape, 1986), p. 4.

11 Maurice Cowling, *The Impact of Labour, 1920–1924: The Beginning of Modern British Politics* (Cambridge: Cambridge University Press, 1971).

protectionism and the revised Prayer Book. Although Baldwin was mostly able to hold the line, the pressure from within the party, and the exaggerated rhetoric that came from parts of it, did not really assist him in playing down a partisanship which was off-putting to many of those who did not identify closely with the party, but who had voted for it in 1924.[12]

This problem was of course compounded by the Liberal revival that followed David Lloyd George's accession to that party's leadership in late 1926. Lloyd George spent vast sums of money in the next two and a half years in sustaining, and where necessary reviving, grassroots party organisation, increasing expenditure both at headquarters and in the regional offices of the party, and in policy development.[13] The significance of the latter is open to question. The work of the Liberal Industrial Inquiry has been carefully analysed, but the extent to which it really affected voters is questionable.[14] Lloyd George's key impact at the 1929 election might simply have been that his cash ensured that there were many more Liberal candidates for whom to vote. Nonetheless, the ambitious plans for job creation included in *Britain's Industrial Future* and *We Can Conquer Unemployment* (the 'Yellow Book') did offer a challenge to the leaders of the other parties which helped to frame the terms on which the election was fought. As Williamson has shown, it was in response to the 'flashiness' of such programmes that the Conservatives deliberately set out their stall as the 'Safety First' party, believing that this emphasis on probity and security would serve very effectively as a counterpoint to images of Liberal crookedness and Labour zealotry.[15]

Labour, however, was playing down any hints of extremism more effectively than at any time since 1918. The party's leaders believed, just as much as Baldwin did, that the key to victory was the political centre ground – they were, in that sense, Downsians before Downs.[16] Howell

---

12 Philip Williamson, *Stanley Baldwin: Conservative Leadership and National Values* (Cambridge: Cambridge University Press, 1999), especially pp. 33–8; Keith Middlemas and John Barnes, *Baldwin: A Biography* (London: Littlehampton, 1969), pp. 279–529, for exhaustive detail on the 1924–29 government.
13 Michael Pinto-Duschinsky, *British Political Finance, 1830–1980* (Washington, DC: American Enterprise Institute for Public Policy Research, 1981), pp. 91–3, 116–19.
14 See especially Michael Freeden, *Liberalism Divided: A Study in British Political Thought, 1914–1939* (Oxford: Oxford University Press, 1986), pp. 105–18; Peter Clarke, *The Keynesian Revolution in the Making, 1924–1936* (Oxford: Oxford University Press, 1988), pp. 81–3.
15 Williamson, '"Safety First"'.
16 Anthony Downs, *An Economic Theory of Democracy* (New York: Addison Wesley, 1957), argued that, in two-party systems, parties would tend to converge on the centre ground in the hope of maximising their support. Of course, Britain in the 1920s was not a

has demonstrated very effectively the means by which they sought to avoid specifics: 'Any conflict would not be between Right and Left but between specificity and generality'.[17] Helped by the circumstances of the fall of the first Labour government and the 'red scare' nature of the 1924 general election campaign, they closed out the Communists to such an extent that significant numbers of the latter were actively seeking to end attempts to work with and through Labour even before the Communist International changed its line to 'class against class' in 1928.[18] Labour's 1929 election manifesto would include towards its end 'An Appeal to the Women', but it was very much women as wives and mothers who were being appealed to, with anything looking remotely like radical feminism being pushed very firmly to the margins.[19] Links with the trade unions could not be wished away, but they were kept out of sight as far as possible, while the word 'socialism', with its 'foreign' connotations, was played down very firmly by party headquarters. Labour could have been expected to stress unemployment as one of the key elements of its attack on the Conservatives, but the fact that the Liberals were also playing it so hard kept them up to the mark. However, perceivedly controversial policies were downplayed. The 1928 programme, *Labour and the Nation*, was a long aspirational wish-list: the manifesto was even more moderate, playing down nationalisation with a pledge to the public ownership of only one industry, coal – an industrial worst case with a strong union which was funding numerous Labour candidates.[20]

The date of the general election (30 May) was announced on 24 April 1929, and Parliament was dissolved on 10 May. Although this allowed only the statutory minimum of three weeks between dissolution and polling, in reality the parties had been limbering up for well over a year. In that sense, it was a long drawn-out affair. This helped to make for

---

two-party system, but it can be applied to the period in the sense that MacDonald and Baldwin largely ignored the Liberals and spoke of politics as if it were essentially a straight choice between their two parties: see Williamson, *National Crisis and National Government*, p. 56.

17 Howell, *MacDonald's Party*, p. 71.
18 Andrew Thorpe, *The British Communist Party and Moscow, 1920–1943* (Manchester: Manchester University Press, 2000), pp. 117–22.
19 Labour Party, *Labour's Appeal to the Nation* (1929 general election manifesto), reprinted in F. W. S. Craig, *British General Election Manifestos, 1900–1974* (London: Macmillan, 1975), pp. 81–6, at p. 85; Pamela M. Graves, *Labour Women: Women in British Working-Class Politics, 1918–1939* (Cambridge: Cambridge University Press, 1994), pp. 114–17, 151–3.
20 Labour Party, *Labour and the Nation* (London, 1928); Labour Party, *Labour's Appeal to the Nation*.

The 1929 general election

what was pretty universally seen as a rather tedious campaign.[21] This was, in many ways, what Baldwin had hoped for – a long campaign would allow time for Liberal and Labour plans to come under critical scrutiny, and for divisions within those parties to come to the fore. But for this to happen, there needed to be close media – or, more precisely, newspaper – scrutiny of those plans. Much of the 'Conservative' press, though, was not altogether enthusiastic about the record of Baldwin's government or the prospect of its re-election. This was particularly so for the mass-circulation papers like the *Daily Express* and *Daily Mail*, owned by Lords Beaverbrook and Rothermere respectively. While there was not as yet the depth of hatred towards Baldwin in those papers that there would be by 1930–31, it was nonetheless the case that they did little to help the Conservative cause: indeed, the Beaverbrook press spent much of its effort during the 1929 campaign pressing for larger goods wagons to be used on Britain's railways.[22] It was no wonder at all that Baldwin and leading figures at Conservative Central Office despaired of the supposedly 'Tory' press.[23] Worse still, the 'red scare' propaganda that had worked so well in 1924 in the context of the 'Campbell case' and the Zinoviev letter was notably absent in 1929: indeed, Labour looked positively respectable, and its leaders were well known national figures who had experience of government and seemed to know what they were doing and talking about.

What did contemporaries expect to happen? The Conservatives expected, by and large, to win. Of course there were those like the Colonial and Dominions Secretary, Leo Amery, who took a stringent view of the late government, and suggested that it perhaps did not deserve to emerge victorious: 'I remain convinced', he wrote shortly afterwards, 'that our defeat has been due to our complete failure to have a policy which would create enthusiasts on our side'.[24] But most ministers, while expecting a tough fight, were also planning their post-election ministries: Neville Chamberlain, famously, was looking forward to a move from Health to

---

21 The campaign has been described as 'sedate' by David Marquand, *Ramsay MacDonald* (London: Jonathan Cape, 1977), p. 486, and as 'dull', by Charles Loch Mowat, *Britain Between the Wars, 1918–1940* (London: Methuen, 1955), p. 351; while John Campbell said 'the sense of apathy was universal', in *Lloyd George: The Goat in the Wilderness, 1922–1931* (London: Rowman and Littlefield, 1977), p. 236.
22 A. J. P. Taylor, *Beaverbrook* (London: Hamish Hamilton, 1972), p. 260.
23 Mackenzie King, Diary, 8–9 September 1928, in Philip Williamson and Edward Baldwin (eds), *Baldwin Papers: A Conservative Statesman, 1908–1947* (Cambridge: Cambridge University Press, 2004), p. 209.
24 John Barnes and David Nicholson (eds), *The Leo Amery Diaries, Volume I: 1896–1929* (London: Hutchinson, 1980), p. 597 (3 June 1929).

the Colonies.[25] Indeed, it is only by reference to the general expectation that they would win that we can really understand the scale and duration of Conservative disunity after their defeat. The Liberals, for their part, did not expect to win the election. In public, of course, they talked up the prospects for a new Liberal government. In private, however, they were a good deal more realistic, seeing 80–100 seats as a likely total and believing that this ought to put them in a position to force through a serious reform of the electoral system so as to ensure they could at least shore up their present and future parliamentary position.[26]

Labour expectations are more difficult to assess. Clearly there was a great deal of optimism around, based on a belief that the party was developing well, that it had a strong leadership and appealing policies, and that the Conservative government had been a woeful failure. Sidney Webb expected Labour to emerge as the largest party, although without an overall majority; Beatrice Webb went so far as to write privately that 'there may be a landslide' for Labour.[27] However, party leaders and managers were very concerned, until shortly before the election, about the Liberal threat, and while this concern tailed off somewhat in the months immediately before polling, there remained uncertainty as to the effect that Lloyd George's appeal might have on the electorate.[28] The Labour Party has been much criticised for *Labour and the Nation* and the election manifesto that flowed from it. Indeed, R. H. Tawney, who drafted it (albeit under close supervision from party leaders), later denounced it as 'a glittering forest of Christmas trees, with presents for everyone', although it is moot as to whether his by-then preferred approach – a sect-like existence not unlike that of the early Christians, in which Labour would declare its 'creed' and

---

25 Neville to Hilda Chamberlain, 12 April, 5 May 1929, in Robert Self (ed.), *The Neville Chamberlain Diary Letters, Volume III: The Heir Apparent, 1928–33* (Aldershot: Ashgate, 2002), pp. 132, 136; A. Duff Cooper, *Old Men Forget* (London: Hart-Davis, 1957), pp. 155–7. The Labour politician H. B. Lees-Smith told Hugh Dalton in October 1928 that Conservative headquarters was expecting an overall majority of 30 'at worst', and that it expected to 'probably do better than this': see Ben Pimlott (ed.), *The Political Diary of Hugh Dalton, 1918–40, 1945–60* (London: Jonathan Cape, 1986), p. 46 (16 October 1928). This tallied with Baldwin's own expectations in the campaign itself, whereas by then Central Office was expecting a majority of 50: see Middlemas and Barnes, *Baldwin*, p. 526.

26 Sir Herbert Samuel, Memorandum, 2 February 1929, Samuel Papers, Parliamentary Archives, London, A72; Sir Donald Maclean, Memorandum, February 1929, Maclean Papers, Bodleian Library, Oxford, dep. c.468.

27 M. I. Cole (ed.), *Beatrice Webb's Diaries, 1924–1932* (London: Longmans, Green and Co., 1956), p. 193 (30 May 1929).

28 Marquand, *Ramsay MacDonald*, pp. 463–5; for the Liberals tailing off, see Sidney Webb's views reported in *Political Diary of Hugh Dalton*, p. 45 (20 July 1928).

then wait for other true believers to join it – would have brought better results.[29] But it may be that party leaders did not really expect to form the next government. For example, Hugh Dalton, a member of Labour's National Executive Committee and soon to become a junior minister at the Foreign Office, predicted that the Conservatives would win 287 seats, Labour 268, the Liberals 55 and Independents 5.[30] Counterfactually, had Labour increased its number of seats to only around 250, and Baldwin been re-elected with a small majority, then they would have had three or four years in which to work out a more streamlined set of policy proposals.

Nineteen twenty-nine represented a huge reversal of electoral fortunes. The 1924 general election is the forgotten landslide of the twentieth century, as convincing a Conservative victory as either the Liberal win in 1906 or Labour's 1945 triumph: indeed, in neither of those cases did the winning party take as many seats as the Conservatives' 1924 figure of 412. Those 412 seats represented 67 per cent of the 615-strong House of Commons, as opposed to the Liberals' 60 per cent in 1906 and Labour's 61 per cent in 1945. This meant that the Conservatives would need to lose more than 100 seats at the subsequent election merely to be relieved of their overall majority. But lose them they did, and more. Almost two seats in every five were lost. The party's share of the vote fell by a fifth. Labour made a mild advance in terms of its poll share, rising from the 33.3 per cent of 1924 to 37.1 per cent, a share increase of a little over 11 per cent. This mild gain was exaggerated, however, by a significant increase in seats: the 151 MPs of 1924 became 287 in 1929, an increase of 90 per cent on the back of the 11 per cent increase in poll share. The reason for this was, in part at any rate, the extensive intervention of Liberal candidates. In 1924, 339 Liberal candidates had managed 17.8 per cent of the votes cast; now, 513 took almost a quarter of the poll (23.5 per cent). This was an increase of almost a third on the poll share in 1924. However, whereas Labour's seats tally was hugely flattering given its poll share, the reverse operated for the Liberals. They managed to get only 59 MPs elected (Table 1), one of whom defected almost immediately to Labour.

Since 1945, psephological analysis has become increasingly sophisticated, with the aid of ever more elaborate surveys and opinion polling. Such techniques were not in existence in the 1920s, of course; and it is notoriously difficult to reconstruct 'public opinion', let alone identify variations in the

---

29 R. H. Tawney, 'The choice before the Labour Party', *Political Quarterly*, 3 (1932), pp. 323–45, reprinted in W. A. Robson (ed.), *The Political Quarterly in the Thirties* (London: Allen Lane, 1971), pp. 93–111, at p. 98.
30 Hugh Dalton, *Call Back Yesterday: Memoirs 1887–1931* (London: Frederick Muller, 1953), p. 211.

Table 1 Results of the 1929 general election

	Votes	Per cent	Candidates	Unopposed	MPs
Conservative	8,656,225	38.1	590	4	260
Labour	8,370,417	37.1	569	0	287
Liberal	5,308,738	23.5	513	0	59
Other	312,995	1.3	58	3	9
Total	22,648,375	100.0	1,730	7	615

voting habits of the inter-war electorate. Even so, it is not impossible to make some suggestions as to what was happening. In 1997, perhaps significantly given the then ascendancy of New Labour under Tony Blair, Duncan Tanner argued that it was not enough to see Labour's victory in 1929 as 'simply ... a consolidation of [core] support combined with a measure of good fortune'. Instead, he argued, it was 'less dependent upon its "core" supporters than ever before', and won 'a number of Tory strongholds'.[31] It made advances, he suggested, among lower-middle-class voters, and it did so because it portrayed itself as a party with broad competence, an 'effective party of reform', which in turn gave it 'a general public credibility'.[32] However, this view has been strongly disputed by Ross McKibbin, who has suggested that Labour was not moving much beyond its working-class base, and indeed that it did not need to do so because the working class was so large that votes from it alone could elect a Labour government.[33]

In the remainder of this chapter, the 1931 census is used to illuminate the social composition of the Labour vote to a greater extent than ever previously attempted (1931 is used rather than 1921 because it is closer to 1929). The censuses of England and Wales, and of Scotland, have been mined extensively to produce figures for constituencies based on two measures. The first is male occupations. This measure – avoiding the complex variables around the recording of women's occupations and the more extensive movement of women into and out of the jobs market – offers a fairly robust statistical analysis of the nature of work, and hence social composition; in particular, it shows the degree to which constituencies were middle class, working class, or dominated by single industries such as mining or

---

31 Duncan Tanner, 'Class voting and radical politics: the Liberal and Labour parties, 1910–31', in Jon Lawrence and Miles Taylor (eds), *Party, State and Society: Electoral Behaviour in Britain since 1820* (Aldershot: Ashgate, 1997), pp. 106–30, at p. 120.
32 *Ibid.*, p. 122.
33 Ross McKibbin, *Parties and People: England 1914–1951* (Oxford: Oxford University Press, 2010), p. 73.

agriculture. These complex calculations, involving aggregation of literally thousands of figures for the smaller local government units that made up most parliamentary constituencies, offer important insights into general election results, not just in 1929 but across the period 1918–45. It should be stressed that this involves considerable work in terms of compilation of totals and rendering into percentages: neither the totals nor the percentage figures are readily available in this form in the census reports themselves. The main problem with this method is that because figures are given at local authority level, for large local authorities (especially county boroughs), only a single set of figures is available, and so some way is needed of differentiating between, say, the seven constituencies in Sheffield, or the three in Plymouth. Therefore I have used a second set of statistics derived from the census. These are those for housing and are based on figures of persons per room, with an assumption that the more people per room, the more working class an area would be. The beauty of this set of figures is that they are reducible to constituency level for larger towns and cities which were divided into more than one seat, where the occupation tables give only an overall figure for the local authority as a whole.

While it is true that Labour did advance electorally into new areas geographically in 1929, it is difficult to be sure of the extent to which it was consolidating or moving beyond the working class. If we look at the seats with the highest percentages of middle-class voters, for example, it is clear that Labour in 1929 made at best limited advances (see Tables 2 and 3). In the 50 most middle-class seats as they would be defined by the 1931 census, the Conservatives were almost wholly dominant throughout the inter-war period, with only the 1923 election seeing any real shift, and then towards the Liberals, who won seven of the 50.[34] In 1929, it is true, Labour appears to have won four, but this is misleading, because the way that the census statistics were presented – for whole boroughs – meant that a single set of figures has to be used for towns and cities that were subdivided into a number of constituencies. Thus the four 'middle class' seats Labour won in 1929 were in fact the most heavily working-class areas of Kensington, Portsmouth, Plymouth and Wandsworth. However, Labour fares better when we look, not at the top 50, but at the next 50 most middle-class constituencies, with middle-class populations ranging down to just under 28 per cent. Here, Labour took 16 seats to the Conservatives' 32. While this meant that the latter still had 78 of the 100 most middle-class seats overall, Labour had 20, more than it would achieve at any other inter-war

---

34 Author's calculations, based on the occupation tables of the *Census of England and Wales, 1931*, and the *Census of Scotland, 1931*.

Table 2 Parties returned by the 50 most middle-class constituencies (1931 census)[a] at general elections, 1918–45

Year	Con	Lab	Lib	Ind Con	Ind	Lib Nat
1918	49	0	1	0	0	0
1922	47	0	0	2	1	0
1923	42	0	7	0	1	0
1924	49	0	1	0	0	0
1929	46	4	0	0	0	0
1931	49	0	0	0	0	1
1935	49	0	0	0	0	1
1945[b]	31	22	0	0	0	0

[a] Range: 60.57 per cent middle class (Aldershot) to 34.34 per cent (Richmond, Yorkshire).
[b] Some seats were divided in 1945, hence the total is more than 50.

Table 3 Parties returned by the 100 most middle-class constituencies (1931 census)[a] at general elections, 1918–45

Year	Con	Lab	Lib	Nat	Ind Lab	Ind Con	Const	Ind	Lib Nat
1918	87	2	9	1	1	0	0	0	0
1922	88	4	5	0	0	2	0	1	0
1923	74	8	17	0	0	0	0	1	0
1924	90	7	2	0	0	0	1	0	0
1929	78	20	0	0	0	0	0	2	0
1931	96	1	2	0	0	0	0	0	1
1935	92	7	0	0	0	0	0	0	1
1945[b]	49	54	0	1	0	0	0	0	0

[b] Range: 60.57 per cent middle class (Aldershot) to 27.88 per cent (Dover).
[b] Some seats were divided in 1945, hence the total is more than 100.

election. Of course, it was possible for Labour to win most of these seats without a single middle-class vote, but the fact that it did so well (relatively speaking) in 1929 does suggest it had a broader appeal then than it had had earlier in the 1920s, or was to have in the 1930s.[35]

What is notable about these 'middle class' seats is the Liberals' poor showing in them in 1929: having held 17 of the top 100 in 1923, they did not win a single one in 1929. This is turn shows the extent to which the Liberal Party was becoming a party of the countryside, and falling away in urban and suburban areas except where peculiar local circumstances prevailed. What it also suggests, of course, is that Liberalism could

---

35 *Ibid.*

still make an appeal to the rural population (see Tables 4, 5 and 6). The language of rural radicalism, over which Lloyd George himself had such mastery, still resonated; Labour, by contrast, struggled until the 1930s to make much of an appeal in agricultural areas, outside a few such as North Norfolk. In fact Labour won only four of the 50 most agricultural seats in 1929, the same number as in 1923; it had managed two even in 1918 (and three in 1922). The Liberals' relative success in 1929 owed much to the perceived failings of the Conservative government in relation to agriculture. The 1920s had been a brutal decade for farming; the Baldwin government's failure to do much to help undoubtedly cost it dearly at the polls. In 1924 the Conservatives had won 43 of the 50 most agricultural seats, to the Liberals' six and Labour's one; in 1929, the figures were 31, 15 and 4 respectively. When attention is turned to the top 100 agricultural seats, the Conservatives fell from 87 to 66, with the Liberals rising from 15 to 28; and in the top 150, the figures showed the Conservatives falling from 133 to 103, with the Liberals rising from 17 to 34. This was hardly obliteration, but it was significant: had this rural shift from Conservative to Liberal not occurred, Labour would not have been forming a second government in May 1929. In short, it was rural defections to the Liberals that cost the Conservatives most, not urban middle-class defections to Labour.[36]

Labour did consolidate its working-class support. That said, of course, the working class was the great majority of the population – the average middle-class population per constituency was 21.17 per cent in 1931 – so this is not for one moment to claim that the whole working class was moving over to Labour. This consolidation had begun earlier in the decade, but 1929 saw its maximum inter-war manifestation. In 1929, Labour took 42 of the 50 constituencies with the lowest percentage of middle-class people (up from 36 in 1922, 1923 and 1924), and 71 of the 100 least middle-class (up from 56 in 1924) (see Tables 7 and 8). The latter statistic suggests it was spreading its appeal among the working class. Its real core support, though, was in the mining areas. Fifty constituencies would show at least 27 per cent of their male workforce as miners in the 1931 census. Labour won each one of those 50 constituencies in 1929. Even in the disastrous conditions of 1931, it would hold on to 27 of them (see Table 9).[37]

Tanner set great store by the fact that, in 1929, Labour won 73 seats that it had never won previously.[38] Many of these were in divided boroughs and so it is hard to be sure about their social make-up. However, we can sketch out the social character of 32 of these constituencies on the basis of the 1931

---

36 Ibid.
37 Ibid.
38 Tanner, 'Class voting and radical politics', pp. 120–2.

Table 4 Parties returned by the 50 most agricultural constituencies (1931 census)[a] at general elections, 1918–45

Year	Con	Lab	Lib	Co Ind	Ind Lib	Lib Nat	Ind
1918	28	2	19	1	0	0	0
1922	26	3	21	0	0	0	0
1923	23	4	22	0	1	0	0
1924	43	1	6	0	0	0	0
1929	31	4	15	0	0	0	0
1931	36	0	7	0	0	7	0
1935	36	1	6	0	0	7	0
1945	28	7	9	0	0	5	1

[a] Range: 53.35 per cent agricultural (Leominster) to 32.18 per cent (Holderness).

Table 5 Parties returned by the 100 most agricultural constituencies (1931 census)[a] at general elections, 1918–45

Year	Con	Lab	Lib	Co Ind	Ind	Ind Lib	Lib Nat	Nat Lab	Nat	Ind Prog
1918	59	3	36	1	2	0	0	0	0	0
1922	55	3	42	0	0	0	0	0	0	0
1923	45	5	49	0	0	1	0	0	0	0
1924	87	1	15	0	0	0	0	0	0	0
1929	66	6	28	0	0	0	0	0	0	0
1931	75	0	12	0	0	0	12	1	0	0
1935	74	2	10	0	0	0	12	1	1	0
1945	63	14	13	0	1	0	8	0	0	1

[a] Range: 53.35 per cent agricultural (Leominster) to 23.97 per cent (Westbury).

Table 6 Parties returned by the 150 most agricultural constituencies (1931 census)[a] at general elections, 1918–45

Year	Con	Lab	Lib	Co Ind	Ind	Ind Lib	Lib Nat	Nat Lab	Nat	Ind Prog
1918[b]	97	4	46	1	2	0	0	0	0	0
1922	98	5	47	0	0	0	0	0	0	0
1923	73	9	67	0	0	1	0	0	0	0
1924[b]	133	2	17	0	0	0	0	0	0	0
1929	103	13	34	0	0	0	0	0	0	0
1931	129	0	14	0	0	0	14	3	0	0
1935	117	5	12	0	0	0	14	1	1	0
1945[b]	92	32	13	0	2	0	10	0	0	1

[a] Range: 53.35 per cent agricultural (Leominster) to 15.06 per cent (Kettering).
[b] Plus 1 Co-operative in 1918, 1 Constitutionalist in 1924, and 1 Common Wealth in 1945.

The 1929 general election 29

Table 7 Parties returned by the 50 least middle-class constituencies (1931 census)[a] at general elections, 1918–45

Year	Con	Lab	Lib	NDP/ Co Lab	Ind Lab	Nat Lab	Lib Nat
1918	8	22	18	2	0	0	0
1922	7	36	7	0	0	0	0
1923	8	36	6	0	0	0	0
1924	13	36	1	0	0	0	0
1929	4	42	4	0	0	0	0
1931	20	22	1	0	1	3	3
1935	8	40	0	0	0	0	2
1945	6	43	1	0	0	0	0

[a] Range: 7.03 per cent middle class (Hemsworth) to 12.15 per cent (St Helens).

Table 8 Parties returned by the 100 least middle-class constituencies (1931 census)[a] at general elections, 1918–45

Year	Con	Lab	Lib	Co-op	NDP/ Co Lab	Ind	Const	Ind Lab	Nat Lab	Lib Nat
1918	22	31	41	1	4	1	0	0	0	0
1922	25	54	21	0	0	0	0	0	0	0
1923	17	61	22	0	0	0	0	0	0	0
1924	37	56	6	0	0	0	1	0	0	0
1929	16	71	13	0	0	0	0	0	0	0
1931	49	27	8	0	0	0	0	2	3	10
1935	28	62	4	0	0	0	0	0	0	6
1945	19	75	4	0	0	0	0	0	0	2

[a] Range: 7.03 per cent middle class (Hemsworth) to 13.72 per cent (Saffron Walden).

Table 9 Parties returned by the 50 constituencies with the most mining (1931 census)[a] at general elections, 1918–45

Year	Con	Lab	Lib	Co Lab	NDP	Lib Nat	Nat Lab	ILP
1918	5	24	18	1	2	0	0	0
1922	3	44	3	0	0	0	0	0
1923	3	45	2	0	0	0	0	0
1924	6	42	2	0	0	0	0	0
1929	0	50	0	0	0	0	0	0
1931	13	27	2	0	0	4	3	1
1935	2	48	0	0	0	0	0	0
1945	0	50	0	0	0	0	0	0

[a] Range: 68.98 per cent mining (Rhondda East and West) to 27.03 per cent (Chesterfield).

census. Such a sketch shows that only six of the 32 were above the national average for middle-class occupations. The great majority were below, and some were a long way below. This would seem to caution against seeing Labour as making too many advances into the middle-class vote.[39] Furthermore, if overcrowding – represented by residential occupancy per room – is taken as a proxy measure of the social composition of constituencies, then we are able to make some comparisons within the divided boroughs. And this demonstrates, again, the fact that Labour's advances in the larger towns and cities were coming very much in the more working-class areas. Of the seven Birmingham constituencies with the highest room occupancy rates in 1931, for example, five were won by Labour in 1929. Labour also won the top four out of four in Leeds; the top five out of five in Sheffield; the top four out of four in Bristol; and the top five out of six in Manchester. Labour was more successful in the big towns and cities in 1929 than ever before, but it was winning in primarily working-class seats.[40]

One way of looking at the result is to try to see how close Labour came to winning an overall majority. One could argue that it was a close-run thing. If the defecting Liberal MP and an unendorsed Labour MP who later took the whip are counted as Labour, then it could be seen as winning 289 seats, rather than 287. If we then exclude the seats which were in some sense 'undemocratic' – the 12 university seats and the two City of London seats being the most notable examples – then Labour came very close indeed. This example would have given a House of Commons of 601 seats; half of this rounded up would be 301; so Labour (289) had come within 12 of an overall majority. One way of making the story even better was to exclude the 12 Northern Ireland seats, in which case the required figure for a majority would have been 295 – even closer. Better still if seats clearly held by the Conservatives thanks to plural votes, such as Manchester Exchange, are also excluded, or notionally counted as Labour on the grounds that the residents, as opposed to the business people, of such city-centre constituencies were usually solidly working class.

---

39 Author's calculations, based on the occupation tables of the 1931 *Census*.
40 Author's calculations, based on the county tables of the *Census of England and Wales, 1931*, and the *Census of Scotland, 1931*. In the county tables, density of population of housing was given in more detail than were the work occupations in the occupation tables. Density of housing occupation was shown by civil parish or ward, which meant that it was possible to calculate down to the level of individual parliamentary constituencies even in divided boroughs. This was not the case for work occupations, where the lowest level of unit shown was the local authority. This meant that in a county borough like Sheffield, which was a single borough but divided into seven parliamentary constituencies, it was not possible to calculate the percentages working in different occupations at the constituency level.

The problem with all this, of course, was that all these seats *did* send MPs to Parliament in 1929; and not one of them was Labour. And, given the circumstances as they actually existed, focus should not be on how close Labour came to an overall majority, but instead on the fragility of its victory. Many Labour seats were held by small majorities. Assuming no change in levels of Liberal participation and support, a uniform national swing of 1 per cent from Labour to Conservative would reduce Labour from its eventual 289 seats to 266 seats and increase the Conservatives to 283; a 2 per cent swing would put Labour on 250 and the Conservatives on 299; a 3 per cent swing would make the respective figures 233 and 316 (a Conservative overall majority); and a 4 per cent swing would reduce Labour to 211 seats and give the Conservatives 338 (an overall majority of 61).[41]

But it was worse than that. The Liberals were not going to be a neutral factor at the next election: they were bound to impact negatively on Labour. The Liberals' 1929 position was unsustainable. They had been very well financed and relatively united, with a policy which, if not commanding the widespread support that might have been hoped for, did nonetheless have a degree of plausibility. None of these factors would apply subsequently. Lloyd George's political fund was diminishing, and would do so more spectacularly once the stock market crash of late 1929 wiped out much of its value. The levels of expenditure that had been necessary to run over 500 candidates in 1929 could not be kept up, and efforts to place the party on a more self-funding basis were not as successful as might have been hoped, even if the party did not become quite as bankrupt as some of its historians have claimed.[42] Candidates became harder and harder to find.[43] The party's divisions also re-emerged soon after the election: if Lloyd George's enemies had been waiting to allow him to gather sufficient rope with which to hang himself, it was now time to erect the gallows. Furthermore, a risky and unproven economic policy was one thing in times of relative economic stability, but quite another in the severe economic instability that was to unfold from late 1929 onwards. By 1930 most Liberals would be saying very little indeed about expansive

---

41 Andrew Thorpe, *The British General Election of 1931* (PhD thesis, University of Sheffield, 1988), pp. 654–66.
42 Chris Cook, *A Short History of the Liberal Party, 1900–2001* (6th edition, London: Palgrave Macmillan, 2002), pp. 111–12; David Dutton, *A History of the Liberal Party in the Twentieth Century* (London: Palgrave Macmillan, 2004), pp. 120–1. For evidence that the Liberals were not quite as impoverished as is sometimes suggested, see Andrew Thorpe, *Parties at War: Political Organization in Second World War Britain* (Oxford: Oxford University Press, 2009), pp. 268–9, 275.
43 Ramsay Muir to Sir Herbert Samuel, 9 February 1931, Samuel Papers, Parliamentary Archives, London, A155(VIII).

schemes to cut unemployment, and a great deal about the need for significant public expenditure cuts to reassure the markets.[44] In short, the events of 1929–31 would erode the Liberal Party as inexorably as acid rain falling onto a rock, eating into its fault-lines to such an extent that by 1931 the Liberal Parliamentary Party (LPP) would be hopelessly and intractably divided. The idea that the LPP could have been dragooned by Lloyd George into supporting a Labour government pursuing interventionist policies along the lines of the Yellow Book is now utterly discredited, a product of the myth that Liberals are inherently 'progressive'.[45]

The Conservatives, for their part, did have serious difficulties as a result of their 1929 defeat. At times, those difficulties seemed to threaten the party leader, and even the very existence of the party itself. The press barons were, in some ways, just the noisiest manifestation of a much wider malaise. Yet Baldwin was able to win at the crucial points, and by the time of his most noted intervention – the Westminster St George's by-election of early 1931 – was already back in control of the situation.[46] By that time, as Ball has shown, the Conservatives were once more largely united around a programme of public economy, tariffs and imperial preference, and state help for agriculture.[47] With by-elections going strongly in their favour, for the most part, they appeared by the spring of 1929 to be on track for a significant victory at the next general election, whenever it might come.

Crucially, the Liberals' problems were always likely to benefit the Conservatives more than Labour. Many Conservatives blamed the extensive Liberal interventions in 1929 for their party's defeat – there was a sense that Liberals had stood with no hope of victory, but with the ability to split the anti-Labour vote to the extent of allowing Labour to win the seat. This may have been fanciful – as Chamberlain put it at the time, '[n]early all' defeated MPs 'ascribe[d] their misfortunes in the first place to Liberal intervention, but I fear they assume that in the absence of a Liberal candidate, Liberal votes would have been given to them, which seems to me very doubtful' – but it was deeply felt by many.[48] And, if they were

---

44 See for example the Yorkshire Liberal Federation, council meeting, 25 January 1930, Yorkshire Liberal Federation Papers, 2, West Yorkshire Archive Service, Leeds.
45 Robert Skidelsky, *Politicians and the Slump: The Labour Government of 1929–1931* (London: Macmillan, 1967); for a convincing rebuttal see R. I. McKibbin, 'The economic policy of the second Labour government, 1929–1931', *Past and Present*, 68 (1975), pp. 95–123.
46 Stuart Ball, *Baldwin and the Conservative Party: The Crisis of 1929–1931* (New Haven: Yale University Press, 1988), pp. 140–3.
47 *Ibid.*, pp. 165–71.
48 Neville to Hilda Chamberlain, 9 June 1929, in *Neville Chamberlain Diary Letters, Volume III*, p. 145.

right and Chamberlain wrong, then the converse of this was that, where a Liberal did not stand again at the next election, those seats ought to have been retrievable by the Conservatives. This electoral arithmetic helped to account for many of Labour's gains in 1929; it also explained why such seats were lost in 1931 and also why they were not then recovered in 1935, when there were far fewer Liberal candidates than in 1929. In addition, if the Liberal vote as a whole were to collapse at the next general election after 1929, the Conservatives would benefit disproportionately – not only had they come second in 40 of the 59 Liberal seats, but they had done so in 7 of the 10 most winnable, 17 of the 20 most winnable, and 31 of the 40 most winnable. Even in defeat, then, the Conservatives were in a relatively strong position, even if they did not see it in the face of an unwelcome and unexpected electoral reverse, and given the total lack of anything approaching serious psephological analysis in either politics or academia.

For Labour, winning the 1929 general election was a blessing that soon became a curse. The bright start that followed its election halted with the economic downturn of autumn 1929. Although they were able to sustain their minority government with more or less tacit Liberal support (at least to the extent of not voting with the Conservatives to oust the government), ministers faced a miserable time as they tried to wrestle with the problems outlined in other chapters in this volume.[49] Their moderate 1920s strategy of seeking to maximise support through playing up broad areas of consensus and playing down distinctive policies (like the capital levy or nationalisation) that looked partisan or divisive had brought success. But it also meant that there had been a neglect of the kind of detailed work on policy that might have given Labour more of an idea of how to face the perils of office, although, that said, the problems it faced from 1929 onwards were much deeper than anyone had expected, and it is hard to see how Labour could have successfully come through its period of office in such a difficult time. After all, it was hardly unique among western governing parties in being baffled in the face of, and eventually swept from power by, the crises of 1929–33. As stated above, it may also be that many leading Labour people did not really expect to overturn the 1924 general election in one go, and that they hoped only to increase Labour representation and build a platform for a serious push for power at the *next* general election. If that was the case, then a strategy based on avoiding detailed policy commitments, and relying on broad ethical appeals, was, in many ways,

---

49 The best single-volume treatment of the government is Neil Riddell, *Labour in Crisis: The Second Labour Government, 1929–1931* (Manchester: Manchester University Press, 1999).

the right one; what went wrong was that it worked too well, in the sense of propelling Labour into government before it was ready.

Be that as it may, Labour was in office, and faced an uncertain future. Just like the Conservatives, Labour's leaders may not have been able to conduct their own psephological analysis, or to get anyone else to do it, but they were aware in broad terms of the underlying weakness of their electoral position. One way of dealing with this would have been to call a further general election very rapidly after May 1929, in the knowledge that they were in their honeymoon period, that the Conservatives were crotchety with Baldwin, and that the Liberals would be unable to run as many candidates as in May 1929. But the results of this would not necessarily have been favourable, given that any Liberal collapse might well have helped even a divided Conservative Party more than it would have done Labour. And, in any case, it ran up against a major problem for Labour throughout the period from the early 1920s to the early 1940s – money. General elections were expensive, and Labour's finances were in poor shape, with the restrictive financial effects of the 1927 Trade Disputes Act having dramatically compounded an ongoing fall in revenue from union sources due to falling membership (itself the product of high levels of unemployment).[50] MacDonald's oft-quoted call for Parliament to consider itself 'more as a Council of State and less as arrayed regiments facing each other in battle' – often seen, after the event, as an early indication of his desire for, or at least propensity towards, some kind of coalition with the Conservatives – can be read instead as a plea to avoid an early election on these grounds (although it can also be compared to the kind of conciliatory comments about agreement that often characterise the early days of new party leaders or Prime Ministers, in which they try to box their opponents into a position in which they look partisan and sectional).[51]

Labour therefore made avoidance of a further general election a central plank of its statecraft. For most of the time from October 1929 onwards, its leaders knew that an election would see them heavily defeated. There were, though, brief periods of hope: David Marquand has shown very well how even the mildest pieces of economic good news could revive ministerial spirits for a time.[52] MacDonald appears to have come round to thinking that protectionism could provide a remedy, as when he alarmed

---

50 Labour Party, *Report of the 31st Annual Conference* (London, 1931), p. 79.
51 *House of Commons Debates*, fifth series, 2 July 1929, 229, col. 65, MacDonald. For views of his speech, see for example Mowat, *Britain Between the Wars*, pp. 355–6. For a more recent example of apparent cross-partisanship with a partisan edge, see *House of Commons Debates*, sixth series, 440, 7 December 2005, col. 861, David Cameron.
52 Marquand, *Ramsay MacDonald*, pp. 518, 597, 603.

his free trade Chancellor of the Exchequer, Philip Snowden, while sitting in the House of Commons one day in 1930, by saying that he thought they should go to the country soon on a programme of maintaining social services, 'a forward programme on unemployment' and a revenue tariff.[53] But although free trade was rapidly losing its lustre as protectionist feeling grew in all quarters, it remained strong enough among Labour ministers, MPs, members and supporters to thwart MacDonald's hopes.[54] Labour's leaders realised that to leave office would mean defeat and the election of a Conservative government committed, increasingly as the period after 1929 wore on, to swingeing cuts in public expenditure and to protective tariffs, both of which, they believed, would impact hardest and most negatively on the working-class people they had come into politics to represent and protect. It would mean an end to what was generally seen as Labour's good work in international affairs, and might prove a body blow to the much-anticipated world disarmament conference, due to start in Geneva in February 1932. There was also a feeling, by no means unjustified, that even if Labour had not been able to make sweeping reforms, still less introduce 'socialism', it could make significant gains for at least some of the people it represented. Cutting half an hour off the miners' working day in 1930 pleased no one in politics or the unions very much, but it did give the men themselves a little more time away from the pit and a slightly better life.[55] Allowing local authorities to make information available on artificial contraception was hardly the socialist millennium, but it was a bold move in the circumstances and it undoubtedly prevented unwanted pregnancies and, in an era of stubbornly high maternal mortality and disablement, allowed significant numbers of women to live longer and better lives than they might otherwise have been able to do.[56] To say that the second Labour government was unsuccessful and, indeed, that on balance Labour deserved to be defeated at the next general election does not mean that it achieved nothing at all.

Much work remains to be done on the British general election of 1929. It has not been possible, in a contribution of this length, to penetrate

---

53 Philip, Viscount Snowden, *An Autobiography* (London: Ivor Nicholson and Watson, 1934), vol. 2, p. 923.
54 Frank Trentmann, *Free Trade Nation: Commerce, Consumption, and Civil Society in Modern Britain* (Oxford: Oxford University Press, 2008), pp. 316–30; Andrew Thorpe, 'The industrial meaning of "gradualism": the Labour Party and industry, 1918–1931', *Journal of British Studies*, 35:1 (1996), pp. 84–113, at pp. 101–2.
55 Barry Supple, *The History of the British Coal Industry, Volume IV, 1913–1946: The Political Economy of Decline* (Oxford: Oxford University Press, 1987), pp. 332–41, p. 429.
56 Audrey Leathard, *The Fight for Family Planning: The Development of Family Planning Services in Britain, 1921–1974* (London: Macmillan, 1980), pp. 44–50.

to the constituency level, to make a detailed analysis of the state of organisation, to investigate in detail the political culture and language of electioneering, or to offer the kind of analysis of the press so beloved of the Nuffield model. It would be valuable, in particular, to have some detailed case studies of constituencies that looked at how the key issues were mediated by the parties in various places. To take just one example, we know from Garry Tregidga's work the extent to which the Liberal clean sweep of the five constituencies in Cornwall was due to 'old' and not 'new' Liberalism, and especially to a resurgent Free Church reaction to the perceived Anglicanism of the Conservative Party in the light of, among other things, the 1928 Prayer Book controversy.[57] It would be good to have a much clearer sense than we do, in addition, of the mood of Labour people in 1929. For them, it appears, May 1929 was a moment of hope every bit as much as July 1945, October 1964 or May 1997 were to be, and the fact that that hope was soon thwarted should not make it any the less worthy of investigation.

It is clear that 1929 was a significant general election. It represented the maximum that Labour could achieve in the electoral context of interwar Britain. It was, in that sense, a remarkable result. The fact that it came little more than a decade after the rather disappointing outcome of 1918 was all the more remarkable. It was a result of which MacDonald and his colleagues could be proud, and had MacDonald himself died shortly afterwards, he would be recalled today in Labour folklore not as the 'traitor' of 1931, but as one of the great founders of the party: many of the 'MacDonald Halls' that were hastily renamed in 1931 would probably still bear his name today. But events turned out very differently. In the event, 1929 opened the way to a very difficult period for Labour, rather than being the staging post to the early overall majority for which most of the party's adherents had hoped in the immediate aftermath of victory.

---

57 Garry Tregidga, *The Liberal Party in South-West Britain since 1918: Political Decline, Dormancy and Rebirth* (Exeter: University of Exeter Press, 2000), pp. 45–50. For the controversy itself, see John Maiden, *National Religion and the Prayer Book Controversy, 1927–1928* (Woodbridge: The Boydell Press, 2009).

3
Labour dealing with labour: aspects of economic policy

CHRIS WRIGLEY

There was an expectation in the 1920s, which was still present in the 1960s and 1970s, that Labour in office would have special skills in handling labour issues. This view was expressed in relation to unemployment insurance at the 1929 Trades Union Congress (TUC) by Arthur Hayday, a Nottingham MP who was on both the Parliamentary Labour Party executive and the General Council of the TUC: 'A Labour government having presented the ideal which is the result of thorough investigation and practical knowledge, is in a better position than anybody else to implement at once the instruments which they have created....'[1] Even more so, it was expected in industrial relations. The record of the second Labour government's handling of the trade unions has been reviewed most notably by Vic Allen, Hugh Clegg, Lewis Minkin, Neil Riddell and David Howell.[2] However, such wider issues as aspects of the labour market and economic policy also deserve reconsideration. In these areas, leading figures in the TUC developed piecemeal economic responses to worrying economic circumstances from at least 1927. The views of the TUC leaders and Ramsay MacDonald and Philip Snowden moved apart as economic conditions worsened during 1930–31. By the time of the final crisis in

---

1 TUC, *Report of the Sixty-First Annual Trades Union Congress* (London, September 1929).
2 Vic Allen, *Trade Unions and the Government* (London: Longmans, Green, 1960); H. A. Clegg, *A History of British Trade Unions since 1889, Volume II: 1911–1933* (Oxford, Clarendon Press, 1985); Lewis Minkin, *The Contentious Alliance* (Edinburgh: Edinburgh University Press, 1991); Neil Riddell, *Labour in Crisis: The Second Labour Government, 1929–1931* (Manchester: Manchester University Press, 1999); and David Howell, *MacDonald's Party: Labour Identities and Crisis 1922–1931* (Oxford: Clarendon Press, 2002).

August 1931 Snowden was dismissive of the TUC, observing that it failed to see the need for public expenditure cuts.

MacDonald's distaste, even contempt, for most trade union leaders is well known, as is Ernest Bevin's reciprocal feelings for MacDonald. Bevin, leader of the Transport and General Workers' Union (TGWU), which had some 300,000 members in 1922, sought to replace MacDonald with Arthur Henderson as Labour Party leader in the autumn of 1924, after the first Labour government. MacDonald had taken great exception to trade union action in 1924 to recover some of the wage cuts of 1921–22, feeling that the trade union leaders were being disloyal to his government. Moreover, Philip Snowden, as Chancellor of the Exchequer in both the 1924 and the 1929–31 Labour governments, was also hostile to trade unions and in his budgets displayed a propensity towards surpluses and deflation, in contrast to economic policies more favourable to labour.

By the later 1920s Bevin, Walter Citrine and some other leading TUC figures, faced with adverse economic conditions, were very concerned about both international economic pressures on British industry and the power of economic orthodoxy. The return to the gold standard had been approved in principle by the Lloyd George coalition government (1916–22) in autumn 1919 and when that return took place in 1925 at the pre-war parity with the dollar, it raised expectations among bankers and economists that, with unemployment high, wages would be pressed down. Bevin and other trade union leaders were no more willing to accept an economic orthodoxy which would ensure economic sacrifices would be made by working people and those unemployed than had trade union leaders during the adverse labour market conditions of the third quarter of the nineteenth century.[3] Trade union reappraisals of economic policies were encouraged not only by the 1925 return to the gold standard and the General Strike of 1926, but also by the realisation that there would be no quick return to the expansionary times of 1910–14, let alone the boom years of 1919–21.

That recovery would be slow after 1921–22 was not immediately apparent. The Great War had boosted agricultural production in North and South America, Australasia and elsewhere, industrial production in the United States and Japan and, in effect, protected markets elsewhere, such as India and South Africa. This extra capacity was there when war-torn European countries resumed production. Alongside a problem of excess capacity there was a much slower rate of growth of demand in

---

[3] G. D. H. Cole, 'Some notes on British trade unionism of the third quarter of the nineteenth century', *International Review of Social History* (1937), 2, pp. 1–27.

international markets compared with 1870–1914. As a result, competition was fiercer and, with international prices falling, there was immense pressure to cut labour costs (less pay, longer hours) at a time when employers could argue that real wages (pay against the cost of living) were falling far less than cash wages. That many of Britain's economic problems were not temporary took time to be accepted.

The scale of the economic readjustments of the early 1920s was very substantial, much greater than in 1931–33 or 2008–10. The overall drop in gross domestic product (GDP) at factor cost from the 1920 boom to 1923 was 30.0 per cent. The recovery of 1923–24 only saw a 1.5 per cent rise in GDP, and even from 1923 to 1929 the recovery was just 8.1 per cent. Coal mining was one of the sectors which suffered badly, with a 25.7 per cent drop in gross trading profits in 1920–23, and as 1923 was an exceptionally good year after 1920, profit levels worsened markedly from 1924 until 1929, recovering only in 1937–38. Indeed, the coal industry weakened until 1935, with a substantial fall in employment.[4]

British trade union membership fell somewhat similarly to GDP over 1920–23, dropping 34.8 per cent (from 8,253,000 to 5,382,000) and with only a 3.9 per cent recovery in 1923–24 (a gain of 210,000 members). In contrast, from 1929 to the worst level in 1933, the drop in membership was only 9.5 per cent. This much smaller fall owed much to the fact that trade union membership in 1929 was still only at 58.2 per cent of the level of 1920.[5]

While trade unionism generally was weakened after 1920, within sectors there were big variations. This was notably so in transport. In terms of percentages of insured workers unemployed, rail and tram/bus workers suffered least, levels fluctuating between 6.0 and 6.9 per cent for the former and 3.0 and 3.8 per cent for the latter between 1923 and 1930 (excluding 1926, the year of the General Strike). In contrast, unemployment in the docks and harbours rose from 27.5 per cent to 33.4 per cent between 1923 and 1930, while in other road transport, a growth area in the 1920s, unemployment steadily dropped from 17.3 per cent in 1920 to 11.7 per cent in 1928, before going up to 14.8 per cent in 1930.[6]

Bevin's own leadership and the survival of his huge amalgamation, the TGWU, created in 1921, had been very much under threat in the early

---

4 C. H. Feinstein, *National Income, Expenditure and Output of the United Kingdom, 1955–1965* (Cambridge: Cambridge University Press, 1972), T11, T72.
5 George Sayers Bain and Robert Price, *Profiles of Union Growth* (Oxford: Blackwell, 1980), p. 39.
6 B. R. Mitchell, *British Historical Statistics* (Cambridge: Cambridge University Press, 1988), Labour Force Table 11, p. 129.

1920s. As Alan Bullock has observed, 'The Union could hardly have been founded at a worse time'.[7] Bevin experienced the wrath of members who suffered negotiated wage cuts in 1921–23, but he rightly believed restitution would be secured when business recovered. Hence he did not hesitate to call strikes for pay rises when trade improved in late 1923 and in 1924.

However, following the 1921–22 recession, labour markets remained far from robust, and in such unfavourable circumstances reliance on trade union strength in lock-outs and strikes on several occasions had poor results, most notably in the case of the miners in 1926. In contrast, in the case of the wool, Ben Turner and other trade union leaders in the industry had lessened and delayed cuts through negotiation with employers on the Joint Industrial Council for the wool and allied textile industry.[8] In a period when financial opinion in the persons of bankers and economists was pressing for further 1921/22-style readjustments of wages in line with prices and relatively poor industrial output, Bevin and other trade union leaders were willing to turn to moderate employers to negotiate better terms than the grim remedies of orthodox finance.

Even during the 1910–21 era of industrial confrontation, a major feature of much trade unionism had been the more moderate approach of joint, and even tripartite, negotiating. This had been so with the Industrial Council, 1911, the National Industrial Conference, 1919, and the Whitley Committees. In addition, the experience of state intervention in the First World War had shown clearly the benefits of rationalisation in the railways, shipbuilding, engineering and other sectors and this had impressed many trade unionists and some employers.[9] Encouraged by Walter Citrine, the TUC Secretary, the TUC President, George Hicks (of the Amalgamated Union of Building Trade Workers), called at the 1927 TUC for 'Much fuller use ... of the machinery for joint consultation and negotiation between employers and employed', both at local and at national level, in order to 'bring both sides face to face with the hard realities of the present economic situation', as this 'might yield useful results in showing how far and upon what terms co-operation is possible in a common endeavour to

---

7 Alan Bullock, *The Life and Times of Ernest Bevin, Volume 1: Trade Union Leader 1881–1940* (Oxford: Heinemann, 1960), p. 219.
8 Chris Wrigley, *Cosy Co-operation Under Strain: Industrial Relations in the Yorkshire Woollen Industry 1919–1930* (York: Borthwick Institute, 1987). J. A. Jowett and K. Layborn, 'The wool dispute of 1925', *Journal of Local Studies*, 2, 1 (1982), pp. 10–27.
9 See, for instance, Leslie Hannah, *The Rise of the Corporate Economy*, 2nd edition (London: Methuen, 1983), pp. 26–40.

improve the efficiency of industry and to raise workers' standard of life'.[10] This suggestion was taken up by the Mond group of employers.[11]

Bevin and other trade union leaders were very aware that the adverse labour market conditions after 1920 were not peculiar to Britain. The fortunes of Labour movements in Europe and other parts of the world had been greatly affected by the boom in the international economy in 1915–20 and in most countries by the severe recession of 1921–22.[12] British trade union leaders discussed how to respond to international economic trends at the various international trade union bodies for particular sectors, such as those for transport workers and miners, that operated in the inter-war years. In addition, the TUC played a substantial role in the International Federation of Trade Unions, with Walter Citrine as its President from 1928 to 1945.[13]

Bevin, like David Lloyd George, had something of a magpie mind. He took glittering ideas from wherever he found them. A. J. P. Taylor wrote of him,

> He remained all his life a casual labourer, ready to turn his hand to anything and without much belief in the trained expert. An engine-driver or a maker of precision-tools would never have challenged the bankers as ruthlessly as Bevin did at the time of the Macmillan Commission [Committee]. He would have been taken in by them and assumed that, as experts, they knew what they were talking about.

Taylor, however, added, 'His mind ran over with cock-eyed ideas; and his rambling talk, if taken down, could have gone alongside Hitler's *Table Talk* as an intellectual curiosity.' Bevin and the other trade union leaders came to the economic problems of the late 1920s with a mix of ideas, ranging from the Gladstonian free trade economics to the Independent Labour Party's radical ideas. Bevin himself alluded at the 1927 TUC to his varied intellectual past, which included the Bristol Socialist Society, an affiliate of the Social Democratic Federation.[14] Bevin eagerly sought

---

10 Speech, 5 September 1927, in *Report of the Fifty-Ninth Annual Trades Union Congress* (Edinburgh, 1927), pp. 66–7.
11 See G. W. MacDonald and H. Gospel, 'The Mond–Turner talks, 1927–1933: a study in industrial co-operation', *Historical Journal*, 16:4 (1973), pp. 807–29.
12 See, for instance, Chris Wrigley, 'Organised labour and the international economy', in C. Wrigley (ed.), *The First World War and the International Economy* (Cheltenham: Edward Elgar, 2000), pp. 201–15.
13 Geert Van Goethem, *The Amsterdam International: The World of the International Federation of Trade Unions (IFTU), 1913–1945* (Aldershot: Ashgate, 2006), especially pp. 96–7, 121–3.
14 A. J. P. Taylor, 'Nobody's uncle', in *Politicians, Socialism and Historians* (London:

confirmation of his embryonic economic ideas on the TUC's economic committee and especially on several government committees during the second Labour government.

Bevin was aware that there had been some recovery of domestic demand in Britain but that generally the sluggish levels of demand in the international economy were a problem. In going to the United States in the autumn of 1926 as part of a government commission to study industry and industrial relations he was interested in levels of demand there as well as industrial efficiency. Bevin wrote in a notebook early on in his visit that it was confirming his view that Britain needed to be part of a larger trading area, within either the Empire or Europe. In favouring Europe he may have been impressed by the arguments of Edo Fimmen, the former Secretary of the International Federation of Trade Unions and a colleague of Bevin on the International Transport Workers' Federation when it had been reconstituted in 1919. Notions of a 'Greater Britain' (Britain plus Empire) went back to at least Sir Charles Dilke and J. R. Seeley over 50 years earlier and had been advocated later by Joseph Chamberlain when he was seeking means by which to maintain Britain as a world power in the twentieth century. Bevin developed his interest in imperial development while on the government's Colonial Development Advisory Committee, in 1929–31.[15] Bevin, when in the United States, predicted that that country would suffer an economic crisis within three years, on the basis of his assessment of the contrast between the increased wealth of the United States since 1919 (which he believed to have grown by 89 per cent) and the much smaller increase of wealth accruing to working people (only 6 or 7 per cent).[16]

Bevin and the TGWU focused on international economic issues at the 1927 TUC. They secured debates on three motions. Those called for the TUC to investigate the impact of tariffs on trade and employment, and the impact of international trusts and cartels, and to promote European economic unity. Bevin explained his union's considerable concern: 'Anyone

---

Hamish Hamilton, 1980), pp. 124–5. For the policies of the Independent Labour Party, see Daniel Ritschel's chapter in the present volume (chapter 4). See also Noel Thompson, *Political Economy and the Labour Party: The Economics of Democratic Socialism* (London: UCL Press, 1996), pp. 55–79. *Report of the Fifty-Ninth Annual Trades Union Congress*, p. 396 (7 September 1927).

15 Fimmen published in 1924 an essay entitled 'Labour's alternative: the United States of Europe or Europe Limited'. See Van Goethem, *The Amsterdam International*, p. 117; Marjorie Nicholson, *The TUC Overseas: The Roots of Policy* (London: Allen and Unwin, 1986), pp. 177, 190–2.

16 Bullock, *The Life and Times of Ernest Bevin*, pp. 356–63; Trevor Evans, *Bevin* (London: Allen and Unwin, 1946), pp. 110–11.

who has had to follow the transport trades of the world realises that while you may satisfy political ambitions by the establishment of boundaries, the economic development of the world is often in total conflict with national aspirations.' As a result he felt that 'we have got to show our people unionism in terms of raw material, in terms of harvests, cycles of trade, and exchange'. Bevin moved the motion calling on the TUC to prepare public opinion to support 'Europe becoming an economic entity', in order to solve the problem of over-production.[17]

Bevin also spoke of international economic considerations and drew on his 1926 trip to the United States when he spoke to the 1928 Trades Union Congress in justification of the Mond–Turner talks. Bevin saw rationalisation of industry and mergers, as in the United States, as inevitable. He told the TUC,

> I shall never forget my experience in America. You talk of rationalisation and great changes in America, but the unions there are outside of it. When I saw the great changes that must come in this country from the war I never rested a moment before the end of the war until now to preach amalgamation, to try to get unity, to try to get a machine and try to create a position that would get us on the inside instead of the outside shouting at them. Company unionism was beginning to take root in this country in many of the great producing factories.... Who will deny that by the specious welfare schemes and in other ways we were being undermined up and down the country? I am going to claim for the Mond Conference that it acted as the greatest check on company union growth that has taken place in this country.[18]

Bevin went on to say that he welcomed rationalisation, as he felt nothing could stop the move from small employers to large. He also drew on information from the US Secretary of Labor, to the effect that for every 100 men employed in 1928 without the technological changes since 1918 there would have been 140 employed. Bevin therefore urged a shorter working week as the necessary response to unemployment.

The TUC sub-committee that participated in the talks with the Mond group of employers agreed to a statement which rejected a return to the pre-war gold standard. The Mond–Turner group perceived the pre-1914 working of the gold standard as playing 'a highly important part in bringing about the long and short term price movements and

---

17 Speech, 8 September 1927, *Report of the Fifty-Ninth Annual Trades Union Congress*, pp. 391–2, 396.
18 Speech, 6 September 1928, *Report of the Sixtieth Annual Trades Union Congress* (Swansea, 1928), p. 448.

industrial fluctuations which seriously disturbed the even flow of our national development, and gave rise to grave social and industrial ills'. Bevin, in particular, was impressed by the need to find a better approach to providing national credit facilities. He warmly agreed with the final Mond–Turner group resolution on the gold reserve and its relation to industry: 'it is essential ... to hold a full inquiry into the best form of credit policy for the country before decisive steps are taken by the government'.[19]

As he had defended the Mond–Turner talks in relation to the gold standard, albeit fairly incoherently, at the TUC, Bevin was not a surprising choice by MacDonald and Snowden for a place on the Committee on Finance and Industry under Lord Macmillan. The Mond–Turner talks very clearly fitted in with MacDonald's and Snowden's views of the role trade unions should play in participating in an industrial consensus, rather than resorting to industrial strife.

Bevin, when defending the General Council again over the Mond–Turner talks at the 1929 TUC, observed,

> Rightly or wrongly, we take the view that if trade unionism confines its work to the mere discussion of wages and nothing else, then we are not performing the function that the needs of the times call upon us to perform in relation to the organisation of the industrial system, and through the function of Parliament to transform into law what we accomplish on the industrial side.

In this, Bevin was elaborating part of the General Council's report: 'It is felt that the currency and banking policy pursued by the Treasury and the Bank of England ought in future be framed in such a way that the special interests of industry are safeguarded and furthered.'[20]

The General Council's view was expounded by the veteran trade unionist and TGWU official Ben Tillett in his speech on 2 September as President at the 1929 TUC, a speech that was drafted at least in part by Citrine. Tillett asserted that the resources of the TUC 'are at the disposal of the nation in a genuine endeavour to promote the regeneration of economic life, to recover lost markets, open new channels of trade, and to modernise our methods of production and distribution'. He reaffirmed the TUC's commitment to the rationalisation of British industry and stated that 'we are as much concerned with world economics as we are concerned with international politics and should be interested in financial movements as any organisation of employers, any bank, company or

---

19 *Ibid.*, pp. 4–51, 230, 449–50.
20 Speech, September 1929, *Report of the Sixty-First Annual Trades Union Congress* (Belfast, 1929), pp. 384–5, 198.

finance house'. Tillett also spoke of the importance of the British Empire as having 'greater potential home consumption than the United States' and urged the trade union movement that it 'must follow with the closest attention the proposals which are being made for the organisation of the British Commonwealth as an economic unit'. In particular, Tillett urged the creation of a state economic council, a tripartite body (state, capital, labour), which 'should have authority in matters of Finance, Banking Credits concerning the State and Industry … and reconsideration of the "Gold Standard" as a basic factor of Trade and Exchange'.[21] Others, notably the Liberal Party's policy groups, had also called for such an economic body. MacDonald's government set up not only the Macmillan Committee but also a tripartite economic advisory committee.

The Treasury minute which stated Snowden's intention for the Macmillan Committee followed closely the views expressed by the Mond–Turner group and by Bevin at the 1928 and 1929 Congresses. It announced the creation of

> a Committee to inquire into banking, finance and credit, paying regard to the factors both internal and international which govern their operation, and to make recommendations calculated to enable those agencies to promote the development of trade and commerce and the employment of labour.[22]

When the Macmillan Committee was set up in November 1929, the proportion of the workforce registered unemployed had risen in Britain by 12.5 per cent from June that year (2.1 per cent per month), to 1.3 million people. Between November 1929 and November 1930 unemployment rose by 78.3 per cent (6.0 per cent per month), to 2.4 million people.[23] Hence the Labour government and the trade unions faced a very rapidly deteriorating situation in 1930.

At the September 1930 TUC another TGWU officer, Jack Beard (formerly of the Workers' Union, now amalgamated with the TGWU), was President. Beard made it clear that the trade unions did not support imperial tariffs, as advocated by Lord Beaverbrook and much of the Conservative Party, but did not 'make a fetish of Free Trade'. He stated:

---

21 *Ibid.*, pp. 63–6. Ben Tillett, *Memories and Reflections* (London: John Long, 1931), pp. 247–8.
22 Minute of appointment, 5 November 1929, Parliamentary Papers (PP) 1930–31 (Cmd 3897), *Committee on Finance and Industry Report*, p. vi.
23 Department of Employment, *British Labour Statistics: Historical Abstract 1886–1968* (London: HMSO, 1971), table 162, p. 308.

> The Trade Union Movement has never been a believer in Manchesterism. Our unions were formed to prevent the so-called free trade in labour. As Trade Unionists and Socialists we believe in interference with the so-called 'immutable economic laws'. We believe in the 'regulation and conscious control of economic factors and forces'.... The opposite of free trade is not tariffs. The opposite of free trade is regulated trade, and there are many methods of establishing economic links with other nations besides the methods of tariffs.[24]

Tariffs were but one controversial economic area that was being explored by the Macmillan Committee.

John Maynard Keynes played a major critical role on the Macmillan Committee, putting the Bank of England's views under scrutiny and offering alternative policies. Keynes briefed Citrine on the progress of the Committee, as did Bevin separately. Keynes wished to secure trade union support for his views. The 1929 general election results, with a disappointing number of seats for the Liberals, showed Keynes the limits of working primarily with Lloyd George, and further encouraged him to try to influence the TUC and Labour Party leaderships.[25]

For the trade union leaders Keynes was a respected economist who offered an alternative understanding of the workings of the economy to that of the Bank of England. The Bank's orthodox economists denied that the return in 1925 to the gold standard at the pre-war parity was damaging the British economy. Instead, the economist W. W. Stewart told the Macmillan Committee that 'wage adjustments [are] as ever so much more important in industry than changes in the Bank Rate or anything bankers can do'. The Bank of England's preferred solutions included (1) reduction of wages, (2) reduction of real social service benefits, (3) redistribution of taxation away from profits and (4) rationalisation.[26] Other than rationalisation, these were policies abhorrent to the trade union leaders. Keynes, in contrast to the Bank of England, was insistent that the high parity of the pound to the dollar after 1925 and the consequent high bank rate were very damaging to industry and the economy generally. Keynes favoured credit

---

24 Speeches, 1 and 2 September 1930, *Report of the Sixty-Second Annual Trades Union Congress* (Nottingham, 1930), p. 71; *The Times*, 3 September 1930, p. 8.
25 See in particular Peter Clarke, *The Keynsian Revolution in the Making 1924–1936* (Oxford: Clarendon Press, 1988), pp. 73–225; D. E. Moggridge, *Maynard Keynes: An Economist's Biography* (London: Routledge, 1992), especially chs 18 and 19; Robert Skidelsky, *John Maynard Keynes: The Economist as Saviour 1920–1937* (London: Macmillan, 1992), especially, pp. 297–40; Lord Citrine, *Men and Work* (London: Hutchinson, 1964), pp. 240–6.
26 Clarke, *The Keynsian Revolution*, pp. 139, 136.

expansion to assist industry as well as public works and tariffs. He did not see wage cuts as an answer. He made this point especially clearly in June 1931 at a Harris Foundation series of lectures and seminars in Chicago. In a discussion on 'Are Wage Cuts a Remedy for Unemployment?' he said,

> With our coal industry we have much reduced our costs.... The labour cost per ton has fallen something like thirty or forty per cent, as much as you could possibly hope for. That has plainly meant competitive wage cutting in all the European suppliers of coal. The amount of coal demanded is rather inelastic, and I think we might have been better off if we had cut wages less.
>
> Equally in the cotton textile industry it is exceedingly doubtful whether we should get any more output, appreciably more output, if we reduce prices by cutting wages. That does not dispose of the point that the cutting of wages might be useful as a means of getting people out of the industry, but that is such a hopeless game in the middle of a depression, because where would they go?[27]

While Keynes dominated the Macmillan Committee, Bevin and Reginald McKenna, the former Liberal Chancellor of the Exchequer (1915–16), played substantial roles in questioning the assumptions underlying Bank of England orthodox views. Bevin and McKenna readily agreed with Keynes on the desirability of reducing unemployment. Bevin emphasised the detrimental effect it had on consumer spending. He gave the Macmillan Committee on 21 March 1930 the example of the coal areas, where he said consumer demand was 'about 42 per cent below what it ought to be'. Without the high unemployment, there would be 'a greater demand for boots for children, and clothes and furniture and luxuries of that kind'.[28]

When Keynes gave his own evidence to the Committee on 20 February 1930 he (Keynes) argued that Britain's return to the gold standard at the old parity in 1925, followed by other countries, 'played a very considerable part' in causing the international fall in price levels. Bevin, who spoke of his experiences seeing German and American industrial production, stated that to expect British industry to make 10 per cent efficiency savings to offset the higher exchange rate was 'giving industry an impossible task'. Keynes agreed with him and added, 'To get back to equilibrium with the gold standard would have meant 10 per cent, but with the subsequent fall of world prices it has meant 20 per cent'. However, he offset part of

---

27 Donald Moggridge (ed.), *The Collected Writings of John Maynard Keynes* (London: Macmillan for the Royal Economic Society, 1973), vol. xiii, p. 373.
28 Clarke, *The Keynesian Revolution*, pp. 122, 124.

this with his guessed estimate that British industry was becoming more efficient by 1.5 per cent per annum, so 'while we were 10 per cent out in 1925 we are 12.5 per cent out now'.

To Lord Bradbury's complaint that money wages had not dropped in the mid and late 1920s as they had earlier, Bevin commented that the move down in money wages in 1921–22 owed much to the over 8 million workers on war bonuses who were subject to sliding scales which operated downwards as prices fell. Bevin said that the problem was that 'those who have been responsible for handling our finance have done it in an exclusive way, without consulting the more modern views of trade unionists and other people who have handled this [working class wages] side of the problem'. He said that the process of reducing wages should have been carried out much more slowly. Keynes pointed to his *The Economic Consequences of Mr Churchill* (1925), in which he had urged a national conference with trade union leaders to secure a reduction in money wages along with income tax rises so that other classes shared the pain.[29]

When the Macmillan Committee on 21 February 1930 discussed with Keynes his views on reforming the gold standard system, Bevin pressed that its considerations should include departure from the gold standard, given that 'the effects of the operation of the monetary system in the last four years on poor people have been very terrible'. However, Lord Macmillan said that 'the consequences of that might be too appalling to contemplate' and at that time Keynes' view was, 'I have given a great deal of thought to what one might do if we were to go off the gold standard. I do not like the look of it.'[30]

Bevin made good use of his membership of the Macmillan Committee to seek better understanding of British and international economic conditions. Like Lord Macmillan, Bevin also sought to extract explanations from the Bank of England officials and associated economists of the reasoning behind the Bank's policies. Faced with statements by the Bank's officials that they felt explaining its actions was dangerous, Bevin vigorously agreed with Keynes' observation, 'The Bank of England by its mystery ... not only retards scientific progress, but, instead of rendering itself less open to popular pressure and to dangerous charges, renders itself

---

29 'Notes of a discussion on Thursday 20 February 1930' (Macmillan Committee), in Moggridge (ed.), *The Collected Writings of John Maynard Keynes*, vol. xx, pp. 38–66, especially 57–9, 61, 65. Lord Bradbury had been Permanent Secretary to the Treasury, 1913–19, British delegate to the Reparations Commission, 1919–25, and an architect of the return to the gold standard in 1925.

30 'Notes of a discussion on Friday 21 February 1930', in Moggridge (ed.), *The Collected Writings*, vol. xx, pp. 66–93, especially pp. 91–3.

more open to those things'. Bevin joined Lord Macmillan in complaining that there should be better economic statistics available not only for the Bank but also for 'the public so that better informed criticism of its action may be brought about'. Bevin, as so often drawing on his trade union experience, added that in collective bargaining 'it is very difficult to get the correct information'.[31]

Bevin joined Keynes in signing an addendum to the main Macmillan report, believing it was otherwise incomplete. For Keynes, Bevin, McKenna, Sir Thomas Allen (of the co-operative movement) and two others, there needed to be additional changes, without which they believed 'we doubt whether it lies within the power of the banking system to restore employment to a satisfactory level'. They believed that 'greater wisdom and prudence' lay in focusing on 'constructive schemes for encouraging national trade and national development rather than on efforts to drive down the general levels of salaries and wages'. Hence they looked to 'the recovery of world prices, the revival of business optimism, the reorganisation of the older British industries and the steady increase of technical efficiency'.[32]

Bevin was joined by Sir Thomas Allen in submitting a statement of reservation to the addendum, in which they argued that if the wholesale price level did not rise internationally 'within a reasonable time' then 'national action of an emergency or short-term character should be tried'. They further stated:

> We should have preferred the course of devaluation because of the effect upon the whole of the dead-weight debt and other fixed charges, but we agree that great weight must be attached to the consideration that to endorse a de facto devaluation is easier than to devalue after a return to pre-war parity.
>
> With regard to the tariff proposal in the Addendum we take the view that, precedent to any tariff, our other recommendation for a large measure of state planning and reorganisation, particularly in the basic industries, with the provision of Transport and Power as State services, should be put into effect. Then, if the alternative remained, tariffs would be preferable to all-round reductions in wages and salaries, provided that at the same time steps were taken to safeguard the export trade and to prevent the exploitation of the consumer.

---

31 'Committee on Finance and Industry, Friday 5 December 1930', in Moggridge (ed.), *The Collected Writings*, vol. xx, pp. 263, 267–8.
32 'Addendum 1', Parliamentary Papers 1930–31 (Cmnd 3897), *Committee on Finance and Industry Report*, pp. 190–209 (quotations at 190, 208 and 209).

Bevin and Allen added that generally they did not believe in tariffs, thinking their effects to be bad. They were enthusiastic about the proposals in this addendum for capital development and a Board of National Investment.[33] Bevin's statement is notable for its support for 'a large measure of State planning and reorganisation' along with the state control or nationalisation of the transport and power sectors.

Bevin, in his and Allen's reservation to addendum 1, was again identifying the root cause of the present discontents to be the return to gold in 1925. In a pamphlet published soon after the fall of the Labour government, he and G. D. H. Cole bluntly stated,

> Ever since 1925, Great Britain has been struggling vainly against the disastrous consequences of this colossal blunder. Our troubles arose, and arise, mainly not from the fact that we went back to the gold standard, but from our folly in doing this by deflation instead of devaluation. The mistake lay in forcing the pound back to its pre-war parity, and so putting on it a value which exceeded its real worth.[34]

In this they joined Keynes.

Bevin and the TUC did not deny there was a problem of British industrial costs being too high. In their view a large part of the population had already paid for this with the wage reductions that had taken place in some sectors of the economy or by being unemployed. As aired before the Macmillan Committee, the question they raised was how to avoid these people paying again if British economic readjustment was affected by deflation. Bevin and the TUC repeatedly sought fairness for those they represented, remedies which involved genuine equality of sacrifice. In a manifesto issued immediately after the fall of the second Labour government, the Labour movement's leaders commented, 'Sacrifices by the workers are intended to be certain, sacrifices by other sections uncertain'. The manifesto then expounded views held by Bevin and Citrine: 'The proposals to economise at the expense of the poor are not only unjust but economically unsound. They will increase unemployment and aggravate the basic problem underlying the present crisis by reducing the consuming power of the masses.' Instead, drawing on Bevin's experiences on the Macmillan Committee and on the thinking behind the capital levy, the labour leaders argued for 'mobilising the country's foreign investment, by a temporary suspension of the Sinking Fund, by taxing fixed interest

---

33 'Reservation' to addendum 1, *ibid.*, pp.209–10.
34 Ernest Bevin and G. D. H. Cole, *The Crisis: What It Is, How It Arose, What To Do* (London: New Statesman and Nation, 1931), p. 18.

Labour dealing with labour

bearing securities and other unearned income which had benefitted from the fall in prices and by measures to reduce the burden of war debt'.[35]

The means to achieve equality of sacrifice was devaluation, which was unacceptable to all but Bevin and Allen on the Macmillan Committee. Keynes altered his position very late in the day, telling Ramsay MacDonald on 5 August 1931 that it was 'now nearly *certain* that we shall go off the existing gold parity at no distant date'. As Peter Clarke has observed, 'By August 1931 the choice was simple: between the orthodoxy of deflation and some form of planning.'[36]

As G. D. H. Cole noted in January 1932, there had been 'a great deal of talk about planning both inside and outside the Labour movement'.[37] Some strands of such thinking went back to at least the First World War, with the Ministry of Munitions, the rationalisation of the railways and other sectors and widespread government controls across the economy, and to some of the Liberal Party's programmes of the 1920s. Others in favour of planning were increasingly influenced by Soviet and Italian fascist planning.

Bevin also used his membership of the Economic Advisory Council to hone his economic ideas. The notion of an economic general staff had derived in part from the planning for reconstruction during and immediately after the First World War. In the 1920s it had been advocated, among others, by the Liberal Party and by Keynes. For MacDonald, the setting up of 'an economic general staff' (a phrase intended to indicate the economic equivalent of the Committee of Imperial Defence) was especially attractive, given his lack of a parliamentary majority. According to Tom Jones, Deputy Secretary to the Cabinet, MacDonald told a preliminary meeting on 9 December 1930, 'I want Labour, Capital and Economics to unite in operating an administrative organ to spur on our industries. It could be the epitome of the country's effort.' Citrine observed that 'The Trade Unionist is weighed down with a sense of insecurity' and believed that an Economic Advisory Council would help 'to create an atmosphere in

---

35 Minutes of the Joint Meeting of the General Council of the TUC, the National Executive Committee of the Labour Party and the Consultative Committee of the Parliamentary Labour Party, 26 and 27 August 1931, Bevin Papers, Churchill College Archives, Cambridge, BEVN 1/5.
36 Clarke, *The Keynsian Revolution*, p. 223.
37 Quoted in Daniel Ritschel, *The Politics of Planning: The Debate on Economic Planning in Britain in the 1930s* (Oxford: Clarendon Press, 1977), p. 98. On the background to planning in the 1930s, including Mosley's plans, see pp. 1–126, as well his chapter in the present volume (chapter 4); see also Richard Toye, *The Labour Party and the Planned Economy 1931–1951* (Woodbridge: Royal Historical Society/Boydell Press, 2003), pp. 1–64.

which employers and trade unionists together could regard the welfare of the country as a whole in a scientific spirit.'[38] The Economic Advisory Council, the first of several twentieth-century bodies set up to provide the government with economic advice, had as well as industrialists, bankers and economists, Bevin and the socialist academics G. D. H. Cole and R. H. Tawney among its non-government members.[39] Tawney, according to Margaret Cole, was complaining by mid-1930 that G. D. H. Cole as well as Keynes were 'veering towards Protection'.[40]

Bevin's presence on the Economic Advisory Council led him to join with G. D. H. and Margaret Cole in a group aiming to come up with new policies for the Labour Party. The other prominent trade unionist involved was Arthur Pugh. It was formally set up as the Society for Socialist Inquiry and Propaganda (SSIP) in January 1931, with Bevin holding the chair and Pugh as one of the vice chairs of its executive committee.[41] In its advertisements the SSIP stated,

> It believes that the present system is rapidly breaking down, and that an alternative system which will satisfy men's aspirations and reason cannot be devised unless the keen Socialists throughout the country give their time and brains to thinking it out in co-operation.

Margaret Cole later recalled of a preliminary conference in the autumn of 1930,

> The highlight (or the prize exhibit!) of the whole conference was Bevin, who took full part in all discussions, formal or informal, and enjoyed himself immensely, holding a kind of court in which he told anecdotes of the past of THE MOVEMENT – he always put it in capitals – to an admiring ring of questioners, and also displaying a grasp of economic and financial essentials which some of the younger intellectuals had scarcely thought to find in a trade union official.[42]

---

38 Susan Howson and Donald Winch, *The Economic Advisory Council 1930–39* (Cambridge: Cambridge University Press, 1977), pp. 7–95; Keith Middlemas (ed.), *Thomas Jones Whitehall Diary, Volume II: 1926–1930* (Oxford: Oxford University Press, 1969), pp. 219–22.
39 Moggridge, *Maynard Keynes*, pp. 481–2.
40 Margaret Cole, *The Life of G. D. H. Cole* (London: Macmillan, 1971), p. 168.
41 G. D. H. Cole, *A History of the Labour Party from 1914* (London: Routledge and Kegan Paul, 1948), pp. 282–4; Margaret Cole, *Growing Up Into Revolution* (London: Longmans, Green, 1949), pp. 139, 144–5; Margaret Cole, *The Story of Fabian Socialism* (London: Heinemann, 1961), pp. 222–5.
42 Margaret Cole, 'The Society for Socialist Inquiry and Propaganda', in Asa Briggs and John Saville (eds), *Essays in Labour History* (London: Croom Helm, 1977), vol. iii, pp. 190–203 (quotation at p. 196).

Labour dealing with labour 53

Bevin readily joined with G. D. H. Cole in writing the pamphlet *The Crisis*, and he gave a public lecture in December 1931 in a series put on by the SSIP, his being entitled 'The Election and the Trade Union Movement'.[43]

Bevin's journey to economic understanding had been slow and often derived from his experiences as a trade union leader. Citrine had come to a similar understanding, and as their economic views encompassed major trade union concerns, other trade unionists were thinking on similar lines or were easily convinced. While Snowden was more susceptible to bankers' arguments and more committed to free trade than MacDonald, the major divergences in views between the Labour government's Prime Minister and Chancellor of the Exchequer and the TUC leaders came as the economic crisis worsened.[44] Bevin on the Macmillan Committee had made it clear that he had started from a free trade position: 'Being a transport worker I am naturally a free trader.'[45] Bevin, as we have seen, moved away from this – and most notably so in 1930. The optimism concerning rationalisation expressed in the Mond–Turner talks and at the TUC dwindled fast as rationalisation led to huge numbers becoming unemployed. TUC leaders, including Bevin, soon found that MacDonald and the government could not, or were unwilling to, discriminate between those unemployed through rationalisation schemes and those out of work for other reasons. Hopes that employers would help those made redundant through rationalisation soon evaporated, not least when in February 1931 the National Confederation of Employers' Organisations publicly called on the government to cut public expenditure, with unemployment benefits to be cut by a third.[46]

With the severity of the 1930–31 economic conditions eliminating the likelihood of 'cosy co-operation' with the employers, Bevin, Citrine and other trade union leaders looked to the state and planning to respond

---

43 Bullock, *The Life and Times of Ernest Bevin*, pp. 502–3.
44 See in particular Duncan Tanner, 'Political leadership, intellectual debate and economic policy during the second Labour government, 1929–1931', in E. H. Green and D. M. Tanner (eds), *The Strange Survival of Liberal England: Political Leaders, Moral Values and the Reception of Economic Debate* (Cambridge: Cambridge University Press, 2007), pp. 113–50, especially pp. 120–4.
45 On 28 February 1930, in Moggridge (ed.), *The Collected Writings*, vol, xx, p. 113.
46 Gordon Phillips, 'Trade unions and corporatist politics: the response of the TUC to industrial rationalisation, 1927–33', in P. J. Waller, *Politics and Social Change in Modern Britain: Essays Presented to A. F. Thompson* (Brighton: Harvester Press, 1987), pp. 192–212, especially pp. 199–205. For more of a focus on unemployment see Sidney Pollard, 'Trade union reactions to the economic crisis', *Journal of Contemporary History*, 4:4 (1969), pp. 101–15.

positively to industries needing to be rationalised. This was to be the means to both efficiency and fairness. The 1931 Labour Party manifesto on key economic issues moved a very long way from that of 1929. On the banking system it declared,

> The Labour Party is convinced, in the light particularly of experience since 1925, that the banking and credit system of the country can no longer be left in private hands.
> It must be brought under national ownership and control.
> The Labour Party further is convinced of the need to form a National Investment Board with statutory powers for the control of domestic and foreign investment.

As for industry, it stated,

> The Labour Party demands efficiency. Any special assistance to industry must be conditional upon the acceptance of the necessary measure of public ownership or control.
> Labour will insist upon the adoption of efficient methods of production so as to secure good conditions of employment for the worker.
> The consumer must be protected by effective regulation of prices.[47]

Bevin and Citrine played the leading roles in evolving a number of alternative economic policies to those held dear by Snowden and, to a lesser extent, by MacDonald. As Philip Williamson has observed, by 1931 'Bevin had become sufficiently confident about monetary questions to doubt that the crisis would result in financial "disaster", and consequently was willing to risk devaluation.' While noting that 'the TUC's thinking was ordered by its sense of social justice', his magisterial account of the politics of national economic crisis is nevertheless severe on the TUC. As Labour Party leader, Henderson, for instance, is castigated for 'capitulating' to the TUC.[48] However, it is quite possible to believe that the level of cuts to be enforced on those among the poorest in society was not essential to managing the economic crisis and that, in part, MacDonald and Snowden 'capitulated' to the forces of economic orthodoxy.

---

47 Labour Party, *Labour's Call to Action* (London, 1931).
48 Philip Williamson, *National Crisis and National Government: British Politics, the Economy and Empire, 1926–1932* (Cambridge: Cambridge University Press, 1992), especially pp. 65, 312–17.

4

Why was there no Keynesian revolution under the second Labour government? A reassessment of Sir Oswald Mosley's alternative economic agenda in 1930–31

DANIEL RITSCHEL

In one highly influential historiographical narrative, the second Labour government stands indicted for thoughtlessly spurning the Keynesian prescription for reflating the collapsing national economy in the crisis of 1930–31. Sir Oswald Mosley, a junior minister who resigned in a dramatic protest against the government's lethargic response, is usually cast in the role of the lone champion of the Keynesian alternative within the MacDonald administration. Mosley's dissident economic platform is depicted as a realistic and feasible option at the time, and a prescient anticipation of the Keynesian economic paradigm behind the social-democratic settlement of the post-war years. The Labour government is thus condemned not only for its own paralysis of will and eventual collapse, but also for thwarting the birth of the progressive economic consensus that the nation (and the Labour Party) would only slowly rediscover over the course of the next decade. Mosley, on the other hand, is portrayed as the tragic 'lost leader' who sacrificed his career by challenging the unimaginative stance of the Labour leadership.[1]

---

1 The classic statement of this thesis may be found in Robert Skidelsky, *Politicians and the Slump: The Labour Government of 1929–1931* (London: Macmillan, 1967) and his *Oswald Mosley* (London: Macmillan, 1975). See also N. Riddell, *Labour in Crisis: The Second Labour Government 1929–1931* (Manchester: Manchester University Press, 1999), pp. 228–9; Peter Clarke, *Hope and Glory* (Harmondsworth: Penguin Books, 1997), pp. 142, 154–5; Noel Thompson, *Political Economy and the Labour Party: The Economics of Democratic Socialism* (London: UCL Press, 1996), pp. 79–86; R. Thurlow, *Fascism in Britain: A History, 1918–1985* (Oxford: Basil Blackwell, 1987), pp. 30–6; D. Marquand, *Ramsay MacDonald* (London: Jonathon Cape, 1977), pp. 474–81, 518–21, 554.

This is a deeply problematic interpretation, not least because Mosley began speculating privately about his turn to the 'continental movement' within six months of his resignation, and declared publicly for fascism only a couple of months after the fall of the Labour government.[2] The usual explanation for this abrupt turn is that it was his extreme frustration at having his ideas rejected by the Labour government and party that, together with a brood of his own personal demons, drove him out of conventional politics.[3] That may be so, and this chapter will not engage with such psychological speculation. However, what is troubling is that the view of Mosley as a 'pioneer Keynesian' is invariably accompanied by the belief that he carried those very same economic ideas straight into his ideology of British fascism. As Robert Skidelsky explains: 'Mosley was a disciple of Keynes in the 1920s; and Keynesianism was his great contribution to fascism.'[4] We are thus left with the implication that the Labour government ought to have accepted a set of policy proposals that were soon to feature as the centre-piece of British fascism. We may accept this interpretation as an illustration of a truly remarkable ideological flexibility that would have made Keynesian economics suitable for application across nearly the entire contemporary ideological spectrum. Alternatively, we are compelled to consider the possibility that the identification of Mosley as a Keynesian may be mistaken, and that we need to think again about the nature of his economics. This chapter will pursue the latter path, by exploring the sources of Mosley's economic ideas in the 1920s, their relationship to the economics of Keynes and position within the Labour political culture, and their role in his turn to fascism. To put it more concisely, what were the economics of the rebellious Labour minister who would so soon re-emerge as the leader of the British Union of Fascists in the 1930s?

The proposition that Mosley was a 'pioneer Keynesian' is generally taken from Skidelsky's influential argument that the expansionist economics elaborated by Mosley in the 1920s and early '30s represented a distinctively Keynesian approach in the otherwise barren policy cupboard of the MacDonald Labour Party. Yet this widely accepted interpretation

---

2   See Oswald Mosley, 'Private and confidential', 30 October 1930, Garvin Papers, Harry Ransom Center, University of Texas, Austin; *The Times*, 15 November 1930; Oswald Mosley, 'Have we a policy?', *Action*, 24 December 1931, pp. 1–2.
3   See Skidelsky, *Oswald Mosley*, pp. 244, 290; Thurlow, *Fascism in Britain*, pp. 30–6, 93.
4   Skidelsky, *Oswald Mosley*, p. 302. See also M. Pugh, *'Hurrah for the Blackshirts!' Fascists and Fascism in Britain Between the Wars* (London: Jonathan Cape, 2006), p. 198; T. Linehan, *British Fascism, 1918–39: Parties, Ideology and Culture* (Manchester: Manchester University Press, 2000), pp. 84–5; Thurlow, *Fascism in Britain*, pp. 146–7, 152; R. Benewick, *The Fascist Movement in Britain* (London: Allen Lane, 1972), p. 62.

rests on extremely shaky grounds. First, there is precious little evidence that Mosley either read Keynes or had any direct contact with the Cambridge economist outside of occasional London dinner parties.[5] Secondly, though Mosley was later happy to accept this attribution in his own efforts to rehabilitate his image, he also insisted at the time and subsequently that his proposals differed fundamentally from, and took him well 'beyond', Keynesian economics.[6] Finally, the underlying premise that Keynes alone offered constructive ideas in the 1920s does great injustice to the richness and diversity of the contemporary policy debate.[7] Indeed, though Mosley (as any other contemporary critic of economic orthodoxy) was certainly influenced by Keynes, a closer look shows that he drew liberally on a number of other ideas and sources, most notably the lively debate on socialist economics he encountered within the Independent Labour Party (ILP) in the mid-1920s.

A socialist apprenticeship

Mosley was a young war veteran and glamorous aristocrat when he first entered Parliament in 1918 as a Unionist supporter of the Lloyd George coalition. He soon grew disillusioned with the broken promises of the coalition government and left its ranks in 1920. After a brief spell as an

---

5 The evidence on Mosley's relationship with Keynes is vague and contradictory. Skidelsky tells us that Keynes had little or no contact with Mosley and that Mosley had not read any of Keynes' major works, though he speculates that Mosley may have read Keynes' popular journalism. See, respectively, Robert Skidelsky, *John Maynard Keynes, Volume II: The Economist as Saviour, 1920–1937* (London: Macmillan 1992), p. 246, and Skidelsky, *Oswald Mosley*, p. 133. Nicholas Mosley, on the other hand, claims that his father had read *The Tract* on his trip to India in the winter of 1924–25 – Nicholas Mosley, *Rules of the Game: Sir Oswald and Lady Cynthia Mosley, 1896–1933* (London: Secker and Warburg, 1982), p. 59. Yet Mosley himself tells us that his encounter with Keynesian economics was 'more in conversation with him than in reading his early writings' – Oswald Mosley, *My Life* (London: Nelson, 1968), p. 178.
6 Oswald Mosley, *Revolution by Reason: An Account of the Birmingham Proposals, Together with an Analysis of the Financial Policy of the Present Government Which Has Led to Their Great Attack Upon Wages* (London: Blackfriars Press, 1925), pp. 11, 12, 14; Mosley, *My Life*, pp. 179, 182, 202. John Strachey, his close collaborator in the 1920s, maintained similarly that their economics took them 'along a road which Mr. Keynes might be unwilling to travel'. John Strachey, *Revolution by Reason: An Account of the Financial Proposals Submitted to the Labour Movement by Mr. Oswald Mosley* (London: Parsons, 1925), p. 53.
7 See P. Williamson, *National Crisis and National Government: British Politics, the Economy and Empire, 1926–1932* (Cambridge: Cambridge University Press, 1992), pp. 13–14.

Independent and a short flirtation with the opposition Liberals, he joined the Labour Party in 1924. His point of entry was through the ILP, and coincided with his growing preoccupation with the post-war slump and related issues of economic policy. Mosley was clearly drawn to the ferment of policy ideas within the ILP and its self-appointed role as the intellectual vanguard of the labour movement. Upon joining, he listed 'the researches of its constructive thinkers', with their 'concrete conceptions of scientific remedies' for Britain's economic ills, as the main attraction of the labour movement.[8] Certainly, though he was to prove extremely selective in his application of socialist economics, much of his own subsequent agenda can be traced back directly to this early context.

The 1920s were a remarkably fertile period for the ILP, as the party engaged in an ambitious rethinking of socialist economic strategy in response to the post-war slump.[9] This response may be divided into three broad categories. The first was based on J. A. Hobson's under-consumptionist critique of capitalism, which traced the violent fluctuations of the trade cycle to the endemic shortfall of purchasing power within the economy due to the uneven distribution of wealth inherent in the capitalist wage system. The remedy was to secure a redistribution of income by means of progressive taxation and higher wages for the working class. As early as 1923, this argument was deployed by the ILP in support of the demand for a 'living wage', a policy theme that was to become the mainstay of its propaganda throughout the decade. For the ILP, the great attraction of the 'living wage' was that it could serve as both a recovery policy to stimulate consumer demand and a political rallying cry to mobilise the working class behind the demand for reconstitution of the economy on socialist lines.[10]

In addition to the under-consumptionist thesis, the ILP debate also featured a sophisticated monetary critique of the post-war attempt to re-establish the gold standard. Here, the slump was attributed to the restriction of credit brought about by the deflationist strategy adopted to drive the pound sterling to the pre-war rate of exchange. In a prolonged discussion of monetary policy between 1923 and 1925, the ILP proponents

---

8 *New Leader*, 11 April and 10 October 1924.
9 See D. Howell, *MacDonald's Party: Labour Identities and Crisis 1922–1931* (Oxford: Oxford University Press, 2002); F. M. Leventhal, *The Last Dissenter: H. N. Brailsford and His World* (Oxford: Oxford University Press, 1985); R. E. Dowse, *Left in the Centre: The Independent Labour Party, 1893–1940* (London: Longmans, Green, 1966).
10 See C. Allen, F. Brockway and E. E. Hunter, *The Socialist Programme: The Constructive Proposals of the Independent Labour Party* (London: ILP, 1923); H. N. Brailsford, J. A. Hobson, A. Creech-Jones and E. F. Wise, *The Living Wage* (London, ILP, 1926); ILP, *The Living Income* (London, 1929).

A reassessment of Mosley's alternative economic agenda 59

of this explanation called for an expansion of bank credit in order to restore monetary demand to the slumping economy. Their ideas on 'socialist credit policy' went substantially beyond the work of the more conventional critics of official monetary policy.[11] At a time when Keynes, Ralph Hawtrey and Reginald McKenna were calling at most for an active bank rate strategy to maintain stable domestic prices, and Keynes suggested only in 1924 that public investment may be needed as a one-time 'jolt' to break the spell of the slump, the ILP's own 'monetary reformers' proposed as early as 1923 that the slump could be cured by a deliberate infusion of additional credit into the economy.[12] Moreover, in a distinctive twist that would later attract Mosley, their version of 'socialist credit control' sought to combine the monetary critique with the under-consumptionist strategy, calling for the distribution of the new credit directly to the working class through a variety of instruments, including social services, public works and credits advanced by the state to industries that could not pay the 'living wage' before their reorganisation.[13] Equally novel was the suggestion that both output and employment could thereafter be managed by monetary and fiscal policy by means of 'vigilant and almost imperceptible alterations of inflation and deflation'.[14] Though this new line of thought encountered strong internal resistance, and the ILP eventually shied away from its more dramatic 'inflationist' recommendations, the early discussions of monetary policy were to serve as a major influence on Mosley.[15]

The third important strand of ILP thought on the economy focused on the idea of centralised planning of trade and industry. Drawing on the experience of wartime controls by some of its own leading thinkers who

---

11 See Skidelsky, *John Maynard Keynes, Volume II*, pp. 153–70; L. J. Hume, 'The gold standard and deflation: issues and attitudes in the nineteen-twenties', *Economica*, 30:110 (1963), pp. 225–42; K. Hancock, 'Unemployment and the economists in the 1920s', *Economica*, 27:108 (1960), pp. 305–21.
12 See Allen *et al.*, *The Socialist Programme*, pp. 25–28, 11; H. N. Brailsford, 'Labour and the Bank', *New Leader*, 13 July 1923; H. N. Brailsford, 'The keys to power', *New Leader*, 21 September 1923; ILP statement, 'How to deal with unemployment', *New Leader*, 5 October 1923.
13 'Realist', 'How banks make unemployment', *New Leader*, 28 September 1923; 'Poverty and unemployment', *New Leader*, 29 August 1924; *New Leader*, 19 October 1924; H. N. Brailsford, 'The living wage', *New Leader*, 29 May 1925. See also ILP motion on 'scientific regulation of credit' in Labour Party, *Report of the 24th Annual Conference* (London, 1924), pp. 160–1, 165–6.
14 H. N. Brailsford in *New Leader*, 19 October 1923; ILP resolution on 'Unemployment' in ILP, *Report of the Annual Conference* (London, 1925), p. 73.
15 For the ILP's far more moderate approach to monetary policy, which came to focus mainly on the maintenance of stable prices, see Brailsford *et al.*, *The Living Wage*, pp. 13–19.

had served as administrators during the war, the ILP developed by the mid-1920s an elaborate design for a planned economy that foreshadowed much of the socialist thinking on the subject in the inter-war period. As early as 1922, the ILP constitution called for a 'central body, representative of the people' to oversee industry and 'decide the amount and character of communal production and service necessary'.[16] By the following year, this became a 'Committee on Production', with powers to institute a 'complete national stocktaking' and to manage trade and government orders 'so as to regulate demand for labour'.[17] Discussions in 1923–24 introduced the subject of 'regulated trade' through import control boards and bulk purchases agreements for foodstuffs and essential commodities.[18] Increasingly, the notion of planning focused on the tasks both of distributing resources in line with social priorities and of aligning the aggregate factors of production, investment and consumption. One early contributor to the debate described the objective as 'centralised control of production and distribution ... to meet the real needs as ascertained by centralised statistics'.[19] By 1925, an ILP pamphlet drafted by G. D. H. Cole called for a 'Central Board of Control' to allocate resources, industrial production, investment and manpower in order to 'ensure a balanced and socially desirable development in every field of industry'.[20] This culminated in a 1926 ILP report entitled *The Industrial Aspects of Socialism*, which charged a 'National Industrial Commission' with the task of aligning 'productive capacity to public requirements', including allocation of manpower, investment, trade, wages and prices.[21] While this dimension of the ILP programme has been overshadowed by the under-consumptionist strategy of the 'living wage', the party was clearly developing an ambitious vision of a planned economy. As H. N. Brailsford, one of the leading contributors to the proposals, explained at the time: 'Socialism means equality, but it also means national planning'.[22]

---

16 ILP, *Report of the Annual Conference* (London, 1923), p. 151.
17 *New Leader*, 5 October 1923.
18 ILP, *A Socialist Policy for Agriculture* (London, 1924); H. N. Brailsford, 'The state as middleman', *New Leader*, 27 June 1924, p. 9; 'Realist', 'The British farmer and world markets', *Socialist Review*, March 1925, pp. 100–16; H. N. Brailsford, *Socialism for To-day* (London: ILP, 1925), pp. 99–102.
19 E. M. H. Lloyd, 'Monetary policy: notes for discussion only', not dated but 1923, Lloyd Papers, British Library of Political and Economic Science, London, 7/14. See also Allen et al., *The Socialist Programme*, pp. 21–4; Brailsford, *Socialism for To-day*.
20 G. D. H. Cole, *Industrial Policy for Socialists* (London: ILP, 1925).
21 See 'The industrial aspects of socialism', *Socialist Review*, November 1925, pp. 193–202.
22 H. N. Brailsford, 'Through prosperity to socialism', *New Leader*, 8 October 1926, p. 9. Richard Toye has suggested recently that the ILP had not developed a mature concept

Mosley's version

It is at the intersection of these three strategies within the ILP that we can find the origins of Mosley's own attempt to 'weld together the Socialist case with modern monetary theory'.[23] He readily acknowledged the assistance of the 'many leading economists of the Socialist movement', and his ideas certainly confirm this influence.[24] In the 'Birmingham Proposals', unveiled first at the ILP annual conference in April 1925 and published later in the same year as the pamphlet *Revolution by Reason*, Mosley sought to fuse the under-consumptionist and monetary lines of analysis. He identified deflation, with its disastrous consequences of mass unemployment and working-class poverty, as the prime factor behind the crisis of underconsumption that had brought the post-war economy to its knees: 'The trouble is the working-class has no "effective demand".'[25] His remedy also echoed earlier proposals within the ILP, calling for an expansion of bank credit, designed specifically to restart the stalled economic engine by stimulating consumer demand. The first step in Mosley's strategy was to be a special issue of 'consumers' credits', to be disbursed directly to the low-paid and unemployed: 'The first essential of any Socialist planning is to see that the new money goes into the right hands.'[26] Once the economy was on the way to recovery, further injections of additional consumer demand were to be administered (as in the ILP's 'living wage' programme) through state-mandated, incremental wage increases. The higher wages were to be financed initially by 'producers' credits', offered by the state banking system to cash-strapped employers; eventually, they were to be supported out of the growing revenue earned by industry in the rapidly expanding economy. In response to criticism that his scheme would be dangerously inflationary, Mosley insisted that inflation could be avoided

---

of economic planning. See Toye, *The Labour Party and the Planned Economy 1931–1951* (Woodbridge: Royal Historical Society/Boydell Press, 2003), pp. 29–31. However, his argument rests on a definition of Soviet-style planning that would also exclude all other inter-war variants of socialist planning outside of the Communist Party of Great Britain. For more positive accounts of the ILP idea of 'planning', see D. Ritschel, *The Politics of Planning: The Debate on Economic Planning in Britain in the 1930s* (Oxford: Clarendon Press, 1997), pp. 32–3; A. Oldfield, 'The Independent Labour Party and planning, 1920–26', *International Review of Social History*, 21:1 (1976), pp. 1–29.

23 Mosley, *Revolution by Reason*, p. 5.
24 *Ibid.* See also Mosley, *My Life*, pp. 182, 185; John Strachey, *Revolution by Reason*, p. xi.
25 Mosley, *Revolution by Reason*, p. 8.
26 *Ibid.*, p. 12.

if central controls ensured that the new levels of consumer demand in the economy were met by proportionate increases in industrial output.[27]

Such controls were to take the form of 'socialist planning'. Here again Mosley drew on the rich seam of existing ideas within the ILP. A central 'Economic Council', armed with statutory powers over industry and the banking system, was to regulate wages, prices, trade, investment and output levels. The goal was to ensure that steadily rising levels of purchasing power were matched by parallel increases in supply for the growing consumer market: 'The business of this Council will be to estimate the difference between the actual and potential production of the country and to plan the stages by which the potential production can be evoked through the instrument of working-class demand.'[28] The ultimate aim was not merely to relieve unemployment or control inflation, but to mobilise what Mosley described as 'the maximum productivity of the nation'. Mosley was clearly fascinated by the 'vast possibilities of potential production' that were opened up by what he described as an 'invincible alliance of working-class demand with Socialist planning'. He calculated that a combination of current idle capacity and technological improvements since the war left immediate room for as much as 30 per cent growth in gross national income: 'What results might be achieved, if we could mobilise this latent productive capacity!'[29]

In short, relying heavily on available socialist thought, Mosley offered a productivist vision of a high-wage economy, driven to its maximum capacity by central planning of credit, purchasing power and industrial production. In later years and subsequent iterations of his economics, Mosley was to add to and adjust these ideas, but not substantially modify the central thrust of his original vision. One important alteration, unveiled most famously in the Mosley Memorandum of 1930, consisted of the substitution of loan-financed national development projects for the original expedient of 'consumers' credits'. This was undoubtedly influenced by the Keynesian Liberal programme of 1929, but it is important to note that the Memorandum depicted public investment as but a short-term recovery strategy required to re-charge the slumping system before the more fundamental steps towards the planned, high-wage economy were implemented. Significantly, Mosley recommended large-scale public works on the grounds that, by reducing the surplus of unemployed workers

---

27 *Ibid.*, pp. 11–19. See also *The Times*, 20 April 1925; *Birmingham Town Crier*, 19 June 1925.
28 *Ibid.*, pp. 14–16, 19–27.
29 *Ibid.*, pp. 16, 15, 22, 15.

in the labour market, they would facilitate the turn to higher wages by strengthening the bargaining position of the trade unions.[30]

By the time of his open rebellion against the Labour government following his resignation in May 1930, Mosley had also embraced 'trade regulation' or 'scientific protection'. This culminated with his call for 'Commonwealth insulation' in October 1930. Though this has often been interpreted as a move into the Tory protectionist camp, both the rationale and the mechanics of Mosley's 'insulation' drew on the well established school of socialist protectionism within the post-war ILP. In line with such ideas, Mosley rejected the Conservative reliance on tariffs in favour of the 'scientific' methods of commodity boards, licensing of imports and bulk purchase agreements, all developed earlier within the ILP as part of the larger armoury of socialist planning. His conclusion that the insulation of the home market could be extended to include the Commonwealth and Empire also had strong socialist antecedents. In fact, like earlier proposals within the ILP, Mosley's protectionism was linked directly to the goal of a high-wage economy and was meant to safeguard rising domestic standards against low-wage competition from abroad.[31] In return for protection, industry was to accept 'national economic planning' of wages, prices and production levels, and retool its production lines for the expanding home market: 'If the power of the State, which represents the whole community, is to be used ... to protect the manufacturer, the State has the right to ensure that this protection shall benefit the worker as well as the employer ... each year, as production increases, ought to see an equivalent rise in the standard of life of the worker.'[32]

The administrative requirements of 'national planning' also served to justify Mosley's last significant addition to his platform in 1930–31:

---

30 See Ritschel, *The Politics of Planning*, p. 61.
31 On ILP advocacy of closer economic ties with the Commonwealth, see ILP, *Socialism and the Empire* (London, 1926); E. F. Wise, 'A socialist Commonwealth of Nations', *New Leader*, 5 November 1926; H. N. Brailsford, 'Socialism and the Empire', *New Leader*, 19 June 1925; E. F. Wise, 'Labour and free trade', *New Leader*, 18 January 1929. On the protectionist school within the ILP and the Labour Party in the 1920s, see D. M. Tanner, 'Political leadership, intellectual debate and economic policy during the second Labour government', in E. H. H. Green and D. M. Tanner (eds), *The Strange Survival of Liberal England: Political Leaders, Moral Values and the Reception of Economic Debate* (Cambridge: Cambridge University Press, 2007), pp. 122–4, 138–9; D. Howell, *A Lost Left: Three Studies in Socialism and Nationalism* (Manchester: Manchester University Press, 1986); R. W. D. Boyce, *British Capitalism at the Crossroads: 1919–1932* (Cambridge: Cambridge University Press, 1987), pp. 83–90.
32 A. Young, J. Strachey, W. J. Brown and A. Bevan, *A National Policy: An Account of the Emergency Programme Advanced by Sir Oswald Mosley, M.P.* (London: Macmillan, 1931), pp. 17, 22–3.

his dramatic call for an overhaul of government and parliamentary procedure. An 'emergency Cabinet' of five ministers without portfolio was to direct national policy by Orders in Council, while Parliament was to retain only 'general control' through its power to censure and dismiss the government. Depicted as a vital corollary to national reconstruction and planning, the reforms were designed to allow for swift decisions and forceful action by freeing the executive from parliamentary delays and obstruction: 'any programme of fundamental national reconstruction is impossible of fulfilment with the present Parliament and Governmental machine'.[33] Although there had been earlier calls within the ILP for similar use of emergency powers by a socialist government, it is fair to say that this was the one significant instance where Mosley anticipated, rather than followed, left-wing thought, which was to turn to such ideas in earnest only after the experience of the 1931 crisis.[34]

Despite the attention paid to the new elements of Keynesian public investment, imperial insulation and authoritarian reform of the machinery of government, it must be kept in mind that it was the original idea of a high-wage economy, pushed to its maximum capacity by central planning of consumption and output, that was to remain at the heart of Mosley's economic thought. As he told his Birmingham constituents during the 1929 general election: 'Higher wages and greater purchasing power are the bases upon which permanent industrial prosperity must rest'.[35] The 'Mosley Manifesto' made a similar case in December 1930: 'The home market must be the future basis of British trade, and that home market depends on the high purchasing power of the people, which in turn depends on high wages.'[36] The New Party's *National Policy* offered the same equation in March 1931: 'The raising of the standard of life of our own people, the consequent increase of their purchasing power, and the organisation of our productive resources and the mobilisation of our idle workers to meet that increase, these are the true remedies.'[37] In *The Greater Britain*, published two years later as the opening salvo of British

---

33 *Ibid.*, pp. 45–8. See also 'Mosley Manifesto' in *The Times*, 8 December 1930.
34 For earlier suggestions, see Cole, *Industrial Policy for Socialists*, pp. 30–1; James Maxton, 'How I would use the E.P.A.', *New Leader*, 5 November 1926. More generally, ILP proposals for parliamentary reform in the 1920s focused on speeding up legislative procedure by delegating decisions to a committee system. For the more radical socialist schemes after 1930, see Harold Laski, 'The prospects of constitutional government', *Political Quarterly*, 1:3 (1930), pp. 307–25; Sir S. Cripps, *Can Socialism Come by Constitutional Methods?* (London: Socialist League, 1933).
35 *Birmingham Town Crier*, 24 May 1929.
36 *The Times*, 8 December 1930.
37 Young *et al.*, *A National Policy*, p. 15.

fascism, the principal economic goal was to 'raise the standard of life and the purchasing power of the people to the point adequate to absorb the surplus production of present industrial machinery in the home market.'[38] Five years later, the British Union of Fascists continued to highlight the centrally planned, high-wage economy as the centre-piece of the fascist 'economics of plenty'.[39]

A 'pioneer Keynesian'?

How 'Keynesian' was this programme? The link with Keynes rests primarily on the oft-repeated contention that, alone in the Labour Party, Mosley sought a growth-oriented monetary policy rather than the traditional socialist approach of redistribution.[40] There is no doubt, of course, that Mosley's radical departure in the mid-1920s lay partly in his suggestion that monetary credit could be employed to boost consumer demand and thereby to draw out new production, and that inflation would not be a problem until the economy reached its maximum capacity. This in some ways anticipated Keynes' own theory of effective demand by nearly a decade, and constitutes the grounds for Skidelsky's praise of what he calls Mosley's Keynesian 'flash of intuition'.[41] The problem is that this attribution overlooks not only the roots of Mosley's ideas in the earlier discussion on 'socialist credit control' within the ILP, but also that his productivist vision of using monetary credit to stimulate progressive economic growth was simply not shared by Keynes himself at the time. In the depths of the post-war slump in the mid-1920s, Keynes had urged a reversal of prevailing deflationary policy, and even suggested that some expansion of credit and an accompanying rise in prices would be necessary as the economy returned to prosperity. He also came to argue for the deployment of the new credit in loan-financed public works as a way of breaking the entrenched mood of business pessimism. Yet he remained reluctant to recommend such expedients as regular features of monetary policy, and

---

38 Oswald Mosley, *The Greater Britain* (London: British Union of Fascists, 1932), p. 103.
39 'The home market will be expanded by a scientific wage system which equates purchasing power with the power to produce.' A. K. Chesterton, *Oswald Mosley* (London: Action Press, 1936), p. 142.
40 Skidelsky, *Politicians and the Slump*, pp. 42–66, 426–9, and *Oswald Mosley*, pp. 138–41, 150–55, 223; Marquand, *Ramsay MacDonald*, p. 478; Alan Booth and Melvyn Pack, *Employment, Capital, and Economic Policy: Britain, 1918–1939* (London: Wiley-Blackwell, 1985), p. 23; D. S. Lewis, *Illusions of Grandeur: Mosley, Fascism and British Society, 1931–81* (Manchester: Manchester University Press, 1987), p. 12.
41 Skidelsky, *John Maynard Keynes, Volume II*, pp. 246–7.

his more general advice focused consistently on using bank rate policy to *stabilise* domestic prices and employment.[42] The distinction was subtle, and even Keynes met with accusations of 'inflationism', but he himself rejected as an 'inflationist fallacy' the suggestion from both the ILP and Mosley that continuous growth in the economy could be stimulated by regular infusions of monetary credit.[43]

The identification of Mosley as a Keynesian also misses the diametrically opposed positions adopted by the two men on the key issue of high wages. It is well known that Keynes' resistance to the gold standard rested on his complaint that the pursuit of the pre-war exchange rate relied on an impracticable and politically destabilising attempt to reduce money wages. However, Keynes never suggested that the solution to the resulting slump lay in *higher* wages, and was dismissive of explanations that traced the depression to deficiency of consumer demand. For Keynes, the slump was a problem of insufficient private investment, due in large measure to the inflation of labour costs brought about by the return to gold at the pre-war rate of exchange. Thus, where Mosley saw his Keynes-style national development programme in the Memorandum as the first step towards the high-wage economy, nearly all of the policy options Keynes himself laid out before the Macmillan Committee in the same year involved alternative ways of achieving reductions in money wages in a manner less disruptive than deflation.[44] At the same time, he vehemently rejected the idea of higher wages as a wrong-headed recovery strategy that would further depress private investment by placing British exports at a competitive disadvantage and driving capital overseas: 'If we want to better the condition of the working class, it is inexpedient to attempt to do it by the method which reduces the rewards of capital below what is attainable in other countries.'[45]

Mosley, of course, sought to guard against the potentially negative consequences of higher labour costs with the physical controls of central economic planning. Planning was to support the upward spiral of his

---

42 *Ibid.*, pp. 153–170; S. Howson and D. E. Moggridge, 'Keynes on monetary policy, 1910–1946', *Oxford Economic Papers*, 26 (1974), pp. 231–7; Hancock, 'Unemployment and the economists in the 1920s', pp. 308–9.
43 See Keynes to J. Strachey, 9 January 1926, Keynes Papers, King's College, Cambridge, JMK/CO/11/191–192; Keynes to H. N. Brailsford, 27 October 1926, Keynes Papers, JMK/CO/1/100-1. See also Skidelsky, *John Maynard Keynes, Volume II*, pp. 246–7.
44 See Donald Moggridge (ed.), *The Collected Writings of John Maynard Keynes* (London: Macmillan/Cambridge University Press for the Royal Economic Society, 1981), vol. xx, pp. 99–148. See also Booth and Pack, *Employment, Capital, and Economic Policy*, p. 176.
45 Keynes, 'The question of high wages' (1930), in Moggridge, *The Collected Writings of John Maynard Keynes*, vol. xx, pp. 9–16.

high-wage economy by ensuring that the higher costs of production due to higher labour costs were counter-balanced by higher rates of production made possible by the enlarged domestic mass market generated by the higher wage rates. It is here that we find the most dramatic chasm separating Mosley from Keynes. Borrowing from socialist sources, Mosley had crafted a radical scheme for a command economy in direct control of all the major factors of production, consumption and trade. Although, as we shall see, he offered this strategy as a pragmatic alternative to the conventional socialist demands for redistribution and public ownership, even sympathetic observers were taken aback by its radical collectivist implications. J. A. Hobson, for instance, concluded that Mosley's ideas on planning would necessitate 'a measure of control amounting to complete ownership and management of the entire industrial system on the part of the State'.[46] Less sympathetic non-socialist critics complained that his 'bureaucratic machinery of industrial and trade controls' would lead to 'political control' over the economy and socialist-style 'dictatorship through bureaucracy'.[47]

Such ideas obviously took Mosley more than a few steps beyond the position occupied by Keynes in the 1920s. The latter may have been one of the more prominent critics of the assumptions of *laissez-faire*, but he never suggested that the market should be eliminated, nor did he endorse permanent state controls. On the micro-economic level, he favoured large-scale cartels and combinations in private industry as self-regulating alternatives to state controls or intervention.[48] On the macro-level, Keynes championed an active bank rate policy to stabilise prices and employment. Once the return to the gold standard had severely limited the scope of monetary policy, he turned to the 'drastic remedy' of state investment in a national development programme. However, this remedy was for Keynes only a temporary expedient, meant as a one-time stimulant to start a 'cumulative wave of prosperity'.[49] His interventionism in the 1920s was thus a carefully circumscribed affair, meant to restore, not displace, the market economy. Indeed, Keynes was deeply repelled by the economic

---

46 J. A. Hobson, *New Leader*, 27 November 1925.
47 See Ritschel, *The Politics of Planning*, pp. 77–83.
48 See Moggridge, *The Collected Writings of John Maynard Keynes*, vol. ix, pp. 288–90, and vol. xix, pp. 578–637; Skidelsky, *John Maynard Keynes, Volume II*, pp. 258–71, 437–8; D. E. Moggridge, *Maynard Keynes: An Economist's Biography* (London: Routledge, 1992), pp. 449–59; M. Freeden, *Liberalism Divided: A Study in British Political Thought, 1914–1939* (Oxford: Oxford University Press, 1986), pp. 137–42.
49 See Moggridge, *The Collected Writings of John Maynard Keynes*, vol. xix, pp. 219–23, 761–6, and vol. xx, pp. 146–7.

authoritarianism implicit in all ideas of 'state planning', and the alternative of macro-economic demand management that he was to evolve in the next decade was designed deliberately as an alternative to the sort of state-directed command economy envisioned by Mosley and later 'planners'. His goal was to 'modify and condition the environment within which the individual freely operates' without 'superseding the individual' or 'hampering the liberty and the independence of the private person'.[50] In short, Mosley diverged sharply from the Keynesian paradigm, not only on the technical grounds of policy, but also on fundamental ideological principles.

A left-wing socialist?

If Mosley was not a Keynesian, may we then identify his pre-fascist position as that of a left-wing socialist? There is, in fact, some support for what have sometimes been called the 'left-wing roots' of his fascism.[51] As we have seen, Mosley developed his early ideas within the context of the ILP debate on economic policy in the mid-1920s, and he continued to be active within the ILP throughout the decade. He served on a number of its policy committees, campaigned energetically to persuade the party to adopt his strategy for credit expansion, secured election to the ILP's National Administrative Committee in 1927 and 1928, and was even rumoured to be preparing to challenge James Maxton for the ILP chairmanship early in 1929.[52] Mosley also aligned closely with left-wing critics of the MacDonald leadership in their campaign late in the decade to persuade the party to commit to a 'short programme' of specific socialist measures.[53] Following his resignation from the government in May 1930, he drew his support in the party mostly from the ranks of the left, including John Strachey, Aneurin Bevan, W. J. Brown and A. J. Cook. At the time, the *Manchester Guardian* located him on the 'left centre' of the Labour Party, and this was generally accepted by many who occupied that

---

50 See Keynes, 'State planning' (1931), in Moggridge, *The Collected Writings of John Maynard Keynes*, vol. xxi, p. 88. See also Moggridge, *Maynard Keynes*, pp. 454–7; Skidelsky, *John Maynard Keynes, Volume II*, ch. 7 and p. 438; Ritschel, *The Politics of Planning*.
51 See M. Pugh, *'Hurrah for the Blackshirts!'*, pp. 198–203; R. Thurlow, 'The guardian of the "sacred flame": the failed political resurrection of Sir Oswald Mosley', *Journal of Contemporary History*, 33:2 (1998), p. 248.
52 See *Manchester Guardian*, 18 February and 5 March 1929. Mosley, together with Strachey, sat on the ILP Finance Enquiry Committee in 1925 and the ILP Finance Policy Committee in 1926.
53 See Marquand, *Ramsay MacDonald*, pp. 476–81.

position on the ideological spectrum.⁵⁴ G. D. H. Cole, for one, was in close contact with Mosley's rebel group throughout 1930 and described his programme in June as 'broadly on the right lines'.⁵⁵

Yet there were always signs of unease and suspicion about Mosley within the labour movement. Much of this was driven by his elevated social background and arrogant personality, but such sentiments were also mingled with concerns about Mosley's highly selective approach to socialism. Though his early radicalism had been born of his dissent from orthodox economic policy, he had always tempered his strident critique with an explicitly reformist perspective, which focused on pragmatic reforms rather than an entirely new social order. Upon joining Labour, he deprecated the socialist 'habit of discussing ultimate issues' and called instead for 'an immediate programme to deal with immediate issues'. He repeatedly depicted his own approach as that of 'realistic' or 'practical socialism' and lectured his new colleagues that 'we must above all be realists'.⁵⁶ He defined his 'practical socialism' in distinctively technocratic language as the 'scientific intervention of the State' that addressed the 'immediate problems of the day' rather than the distant questions of the 'final evolution of society'.⁵⁷

This pragmatic rhetoric was reflected in the substance of Mosley's policy proposals, which focused on immediate reforms and openly downplayed core socialist aspirations. In *Revolution by Reason*, for instance, Mosley dismissed redistribution as a subsidiary step of ethical rather than economic relevance, and urged instead the importance of general economic growth as the essential first step in his recovery programme: 'The workers' position will only be greatly improved by an increase in the net total wealth production directed to working-class uses. When we have begun this *major* operation, we shall have greater prospect of success in the *minor* attempt to transfer existing demand.'⁵⁸ Similarly, while his ILP colleagues often portrayed the 'living wage' as the 'impossible claim' that would force private enterprise to submit to public ownership, Mosley disparaged their preoccupation with nationalisation as a misguided policy that would only generate resistance and frighten away moderate voters. Indeed, he suggested repeatedly that his alternative strategy of high wages,

---

54 *Manchester Guardian*, 21 May 1930.
55 *Birmingham Town Crier*, 27 June 1930. See also G. C. Catlin, *For God's Sake Go!* (Gerrards Cross: Colin Smythe, 1972), pp. 73, 80–1.
56 *Daily Herald*, 1 and 3 April 1924; Mosley, *My Life*, p. 221; Skidelsky, *Oswald Mosley*, p. 126; Mosley, *Revolution by Reason*, pp. 6, 28.
57 *Daily Express*, 19 February 1929.
58 Mosley, *Revolution by Reason*, pp. 16–17.

credit expansion and state planning would make the 'older conceptions of socialist strategy' if not unnecessary, then at least not immediately urgent. As he explained in *Revolution by Reason*, the great advantage of his scheme was that its benefits would be felt 'long before we have entirely transformed society to a socialist basis'.[59]

Mosley's 'practical socialism' did not mark him out as a heretic within the extremely broad church of MacDonald's Labour Party. Even within the ILP, there were many who cautioned that aggregate economic growth was a precondition for income redistribution to bear fruit, and who cautioned that public ownership alone was no panacea for industrial obsolescence.[60] As David Howell has shown, there was also tacit acknowledgement that the 'living wage' could be applied initially to manage capitalism towards greater prosperity rather than to eradicate it immediately.[61] Moreover, in the midst of widespread disappointment with the first Labour government, Mosley's contemptuous critique of the glacial pace of gradualist assumptions placed him firmly alongside the party's dissident left wing.[62]

Nevertheless, there were always some on the left who complained that Mosley's productivist economics aimed merely to 'stabilise' or 'bolster up' capitalism.[63] Perhaps the most insightful critique came from Brailsford, the editor of the ILP's political weekly, the *New Leader*, and one of the authors of *The Living Wage*. Brailsford had initially been sympathetic to *Revolution by Reason*. If anything, he worried that its recommendations for credit expansion were 'a little reckless', even for the ILP.[64] However, he soon came to voice serious concerns about Mosley's failure to link his high-wage economics with any deeper socialist purpose. While undeniably desirable, higher wages and general economic recovery would not by themselves bring closer the goal of a socialist society. Without a transformation in the status of the workers through the redistribution of income and economic power, Mosley's quest for high wages would be little better than the new American business ethic of 'Fordism'. If successful, Brailsford cautioned, a high-wage economy would improve the workers' conditions, but also entrench the capitalist order: 'We march to defeat if we allow our own army to suppose that our purpose is merely to win for

---

59 Mosley, 'Is John Wheatley right? How to get a living wage', *New Leader*, 1 April 1927; Mosley, *Revolution by Reason*, pp. 16, 20.
60 See *The Living Wage*, pp. 3–4, 10; John Wheatley, *Socialise the National Income* (London: ILP, 1927), pp. 10–13; Brailsford, *Socialism for To-Day*, pp. 96–7, 104–5; H. N. Brailsford, 'The seats of power', *New Leader*, 19 December 1930.
61 See Howell, *A Lost Left*, pp. 270–1, 275.
62 See Mosley, *Revolution by Reason*, p. 28.
63 See *New Leader*, 29 May 1925, 9 October 1925, 26 March 1926, 8 October 1926.
64 See *New Leader*, 2 April 1926.

it an easy material life. Our purpose is to change the motive of work. Our goal is the conquest of power.'[65]

Yet it was precisely this sort of 'practical' approach, one that embraced radical collectivist measures to promote prosperity but stopped short of larger socialist teleology, which became the defining feature of Mosley's position after his resignation from the Labour government in 1930. He urged that the crisis required an 'emergency programme' to rescue the economy, appealed for support from across all parties, and insisted that all discussion of ideological provenance or principles be postponed until after the emergency had been addressed. 'What if it is Socialism?', he challenged Conservative critics of his ideas on planning in July 1930. 'In circumstances like these, surely the practical thing to do is to ask whether it is a right and wise thing to do in the given facts, not whether it means the application of some general principle in which we believe or disbelieve.'[66] Mosley directed a similar plea to socialists: 'Academic questions of nationalisation are excluded by the very emergency of the situation which confronts us.'[67] Such pragmatic appeals for 'immediate action' came to serve as the rationale for the New Party early in 1931: 'the immediate question we are concerned with is not the question of the ultimate form of Social Organisation, but with an emergency in which the whole structure of industry is threatened.'[68]

Mosley's crisis-driven pragmatism helps us identify both the attraction and the potential danger of his position for radical socialists. His 'emergency programme' involved dramatic departures in the direction of centralised state controls and planning, all policies Mosley had developed in the context of radical socialist thought. Yet, both because of the urgency of the situation and in order to attract as wide support as possible for his rescue agenda, Mosley severed the usual association of such interventionist policies with long-term socialist goals. There was to be persistent tension within the 'Mosley group' about the exact ideological balance and duration of this compromise, but it is clear that he initially attracted precisely those left-wingers who were frustrated by the Labour government's sluggish response to the crisis and who shared his demand for immediate action. The problem was that, in a crisis facing a capitalist economy, such pragmatic crisis containment could easily drift into the application of radical collectivist methods to help restore capitalism. Indeed, while the signatories of the Mosley Manifesto insisted in 1930 that they would

---

65 *New Leader*, 29 May 1925, 9 October 1925, 26 March 1926, 8 October 1926.
66 *House of Commons Debates*, fifth series, 16 July 1930, 241, col. 1355.
67 Mosley, 'Private and confidential'.
68 Young *et al.*, *A National Policy*, pp. 6–7.

'surrender nothing of our Socialist faith', they nonetheless acknowledged that their 'emergency programme' was meant to 'make capitalism work'.[69] By early 1931, official accounts of the New Party's platform combined its radical interventionist economics with explicit commitment to 'maintain and renovate capitalism'.[70] This ideological shift was endorsed even by some of those who had come over from the ILP. C. E. M. Joad offered this elucidation: 'It does not, like the old Socialism, propose to supersede private enterprise; it seeks to provide a framework of public control erected in the public interest, within which private enterprise shall operate.'[71] Harold Nicolson's description of New Party economics as 'state capitalism' was perhaps the most accurate shorthand for this emerging ideological hybrid.[72]

This ambiguity at the heart of Mosley's position helps explain why the ILP lent early support to the initial stages of Mosley's rebellion against the Labour government, only to reverse course by the end of 1930 and reject his alternative programme as 'anti-socialist'. The ILP's own early critique of the government's economic policy had anticipated much of the Mosley Memorandum.[73] Fenner Brockway, who had succeeded Brailsford as the editor of the *New Leader*, therefore greeted the Mosley Memorandum on the grounds that it was 'along the lines which have been advocated by the "Left"', and expressed the hope that all the Labour dissidents would work together.[74] Although there were complaints after Mosley's resignation that he was building himself an independent power-base among ILP members, there was also broad acceptance that his position had, as Cole suggested in July, an 'affinity with the views of Mr. Maxton and the ILP'.[75] As late as November, Brockway still found 'a good deal in common' between Mosley's economic ideas and those of the ILP, and again suggested that there were possible grounds for co-operation.[76]

---

69 'Mosley Manifesto', *The Times*, 8 December 1930; John Strachey and Allan Young in *Birmingham Town Crier*, 27 June 1930; Allan Young, 'Unemployment', *New Leader*, 18 July 1930.
70 W. E. D. Allen, *The New Party and the Old Toryism* (London: New Party, 1931), pp. 2, 8.
71 C. E. M. Joad, *The Case for the New Party* (London: New Party, 1931), pp. 8, 7.
72 Harold Nicolson, Diary, 27 September 1931, Balliol College, Oxford.
73 See H. N. Brailsford, 'Enthroning the bankers', *New Leader*, 17 January 1930, p. 4, and 'Will the Cabinet act?', *New Leader*, 14 February 1930, p. 9. See also a series of articles by G. D. H. Cole on 'Mr. Thomas and unemployment', *New Leader*, 6, 13, 20 and 27 December 1929.
74 F. Brockway, 'A review of Parliament', *New Leader*, 9 and 23 May 1930.
75 'An onlooker's diary', *New Leader*, 4 April 1930; G. D. H. Cole, *Gold, Credit and Employment* (London: George Allen and Unwin, 1930), p. 161.
76 'A ferment of ideas', *New Leader*, 7 November 1930, p. 9.

This positive response began to change as Mosley unveiled his plan for 'Commonwealth insulation' in mid-1930. Brockway warned immediately that Mosley appeared to be leaning towards 'Economic Imperialism'.[77] Significantly, the objection was neither to Mosley's transgression against free trade nor to his call for an extension of trade controls to the Empire, both of which were long-standing ingredients of ILP trade policy. Instead, what worried the ILP were the ideological implications of Mosley's suggestion for an *exclusively* imperial trading area. As E. F. Wise explained, the real issue was whether trade controls were to be an 'exclusively Imperial scheme' or whether similar reciprocal trade agreements were to be sought with other countries as well.[78] The danger, as the *New Leader* pointed out, was that without a clear commitment to internationalist principles, Mosley's ideas could easily turn into a 'mere instrument for "Empire Free Trade" and similar imperialist nostrums', while 'masquerading under "Labour" labels'.[79]

It was Mosley's explicit denial of the immediate relevance of socialism in the Manifesto that finally alienated the ILP. In an extended critique of the Mosley Manifesto in December 1930, Brockway noted that many of its individual proposals were extremely familiar: 'Indeed, a number of the specific proposals he puts forward have been before the country in the Living Income Programme of the ILP for the last five years.' However, in Mosley's scheme they were presented as a 'substitute for Socialism' and 'the whole plan oriented in such a way as to make it, if operated, a buttress in the stabilisation of Capitalism'. The real complaint, in fact, was that Mosley sought to utilise the collectivist methods he had poached from the ILP in order to restore capitalism: 'What he proposes is, in effect, the Executive controls of a social order in revolution – but operating for Capitalist purposes in a Capitalist State.'[80] This, according to Wise early in the next year, was not a pragmatic compromise, but a reactionary alternative that would 'use the resources of the State and the growing realisation of the necessity of a national view of our industrial problems to buttress up private capitalism at the moment when it is rapidly collapsing'.[81] By

---

77 'A review of Parliament', *New Leader*, 18 July 1930, p. 6, and 'What we think', *New Leader*, 25 July 1930, p. 3.
78 *House of Commons Debates*, fifth series, 16 July 1930, 241, col. 1406. See also E. F. Wise, 'Socialise food supplies', *New Leader*, 24 October 1930, p. 9.
79 'What we think', *New Leader*, 25 July 1930, p. 3; Brockway, 'A review of Parliament', p. 6. See also A. G. Stock, 'The month at home', *Socialist Review*, August 1930, pp. 174–5.
80 'What we think', *New Leader*, 12 and December 1930.
81 'The discreet buccaneer', *New Leader*, 6 March 1931.

late spring of 1931, the *Socialist Review* identified Mosley's position as 'a sort of watered down and constitutional fascism'.[82]

An early revisionist?

If Mosley's position in 1930–31 was neither Keynesian nor left-socialist, may we then identify him as a pioneer revisionist who crafted a pragmatic synthesis that fell in between Keynes and state socialism? This, at any rate, has been the conclusion offered by a number of historians, who have suggested that his pre-fascist position anticipated the revisionist ideas of the Young Fabians around Hugh Dalton in the 1930s and subsequent social-democratic thought after the war.[83] There is again some evidence to support this proposition. As we have seen, Mosley shared with the later revisionists a pragmatic preference for control over any doctrinaire attachment to wholesale nationalisation; for aggregate growth over left-wing preoccupation with redistribution; and for a combination of monetary management and physical planning that could be applied in either a socialist or a capitalist economy.[84] It is difficult, of course, to establish a meaningful comparison between the two positions, since they were separated by nearly a decade and substantially different circumstances. However, we do have closer to hand a far more contemporary example of Mosley's encounter with an identifiably revisionist approach, in the thought of his own closest political ally, John Strachey.

In the literature on Mosley, Strachey is sometimes dismissed as an intellectually and ideologically unstable figure, who swung wildly from being an ardent admirer of Mosley in the 1920s to become one of the

---

82 'Events at home', *Socialist Review*, April–June 1931, p. 175.
83 According to Skidelsky, Mosley 'anticipated Croslandite democratic socialism' ('Mosley, Sir Oswald Ernald', *Oxford Dictionary of National Biography*, online, accessed 4 April 2006). See also Roger Eatwell, 'The drive towards synthesis', in Roger Griffin (ed.), *International Fascism: Theories, Causes, and the New Consensus* (New York: Oxford University Press, 1998), p. 196; Booth and Pack, *Employment, Capital, and Economic Policy*, p. 24; Hugh Thomas, *John Strachey* (London: Methuen, 1973), p. 51.
84 For revisionist economics, see Noel Thompson, *Political Economy and the Labour Party: The Economics of Democratic Socialism* (London: UCL Press, 1996); Radhika Desai, *Intellectuals and Socialism: 'Social Democrats' and the Labour Party* (London: Lawrence and Wishart, 1994); Nicholas Ellison, *Egalitarian Thought and Labour Politics* (London: Routledge, 1994); Elizabeth Durbin, *The New Jerusalems: The Labour Party and the Economics of Democratic Socialism* (London: Rouledge and Kegan Paul, 1985); Stephen Haseler, *The Gaitskellites: Revisionism in the British Labour Party, 1951–64* (London: Macmillan, 1969).

most outspoken exponents of revolutionary Marxism in the 1930s, only to embrace Keynesian social democracy at the close of the decade.[85] What is overlooked in such characterisations, however, is that Strachey articulated in the 1920s a remarkably sophisticated variant of 'socialist realism' that both served to justify his collaboration with Mosley and foreshadowed the revisionist thought to which Strachey himself was to return shortly before the Second World War. It is also evident that it was Strachey's traumatic discovery in 1931 that, far from accommodating such 'socialist realism', Mosley's position had evolved into fascism that propelled Strachey into the arms of militant Marxism.

Strachey was the Oxford-educated son of the editor of the Unionist *Spectator*, who had converted to socialism and joined the ILP shortly before meeting Mosley in 1924. The two upper-class recruits quickly established a close intellectual and political partnership that was to last until Strachey's abrupt departure from the New Party in mid-1931. In this partnership, Strachey filled the role of the socialist intellectual, who explored in depth the issues and strategies that Mosley addressed on the political stage.[86] Right from the start, he sought to balance his passionate commitment to the ultimate goals of socialism with his equally strong interest in more immediate strategy that would tackle the pressing problems of the day. This was apparent as early as his book-length exploration of the economics of the *Revolution by Reason,* published in December 1925. He defended its proposals with typically fundamentalist language: 'As Socialists, our object must surely be to abolish, not to tame, the Capitalist system.'[87] Yet he also criticised those left-wingers who refused to consider suggestions for more immediate 'economic betterment' and offered Mosley's ideas on credit expansion as 'a chance of finding a solution to our troubles by money regulation, without a transference of ownership'.[88] Indeed, Noel Thompson has described Strachey's position in the mid-1920s as a novel form of 'liberal socialism'.[89]

As the editor of the ILP's political journal, *Socialist Review*, in the second half of the 1920s, Strachey continued to explore the possibilities of revisionist economics. He engaged at length and sympathetically with

---

85 Skidelsky, *Oswald Mosley*, pp. 137–8; Martin Green, *Children of the Sun: A Narrative of Decadence in England After 1918* (London: Constable, 1976), pp. 269–73.
86 See Michael Newman, *John Strachey* (Manchester: Manchester University Press, 1989); Noel Thompson, *John Strachey: An Intellectual Biography* (London: Macmillan, 1993); Hugh Thomas, *John Strachey* (London: Eyre Methuen, 1979).
87 Strachey, letter to *New Leader*, 4 December 1925.
88 Strachey, *Revolution by Reason*, p. 97.
89 Thompson, *John Strachey*, pp. 10–29.

Marxist theory, and left no doubt about his own commitment to 'the socialist prerequisite of the abolition of economic inequality and class distinctions'.[90] Yet he fiercely criticised the communist call for a direct confrontation with capitalism as a 'hopeless insurrectionism' that was dangerously unrealistic, especially at a time when capitalism had clearly recovered its strength after the instability of the immediate post-war years. He was no less disapproving of the 'illusion of democratic omnipotence' that lay behind the gradualist assumptions of the MacDonald leadership. Unless armed with an intermediate economic strategy, a Labour government would only disappoint and disillusion its working-class supporters. Strachey therefore urged the articulation of a 'realistic programme' that would solidify electoral support for the Labour Party by providing 'immediate amelioration for the masses', while also paving the way for the long-term transition to 'true socialism'.[91]

Strachey elaborated this strategy in tandem with Allan Young, Mosley's political secretary and another close collaborator in his circle of ILP supporters. In a series of articles in the *Socialist Review* between 1927 and 1929, they outlined many of the elements of the short-term policy that would reappear in Mosley's subsequent position in 1930, including an expansionary monetary policy and departure from the gold standard, reorganisation of the ailing staple industries and a public spending programme of £150 million annually, designed to stimulate the 'home market' by investing in 'workers' purchasing power', including public housing, family allowances, education, higher school-leaving age and increased pensions. Bulk purchase and barter agreements in international trade, and a tightly focused nationalisation programme in the key utility sectors of banking, transport and energy were to lay the foundations for socialist economic controls in the future. Their administration was to take the form of autonomous 'Public Utility Corporations', which anticipated the technocratic format of the Morrisonian model for socialised management of industry later adopted by the Labour Party in the 1930s.[92] Young described their proposals as 'socialist realism' and its revisionist mix of recovery policies with a long-term socialist agenda was emphasised by Strachey: 'It would, in a sense, reconstruct capitalism, and so, no doubt,

---

90 *Socialist Review*, April 1929.
91 This entire argument was rehearsed by Strachey in a number of editorial articles in the *Socialist Review*. See 'Notes of the month' in September and December 1927, June and September 1928, March and November 1928.
92 See A. H. Hanson, 'Labour and the public corporation', *Public Administration*, 32:2 (1954), pp. 203–9.

would in a sense strengthen it. But in so doing it would strengthen the corresponding parts of the working-class movement quite equally.'[93]

It was this 'realistic' stance that made it possible for Strachey to follow Mosley in his rebellion within and against the Labour Party in 1930–31. He defended Mosley's ideological pragmatism as the sort of ecumenical compromise that could break the 'paralysis of national will' produced by the 'platitudinous inaction' of both the Labour government and the other 'old parties' by rallying all those who were prepared to support an immediate response to the crisis. The New Party, he wrote, was 'the only alternative to sitting and waiting with Mr. MacDonald and Mr. Baldwin for immediate decline and ultimate catastrophe'.[94] However, while Strachey endorsed the compromise formula behind Mosley's 'emergency programme' as a necessary tactical concession to the crisis, he was by no means prepared to abandon his own long-term socialist aspirations. Though he acknowledged that their approach sacrificed 'some of the economic doctrines we have held on these benches (and which I, for example, have held very strongly)', he made persistent efforts to paint their policy in socialist colours. He protested repeatedly that its 'essential conception is collectivist,' and that its emphasis on 'order, planning and conscious control' rested on the 'essential principles which Socialist thought has sponsored'.[95] He also expressed his confidence that, in the process of addressing the crisis, they would be advancing the socialist cause: 'Our appeal is not to "save the nation", but to make a nation worth saving. Let us make no mistake about it: for the worker the past is not worth restoring, nor the present worth preserving. The only task which the worker will undertake, the only task to which we summon him, is the building of a fundamentally new social structure.'[96]

Unfortunately, it gradually became apparent that Mosley's evolving ideas about this 'fundamentally new social structure' diverged dramatically

---

93 John Strachey, 'Notes of the month', *Socialist Review*, November 1928, p. 10. See also Strachey's 'Notes of the month' from April 1927, September 1927 and March 1929. Young discussed 'socialist realism' in 'The struggle for power', *Socialist Review*, January 1929. See also his 'After Norwich', *Socialist Review*, May 1928; 'What do Cook and Maxton mean?', *Socialist Review*, October 1928.
94 'The progress of the New Party', *Week-end Review*, 20 June 1931, pp. 909–10; 'Mosley Manifesto: why we have issued it', *Spectator*, 13 December 1930, p. 930. See also John Strachey, *The Menace of Fascism* (London: Victor Gollancz, 1933), pp. 156–7.
95 See John Strachey in *House of Commons Debates*, fifth series, 29 October 1930, 241, col. 172; 'Socialism and free trade', *Birmingham Town Crier*, 27 June 1930; *Manchester Guardian*, 24 February and 16 March 1931; and 'The progress of the New Party'.
96 'The Mosley Manifesto: why we have issued it'; *Manchester Guardian*, 24 February 1931; *Birmingham Town Crier*, 7 November 1930.

from Strachey's long-term socialist vision. This divergence became evident early in the summer of 1931 as Mosley began to transform the New Party's 'emergency programme' into the permanent ideological framework of the 'Corporate State'. These early discussions of the Corporate State within the New Party are a surprisingly overlooked feature of Mosley's pre-fascist thought, and his corporatism is often treated as simply a derivative set of ideas that he borrowed wholesale from Italy once he decided for fascism.[97] Yet there is clear evidence that Mosley was thinking along the lines of what he then called the 'modern movement' as early as October 1930, and Strachey tells us that he grew aware of the corporatist turn in Mosley's thought by April 1931.[98] We also know that it was this issue that finally drove the two men apart.

As outlined in Mosley's correspondence and various New Party publications over the course of 1930–32, the new corporatist blueprint was assembled from the familiar components of socialist planning that he had long integrated into his thought. As in his previous programmes, there was to be a high-wage economy and centralised planning of an insulated imperial market. Coordination was to be carried out by a network of 'Planning Councils' at the industry and trade levels, representative of workers, employers and consumers, and headed by a central 'Economic Planning Council', charged with the task of overseeing the national economy. The entire framework was to be directed by a streamlined Cabinet, armed with direct legislative authority and constrained only by Parliament's right to voice its disapproval of individual initiatives. The only truly new institutional component was the suggestion of an 'occupational franchise' for elections to Parliament.[99]

It is important to recognise that it was less any departures in individual policy or institutional elements than their assembly in an explicitly new ideological framework that distinguished Mosley's Corporate State from his previous proposals. For the first time, there was an admission of the socially conservative nature of his vision. Representatives of workers were to join employers and consumers on the new Planning Councils, but the goal was to 'reconcile the inevitable conflict of interests' rather than to redistribute power between classes. Mosley did offer a strong critique of inherited privilege, insisted on meritocratic individual advancement, and

---

97 See M. Worley, 'What was the New Party? Sir Oswald Mosley and associated responses to the "crisis", 1931–1932', *History*, 92:305 (2007), p. 58; Gary Love, 'What's the big idea? Oswald Mosley, the BUF and generic fascism', *Journal of Contemporary History*, 42:3 (2007), pp. 450–1, 467; Pugh, *'Hurrah for the Blackshirts!'*, pp. 130–1.
98 See Mosley, 'Private and confidential'; Strachey, *The Menace of Fascism*, pp. 161–2.
99 Mosley, 'Have we a policy?', *Action*, 24 December 1931, pp. 1–2.

A reassessment of Mosley's alternative economic agenda 79

called for a 'newly awakened social conscience' in service to the nation.[100] However, there was no mention of redistribution of wealth or status, and repeated assurances were offered that private capital would be left undisturbed so long as it served the 'national interest'. Indeed, by allocating both industrial and parliamentary representation by function and occupation, the Corporate State was meant to institutionalise the established hierarchies of capitalist society. The goal was not to eliminate, but to make more efficient existing social relations by replacing the dysfunctional 'class war' with a 'machinery which reconciles the conflict of interests and arbitrates and harmonises the differences of class'.[101]

The material benefits offered by the high-wage economy were to dampen class friction and secure popular consent for the new constitution. The new regime was to satisfy working-class aspirations in an economy planned for high wages and continuous economic growth, while ensuring 'a square deal to the differing participants of industry' and safeguarding the interests of the 'community as a whole'.[102] However, where such material rewards proved insufficient to ensure harmony, the Corporate State was to impose its absolute authority. Strikes and lock-outs were to be banned, as were all other private actions 'contrary to the interests of the state'.[103] Mosley readily acknowledged that his vision was 'in essence authoritarian'. The Corporate State was to 'subordinate the individual and the interest to the overriding purpose of the Nation', in order to 'govern Britain in the interest of all Britain'.[104]

The socially conservative and authoritarian nature of Mosley's ideological hybrid thus became for the first time explicit. Its purpose was not to carry out a redistribution of wealth or power, much less a social revolution. On the contrary, the last vestiges of socialist rhetoric were dropped in favour of the Corporate State as an answer not only to 'the collapse of the capitalist system', but also to the menace of the 'communist threat' and 'proletarian revolution'.[105] The new state was to protect 'civilisation' from both by imposing its authority impartially on all classes and by enforcing class collaboration and 'corporate discipline' throughout the community. The ideological ambiguity at the heart of Mosley's 'emergency

---

100 Mosley, 'Private and confidential', p. 32.
101 Mosley, 'Have we a policy?'
102 Oswald Mosley, 'Ancient gentlemen at war', *Action*, 15 October 1931, p. 1.
103 Patrick Noir, 'A brief survey of our policy', *New Times* (New Party), 1:1 (June 1932).
104 Mosley, 'Private and confidential', p. 31; *Action*, 15 October 1931; 'This new movement', *New Times* (New Party), 2:1 (July 1932), p. 2. See also *Action*, 12 November and 24 December 1931.
105 '*Action* looks at life', *Action*, 8 October 1931, p. 4, and 17 December 1931, p. 14.

programme' was thus finally resolved in the firmly anti-socialist vision of the Corporate State. Instead of proletarian emancipation, he offered a prosperous but static social order 'in which each part will be content with its own function and will not aspire to functions better performed by some other elements'.[106]

Was this fascism? At the time and subsequently, Mosley denied vehemently that he was imitating any foreign paradigms, and claimed to have constructed the Corporate State directly from his earlier socialist economics: 'in the Commodity Board system, the National Planning Council, the National Investment Board, and other conceptions of the New Party, we had evolved quite independently the germ of the Corporate ideal in this country long before it was ever suggested we were imitating Italy'.[107] There is no doubt that this claim of a domestic socialist provenance behind his corporatism needs to be given far more credence than it has received in the past. Yet, as Zeev Sternhell has shown in the case of continental fascism, it was precisely the adaptation of socialist economics to nationalist and authoritarian ends by 'revisionists of the Right' that constituted the fascist ideological blend.[108] Certainly, as early as October 1930, Mosley himself acknowledged the close parallels between his evolving position and fascism in a private statement to a Conservative audience: 'The modern movement, like most movements, began on the Continent and comes last to Britain.'[109] Paradoxically, while similar suspicions led some of his socialist supporters to refuse to follow him into the New Party, others, including Strachey, joined the new enterprise even as they acknowledged the potentially fascist 'tendencies' or 'resemblances' of some of its ideas. Their contemporary comments suggest they believed that the party's ideological hybrid would evolve on 'socialist' or 'progressive centre' lines.[110]

Nevertheless, fascism soon reared its ugly head as the Corporate State became the subject of heated debates between Mosley and his socialist followers at internal party meetings early in the summer of 1931. The conflict was evident at one weekend session in June, when a newcomer detected

---

106 'The organic state', *Action*, 15 October 1931, p. 3.
107 'Have we a policy?', p. 1. See also Mosley, *The Greater Britain*, pp. 96–8; Mosley, *My Life*, pp. 332, 362; N. Mosley, *Rules of the Game*, p. 61.
108 See Zeev Sternhell, *Neither Right Nor Left: Fascist Ideology in France*, trans D. Maisel (Princeton, NJ: Princeton University Press, 1995), and *The Birth of Fascist Ideology: From Cultural Rebellion to Political Revolution*, trans D. Maisel (Princeton, NJ: Princeton University Press, 1995).
109 Mosley, 'Private and confidential'; *The Times*, 15 November 1930.
110 See C. E. M. Joad, 'Prologmena to fascism', *Political Quarterly*, 2:1 (1931), pp. 82–99; John Strachey in *Manchester Guardian*, 16 March 1931; C. F. Melville, 'Political upheaval. 1: Sir Oswald Mosley', *Fortnightly Review*, 1 May 1931, pp. 658–67.

an open split between the two wings of the New Party: 'one Fascist in tendency, the other Socialist'. Mosley spoke 'soulfully of the Corporate State of the future', while Strachey delivered 'a good old fashioned Marxian speech'.[111] Another member noted at the time that Mosley 'at the bottom of his heart really wants a Fascist movement, but Allan Young and John Strachey think only of the British working man'.[112] Strachey became increasingly uncomfortable at the corporatist turn in Mosley's thinking and fought back by reaffirming his socialist principles and pledging loyalty to the working class: 'neither I nor any other of the men and women who founded the New Party would ever, or will ever, be connected with any organization which can even be suspected of being anti-working-class in character'.[113] Strachey later recounted his bewilderment at Mosley's new ideological turn: 'I had at that time no clear idea of what the Corporate State might be. But the more Mosley talked about it, the more it seemed to be remarkably like Capitalism: or rather it seemed to be Capitalism minus all the things which the workers had won during the last century of struggle. Our doubts grew and grew.'[114] These doubts finally boiled over late in July, as Strachey and Young stormed out of the New Party, complaining that Mosley was leading the party towards fascism.[115] Mosley did not take long to arrive at that destination. The New Party fought the October 1931 general election on the platform of the Corporate State and openly acknowledged its embrace of fascism in December.[116]

Strachey's subsequent reaction reflected his profound shock at how badly mistaken he had been in his belief that Mosley's ideological pragmatism corresponded with his own socialist revisionism. Almost immediately, his disillusionment led him to reject all possibility of reformism. The New Party, he came to maintain, had been based upon 'an entirely utopian appeal for social compromise' in a 'hopeless attempt at obtaining the agreement of Capital and Labour for a quite impracticable policy of national reconstruction'.[117] This, he confessed, was a 'particularly hard lesson' for him to learn. However, he now realised that this was the 'fatal defect' of the New Party, and was prepared to 'renounce the "gradualist" conception of "making Capitalism work", and accept the

---

111 Jack Jones, *Unfinished Journey* (London: Hamish Hamilton, 1938), p. 264. See also *New Statesman*, 6 June 1931.
112 Nicolson, Diary, 17 July 1931.
113 'The progress of the New Party', p. 909. See also Strachey in *Manchester Guardian*, 11 June 1931.
114 Strachey, *The Menace of Fascism*, p. 163.
115 *The Times*, 24 July 1931.
116 Mosley, 'Have we a policy?', pp. 1–2.
117 Strachey, *The Menace of Fascism*, pp. 159–60, 164.

dynamic Socialist conception of using political power for revolutionary class ends'.[118] Thus almost overnight Strachey transformed from a left-wing revisionist to an outspoken exponent of revolutionary Marxism, a position which he was to maintain throughout the first half of the 1930s with the missionary zeal of the convert. In his writings he concentrated particularly upon explaining why the collectivist rhetoric of fascist corporatism was nothing but a reactionary trap for the unwary socialist: 'an elegant intellectual disguise' for 'monopoly capitalism'.[119]

Neither a Keynesian nor a socialist

This chapter has sought to show that Mosley's economics represented neither a Keynesian nor a left-socialist nor, for that matter, a revisionist alternative during the crisis of 1930–31. Instead, his position resembled most closely the 'revisionism of the Right' that Sternhell has identified as the ideological source of fascism on the continent. Mosley's ideological evolution supports Sternhell's suggestion that inter-war fascism was born of an authoritarian, productivist, technocratic and nationalistic revision of classical socialist strategy by those who rejected liberal political culture and market economics in favour of authoritarian economic collectivism and planning, but who did not share the class-based, egalitarian values of socialism itself. From the early days of his 'practical socialism' within the ILP, through the pragmatic 'emergency programme' of the Mosley group in 1930, to the Corporate State of the New Party, Mosley followed a course that paralleled closely the well known political trajectory of a large number of 'neo-socialists' who turned to fascism on the continent, including Marcel Deat, Hendrik de Man and Benito Mussolini himself.[120]

---

118 'Gradualism is bankrupt', *New Leader*, 2 October 1931, p. 8. See also Strachey, in *New Statesman*, 26 September 1931, p. 370, and 'Opposition policy', *New Statesman*, 19 September 1931, pp. 328–9.

119 John Strachey, *The Coming Struggle for Power* (London: Victor Gollancz, 1932), pp. 242–7. See also Strachey, *The Menace of Fascism*, ch. 6.

120 See Sternhell, *Neither Right Nor Left* and *The Birth of Fascist Ideology*; Sheri Berman, *The Primacy of Politics: Social Democracy and the Making of Europe's Twentieth Century* (Cambridge: Cambridge University Press, 2006); Ian Barnes, 'A fascist Trojan horse: Maurice Bardeche, fascism and authoritarian socialism', *Patterns of Prejudice*, 37:2 (2003), pp. 177–194; Dan White, *Lost Comrades: Socialists and the Front Generation, 1918–1945* (Cambridge, MA: Harvard University Press, 1992); Dick Pels, 'The dark side of socialism: Hendrik de Man and the fascist temptation', *History of the Human Sciences*, 6:2 (1993), pp. 75–95.

Mosley's ideological evolution also offers a highly compelling illustration of Michael Freeden's influential view of political ideologies as contested configurations, built from shared but differently arranged conceptual elements according to the divergent ethical choices and values of their followers.[121] Certainly, despite Mosley's appropriation of what were undeniably radical economic measures borrowed mostly from the large stock of available socialist ideas within the ILP, he put them together in an ideological framework that differed dramatically from any of the other socialist alternatives that drew on this same stock. As in the case of the continental neo-socialists, Mosley's ideological configuration was one that sought to utilise the productivist potential of the socialist economic techniques he had learned within the ILP, but without the underlying values and social goals that held them together within socialist ideology. As he fashioned an aggressive agenda of centralised state planning that was far removed from the moderate interventionism espoused by Keynes, Mosley began to build a socially conservative collectivist alternative that initially downplayed and eventually repudiated core socialist concepts, including redistribution, public ownership, internationalism and working-class emancipation. The ideological nature of this alternative was not immediately obvious to either Mosley or his many socialist admirers in the 1920s, but became gradually apparent after Mosley left the Labour government in 1930. It is a testament to both the novelty of his configuration and the extreme fluidity of all ideological constructs that this emerging hybrid continued for almost another year to attract the support of rebellious left-wingers. However, as Mosley began to evolve his ideas into a more coherent platform for the New Party, they all quickly dropped away. By mid-1931, it became evident that his Corporate State was designed not, as in the socialist prescription, to use state power to change society by redistributing wealth and class power, but to submerge class conflict in functional class collaboration and authoritarian collectivist controls superimposed over the existing social order. Though it is sometimes implied that Mosley's great mistake was to associate his ideas with the foreign creed of 'fascism', it is clear that that decision came only after his own autonomous evolution towards the proto-fascist ideology of the Corporate State.

This is not to conclude that Mosley was rejected by the MacDonald government because they correctly identified his ideological trajectory towards fascism. As Tanner and McKibbin have shown, MacDonald and Snowden spurned Mosley's advice with the same contempt they reserved

---

121 See Michael Freeden, *Ideologies and Political Theory: A Conceptual Approach* (Oxford: Oxford University Press, 1996).

for all dissenting opinion from within the labour movement, and there is little doubt that a truly 'Keynesian' alternative would have received no more favourable hearing than that given to the Mosley Memorandum or the ILP's *Living Wage*.[122] But it should be recognised that, far from offering a feasible progressive alternative that could have rallied effective opposition to MacDonald and Snowden, Mosley had crafted by early 1930 an idiosyncratic ideological hybrid that was less than a year removed from its metamorphosis into the proto-fascist Corporate State and less than two years from his public embrace of fascism itself late in 1931. If he was, indeed, a 'lost leader', this may not have been as great a tragedy as had once been thought.

---

[122] See D. M. Tanner, 'Political leadership, intellectual debate and economic policy during the second Labour government', in E. H. H. Green and D. M. Tanner (eds), *The Strange Survival of Liberal England: Political Leaders, Moral Values and the Reception of Economic Debate* (Cambridge: Cambridge University Press, 2007), pp. 113–50; Ross McKibbin, *Parties and People: England 1914–1951* (Oxford: Oxford University Press, 2010), pp. 69–86.

5

A 'reef of granite' or 'damp cement': conflicting loyalties inside the Parliamentary Labour Party, June 1929–September 1931

ROBERT TAYLOR

> We find ourselves caught between two loyalties – our loyalty to the party and our anxiety not to make difficulties for our leaders nor to engage publicly in any pressure for amendments which could in any way be regarded as a 'revolt' or a 'split'; and on the other our loyalty to our supporters.[1]

The Parliamentary Labour Party (PLP) has often been criticised for its supine behaviour during the period of the second Labour government. Jennie Lee, Independent Labour Party (ILP) member for North Lanarkshire, even suggested the PLP should bear 'a very heavy burden of responsibility' for MacDonald's decision to form the National Government in August 1931. 'In the PLP it was not the shepherds who frightened me', she recalled. Neither was it the 'plain, ordinary party hacks', as every party 'has a percentage of ambitious people ready to do anything that carries the hope of promotion'. She said that she was 'prepared for that'.

> But what I was totally unprepared for was the behaviour of the solid rows of decent, well intentioned unpretentious Labour backbenchers. In the long run it was they who did the most deadly damage. Again and again an effort was made to rouse them from their inertia. On every occasion they reacted like a load of damp cement. They would see nothing, do nothing, listen to nothing that had not first been given MacDonald's approval.[2]

---

1 Cecil Malone to J. R. MacDonald, 18 November 1929, MacDonald Papers, The National Archives/Public Record Office, TNA/PRO, 30/69/1174.
2 Jennie Lee, *This Great Journey* (London: MacGibbon and Kee, 1963), p. 112.

In March 1931 W. J. Brown, ILP member for Wolverhampton West, resigned the Labour whip and wrote an angry letter to MacDonald to explain why. 'The PLP meets on the average about once a week for about an hour. It cannot deal with one tenth of the business which is to come before Parliament in the subsequent week.' Brown described the PLP as a caucus that imposed collective discipline and reduced Parliament to 'a position of almost complete irrelevance'.[3]

Bitter comments about the behaviour of the PLP in the 1929–31 Parliament came mainly from a handful of ILP militants. But Labour MPs faced a genuine conflict of increasingly divided loyalties in the Commons. On the one hand, they recognised and accepted that their primary task was to sustain their government in office through the lobbies. On the other, many believed they shared a moral responsibility to protect and improve the welfare of their working-class constituents, whom they saw as the hapless victims of the growing depression.

Their behaviour could not so easily be dismissed as subservience to an over-centralised and timid government. Most of the 287 Labour MPs elected in June 1929 were well aware of the formidable obstacles they faced as their government, without an overall majority, sought to rule through the vagaries of a hung Parliament. They were confronted across the chamber by 260 Conservatives, 59 Liberals and 9 Independents. Without any formal or informal support or at the very least acquiescence from either of the other two main parties, Labour could not hope to survive in office for very long unless it accepted the need to compromise and accommodate, in a hand-to-mouth existence, issue by issue.

The Conservative leader Stanley Baldwin might offer occasional emollient words of goodwill but he and his party were intent on bringing down the government at the earliest opportunity. For their part the Liberals were less clear or united about their parliamentary intentions. Their leader, David Lloyd George, had fought his party's election campaign in 1929 on an ambitious programme to conquer unemployment. It might have been supposed the all-consuming question of how to shorten the dole queues would have brought at least a Labour–Liberal understanding or pact in Parliament. This did not happen. Lloyd George and his party were regarded by MacDonald and most of his PLP colleagues as potentially unreliable allies. The Labour leader, when in opposition, wrote to David MacKay, the party's candidate for Inverness in April 1929. He pointed out that during the whole of the 1924–29 Parliament the Liberals 'never cast a united vote on

---

3   W. J. Brown to J. R. MacDonald, 4 March 1931, MacDonald Papers, TNA/PRO, 30/69/1310.

any subject of importance nor put their strength into the division lobbies'. Even in their attitude on how to respond to the unemployment crisis MacDonald believed the Liberals were 'invariably split'.[4]

The Liberal Party's internal divisions were confirmed during the course of the new Parliament. The Liberals remained divided, without discipline. Many feared that Labour posed a dangerous threat to their parliamentary survival and believed its collectivist values were alien to their own beliefs. 'Thorns and thistles appeared in the Labour field almost as soon as the crop was sown for the two oppositions once again began the old congenial task of goading and defaming Labour ministers and taunting the members with incapacity and cowardice', recalled Harry Snell, Labour MP for Woolwich East and chairman of the PLP's newly formed Consultative Committee, the body that attempted to liaise between the government and its own backbenchers.[5]

It is unsurprising that MacDonald questioned aloud in his opening speech to the new Parliament whether all the parties ought to see themselves 'as a Council of State and less as arrayed regiments facing each other in battle'.[6] He believed 'the condition of the Commons should encourage cooperation between the parties' on agreed policies. Labour critics later saw such a plea as early evidence that MacDonald's ultimate purpose was to form and lead a National Government of all the parties. In fact, his observation was an accurate reflection of the parliamentary realities once Labour had agreed to form a second minority administration.

But despite the obvious difficulties for the party, Labour MPs assembled in a buoyant mood at Westminster in July 1929. For the first time in their party's history, Labour had won the largest number of seats in Parliament. Moreover, the party had been elected on an ambitious manifesto that promised a programme of 'national development and reconstruction leading towards the socialist and cooperative commonwealth' as 'the only alternative to reaction and revolution'.[7] Fenner Brockway, newly elected ILP MP for East Leyton, captured the PLP's mood of the moment:

> The opening day of the new Parliament was like the first day of term at school; it was a reunion rather than an initiation. The members' lobby was crowded with comrades whom I had been associated with in all parts of the country. The Tory and Liberal MPs found themselves alien in their

---

4   J. R. MacDonald to D. MacKay, 16 April 1929, MacDonald Papers, TNA/PRO, 30/69/74.
5   Harry Snell, *Men, Governments and Myself* (London: Dent, 1936), p. 227.
6   *House of Commons Debates*, fifth series, 2 July 1929, 229, col. 65.
7   J. R. MacDonald to D. MacKay, 16 April 1929, MacDonald Papers, TNA/PRO, 30/69/74.

own House. They looked askance at this invading host, so boisterous, a big family rather than a political party. They slunk to the smoking rooms to discuss whether this really meant the revolution and to drown their gloom in drinks.[8]

Most Labour MPs were uncritical admirers of MacDonald. To them he was a revered man of destiny. Labour's victory was regarded as his personal triumph. The idolatry for MacDonald was apparent in their response to his appearance as Prime Minister at the first PLP meeting of the new Parliament. He won a standing ovation before he had even risen to speak. MacDonald promised Labour MPs that the government 'would realistically serve the working class in the large field of beneficial reform which was practicable with minority support'. He added that the party in office would prove once again, as it had done in 1924, that it knew how to govern effectively. But he warned the one thing that would destroy their government would be 'sniping from within'. 'A roar of cheers resounded round the room at this comment', noted Hugh Dalton.[9]

However, already at that first PLP meeting, some members expressed doubts about the wisdom of the party leadership's decision to form another minority government. John Wheatley, ILP MP for Glasgow Shettleston, and one of the few ministerial successes of the 1924 government, was deliberately excluded by MacDonald from his new Cabinet. Now he questioned whether the Prime Minister should have agreed to form another administration without having an overall Commons majority. Prophetically, Wheatley warned the PLP meeting that the current crisis of capitalism would force the government – whether it wanted to do so or not – to reduce the living standards of the working class in response to the demands of international finance, with savage cuts in public expenditure and in particular unemployment benefits. It would be better – he reasoned – for the Conservatives and the Liberals to shoulder the responsibilities of government in the current circumstances while Labour remained in opposition until the party secured an overall parliamentary majority in a further general election. Then, in government, it could implement the transition from capitalism to socialism to which all of the party was committed.

An alternative strategy for the Labour government in 1929 was to pile up legislative proposals for enactment and challenge the opposition parties to defeat them and thereby force an early general election. But

---

8 F. Brockway, *Inside the Left* (London: Allen and Unwin, 1942), p. 196.
9 Ben Pimlott (ed.), *The Political Diary of Hugh Dalton 1918–40, 1945–60* (London: Jonathan Cape, 1986), p. 62.

Brockway provoked loud protests from many Labour MPs when he suggested such a course of action. And yet he reasoned if the government was forced to do only whatever the Liberals and Conservatives allowed them to do, they would be driven from compromise to compromise and finally humiliation and defeat, which would cast Labour into the political wilderness for a decade.

Doubts about the wisdom of forming another minority government were not confined to ILP members. Herbert Morrison, MP for Hackney South and a loyal MacDonald supporter, admitted later there was a 'good deal to be said' for Labour staying out of power.[10] However, he concluded the party had been 'elected as a minority government and democracy required' they would have 'to accept the consequences' and do the best they could 'in the hope that the Labour minority government could pass some beneficial measures'. Ernest Bevin, General Secretary of the Transport and General Workers' Union (TGWU) and no friend of MacDonald, also cast doubt on the sense of forming another Labour minority government. His union had been almost alone at the 1924 Labour Party conference in urging Labour not to take office again until it won an overall Commons majority. His union had not changed its mind since then. 'We are confident that if that position had been adopted and adhered to the country would have given us the necessary majority with the power such a majority commands', the TGWU executive council noted.[11]

Overwhelmingly, however, Labour MPs supported MacDonald in his decision to form a minority government again. What was to anger and weary them over the party's troubled period in office was the behaviour of ILP leader Jimmy Maxton and his tiny band of followers. 'They were never without a grievance and they could never be appeased. They had not the slightest sense of team work and their sole method of getting *Socialism In Our Time* was to try and embarrass the only political party that aimed to get it at any time', Snell reflected.

> Their amendments and resolutions were usually pressed to a division for the apparent purpose of providing material for denouncing in the constituencies the loyal members of the party who did not support them. The Tory and Liberal parties quite naturally gave to these party rebels every possible encouragement. The cartoonists and journalists of the capitalist press gave them the publicity they desired. Liberal and Tory members in the House of Commons assured them that they were great fellows; a

---

10 Herbert Morrison, 'Autobiography' (original manuscript), Morrison Papers, Nuffield College, Oxford, box A, folder 8, p. 33.
11 Transport and General Workers' Union (TGWU), *Annual Report* (London, 1929), pp. 8–9.

tribute which was so much in accordance with their own convictions, that they 'fell for it' and purred like petted cats.[12]

By contrast, Snell highlighted what he regarded as the sterling character of the vast majority of Labour working-class backbenchers:

> Taking them man for man they were equals in capacity to those of the other parties in the House. They had both the qualities and the shortcomings of their class; they were at once stubborn and generous, impatient and loyal, tough minded and emotional and they were as straight and clean as a drawn sword. To have won their trust and regard was a sufficient reward for any man.

A significant number of the newly elected Labour MPs came from the professions – law, teaching, medicine and public administration. Some were distinguished arrivals from the Liberal Party, such as Charles Trevelyan, Christopher Addison and Arthur Ponsonby. They reflected the PLP's widening social and occupational base as the party became more broadly representative of the nation as a whole. But the PLP's solid core lay with its 115 trade union-sponsored manual working-class members, who organised themselves as a distinctive parliamentary group. An editorial in the journal of the National Union of General and Municipal Workers (NUGMW) praised those MPs for bringing their experience of manual work into Parliament:

> The greater number [of the PLP] have worked with their hands for weekly wages and have known but too well the haunting insecurity of the wage earners' lot. Such experiences are in themselves a qualification for the serious politics of these days. There are permanent representatives of organised labour in practically every industry – mining, railways and all forms of transport, textiles, engineering, iron and steel, boots and shoes, agriculture, woodworking, municipal employment, the general workers.[13]

Those Labour MPs shared not only their manual working-class roots and experiences of previous service as trade union officials, local councillors and justices of the peace but also their common values of collective loyalty to both the government and the wider movement, solidarity and stoical self-discipline. Trade union disciplines reinforced a sense of fraternity in hard times. It was unsurprising that the majority in the whips' office were sponsored MPs from the Miners' Federation, a bastion of trade union strength inside the PLP and a power base for MacDonald.

---

12 Snell, *Men, Governments and Myself*, p. 231.
13 NUGMW, *Journal*, August 1929, p. 302.

In his message to the 1930 NUGMW congress, J. R. Clynes, his union's President and Home Secretary, contrasted the 'unreasoning individualists' of the ILP with the trade union MPs who accepted 'collective decisions' and the 'democratic practice of all working class bodies'. Although he warned the government of which he was a member that it 'must not expect a submissive and uncomplaining body of followers', Clynes emphasised that Labour MPs needed to display 'team work and loyalty to those who were required to lead the party'.[14]

But from the outset of the 1929 Parliament the relationship between Labour backbenchers and the government proved fractious. 'The government could not adopt a policy such as would have satisfied its own members who were consequently deeply and frequently humiliated by the necessity of having to vote against their own convictions', Snell recalled. 'The government had to emasculate its own measures and accept amendments which still further reduced their political significance and the hearts of the members of the PLP were slowly but surely broken'.[15]

Managing the PLP was not made any easier by MacDonald's solitary style of leadership. In the privacy of his diaries the Prime Minister vented growing exasperation, even contempt for Labour backbenchers. His bitter feelings were not confined to the usual ILP suspects either, but included the trade union-sponsored members. Moreover, he made little effort to keep in close personal touch with the PLP. Arthur Henderson and Clynes were given the thankless task of acting as intermediaries between the Cabinet and the PLP, to calm feelings and call for loyalty. MacDonald was conspicuous mostly by his absence from PLP meetings, as was Philip Snowden, the increasingly acerbic Chancellor of the Exchequer, whose deflationary economic policies were beginning to alarm a growing number of Labour MPs. Such behaviour left the understandable impression that the Prime Minister took them too much for granted. MacDonald's 'habitual absence from party meetings slowly undermined his influence over his followers', admitted Snell. He wrote of MacDonald's 'aloof and baffling personality' and his 'lack of spontaneous geniality'. In Snell's opinion this 'undoubtedly led the rank and file of Labour members to believe that he regarded them with disdain'.[16] But, despite such apparent indifference to the PLP's feelings, Snell continued – like most of his parliamentary colleagues – to hold MacDonald in high regard. Herbert Morrison – who joined the Cabinet in March 1931 as the Minister of Transport – later recalled that the Prime Minister became 'rather cross, irritated, and bad

---

14 NUGMW, *Congress Report*, 9 June 1930.
15 Snell, *Men, Governments and Myself*, p. 253.
16 *Ibid.*, p. 226.

tempered' with the PLP and came to believe he was 'surrounded by conspiracies against him when there were none'.[17]

But the PLP's loyalty to MacDonald's government was never unconditional. It is true only a handful were prepared to throw their support behind the patrician Labour MP for Smethwick, Sir Oswald Mosley, in June 1930 when he resigned melodramatically from the government and called on Labour MPs to back his radical plans to cut unemployment. And yet, as J. C. Welsh, Labour MP for Coatbridge, noted in a letter to MacDonald at that time:

> No one believes the government under existing conditions can cure unemployment. But most people are convinced that something more can be done than has so far been attempted. I should like to hear a reasoned case put up against Mosley's proposals. Certainly the case as put from the Front Bench last week in reply to the vote of censure will not do.[18]

Welsh wrote about the 'deep disquiet' among Labour MPs at the government's 'ineffectiveness'.

The inexorable rise in the number of registered unemployed – from 1,630,000 in June 1929 to 3,000,000 in September 1931 – concentrated the PLP's mind throughout most of the Parliament. Mary Hamilton, the Labour MP for Blackburn 1929–31 and the biographer of both Ramsay MacDonald and Arthur Henderson, later wrote, 'There was no single issue on which feeling in the PLP was so decisive and so unanimous – while the rank and file would tolerate other sacrifices, if they were assured they were necessary, sacrifices at the expense of the unemployed they would not tolerate'.[19] Hugh Dalton, Labour MP for Bishop Auckland, likened the PLP's attitude towards unemployment to a 'reef of granite'.[20] Labour MPs expected decisive government action to deal with the growing crisis. After all, they reasoned, they had been elected on an ambitious manifesto that promised the party, if elected, would give 'an unqualified pledge to deal immediately and practically with mass unemployment'.

But the PLP was soon forced onto the defensive as it sought to protect the unemployed and maintain their existing meagre living standards from the growing threat of cuts to state benefits emanating from a cost-conscious Treasury, aware of the country's perilous financial position and

---

17 Morrison, 'Autobiography', p. 36.
18 J. C. Welsh to J. R. MacDonald, 19 April 1930, MacDonald Papers, TNA/PRO, 30/69/117.
19 M. Hamilton, *Arthur Henderson* (London: Heinemann, 1938), p. 362.
20 H. Dalton, *Call Back Yesterday: Memoirs 1887–1931* (London: Frederick Mueller, 1953), p. 265.

the need to reassure the money markets. Many Labour MPs knew from their own harsh experiences of what life had been like for them in their earlier years. 'I have walked the streets unemployed, heartbroken and foot sore and although I have now forgotten the hungry days and the physical privations the spiritual depression and more agony of it all remain indelibly written upon my memory', Snell told the Commons.[21] He later recalled that the PLP's Consultative Committee needed to display 'hourly labour and infinite patience' with backbenchers over how they should respond to the intractable unemployment issue. 'Constant efforts had to be made to revive their dropping spirits, to dispel their doubts and to keep them in good heart'.[22]

One of the most influential PLP backbench figures who closely allied himself with the cause of the unemployed was Arthur Hayday, Labour MP for Nottingham West, Senior National Officer in the NUGMW, member of the General Council of the Trades Union Congress (TUC) and President of the TUC in 1931. A strong disciplinarian and instinctive loyalist, he reflected the divided loyalties of many Labour backbenchers. Hayday warned his colleagues they must keep a close eye on the trend of events to make sure the administration was helped and encouraged to become an instrument for assistance rather than a soulless machine. Ever a pragmatist, he urged the government to introduce a legislative programme of practical measures, designed to reassure the manual working classes and improve their living standards. But Hayday was also a genuine labour socialist. In this he shared the hatred of his fellow working-class Members of Parliament for the iniquities of the free market system. He believed that the predatory tendencies of capitalism must be held in check. Hayday insisted that workers should have the self-confidence and determination to demand a bigger share in prosperity. He told the 1930 NUGMW conference:

> The trade union group within the Labour Party in the House of Commons have found that they must now become more emphatic in pressing the industrial point of view than others hitherto. They must remind the idealists who are attracted to the Labour Party that the trade unionists are the heaviest contributors towards the political machine and in consequence they intend to press home upon the government the necessity whatever opposition might come from the Liberals and Tories, for industrial legislation.[23]

---

21 *House of Commons Debates*, fifth series, 2 July 1929, 229, col. 52.
22 Snell, *Men, Governments and Myself*, p. 230.
23 NUGMW, Biennial conference, June 1930, p. 48, quoted in David Howell, *MacDonald's Party: Labour Identities and Crisis 1922–1931* (Oxford: Oxford University Press, 2002), pp. 167–8.

Hayday made himself a recognised expert on the complexities and inequities of social insurance and a champion of the jobless. He led a successful revolt inside the PLP in the autumn of 1929 against Margaret Bondfield, the Minister of Labour and a member of his own union, when she sought to tighten the existing rules under which the unemployed were entitled to benefit. Many Labour MPs feared she was too much under the grip of her senior civil servants in what they regarded as an unbending official attitude towards the unemployed. On the second reading of the government's Unemployment Insurance Bill in November 1929 not a single Labour MP backed the measure in the debate. At PLP meetings Bondfield came under withering criticism from Hayday and others for her stubbornness. During its committee stage the measure came under further backbench attack, especially over her insistence on maintaining the previous Conservative government's rule that unemployed people had to prove they were 'genuinely seeking work' before receipt of benefit. Bondfield backed down eventually, following MacDonald's intervention. But it was the PLP's trade union group that was really responsible for her unseemly retreat.

Despite continuing public concern about Labour's policies towards the unemployed, the trade union-sponsored MPs never saw themselves as a threat to the government. On the contrary – despite their fears and frustrations – they remained loyal to the end. Nor was any attempt made by the national trade unions that sponsored them from outside Parliament to subvert the government through applying pressure on their sponsored MPs. Bevin was increasingly hostile to the government's economic policy but he did not seek to use his revamped TGWU parliamentary group to threaten MacDonald's policies. Instead he looked to the lobbying of the General Council of the TUC as the most effective means for influencing the government. His union took only a limited view of what trade union MPs should concern themselves with:

> The greatest work that can be done is not so much the delivering of speeches on the floor of the House of Commons as the acquiring of knowledge and the utilisation of such knowledge in the committee stages of Bills, in departmental work and in the general detailed service they are able to render. In fact with the Labour government in office, the most efficient MP is the one who, by talking the least, helps get the business through.[24]

Bevin treated the PLP like a rest home for veteran casualties of his own trade union merger offensive. In the 1929 Parliament were men like Sir James Sexton, Ben Tillett, Harry Gosling and Charles Duncan – all former national union leaders with illustrious industrial careers behind them and

---

24 TGWU Executive Council, *Report* (London, 1930), p. 117.

now absorbed inside his mighty TGWU. But Bevin did not use or ask them to cause trouble or embarrass the government. He saw trade union MPs not as a 'cave' or faction but sensitive to the needs of the government, who could prove of use to the trade unions through the provision of detailed private advice and consultation with government departments.

A similar view of the limited role for trade union-sponsored MPs in the PLP was taken by the Miners' Federation, with its 44 sponsored MPs. Only the young Aneurin Bevan, newly elected MP for Ebbw Vale, was a prominent parliamentary rebel among them. Most of the miners' group remained loyal to MacDonald, although they often were so through gritted teeth. Moreover, their activities behind the scenes brought some success in efforts to further the interests of the miners, despite the government's determination not to be seen as beholden to their interests. Their warm relationship with Willie Graham, President of the Board of Trade, proved particularly fruitful in shaping the content of the Coal Mines Bill. But the miners' MPs were never a silent or servile 'lump' inside the House. Stalwarts like Jack Lawson, who served as a junior minister at the Ministry of Labour, and William Whiteley were later to become important pillars of strength to the parliamentary leadership during the 1930s and beyond. Ebby Edwards, Labour MP for Morpeth, later Secretary of the Miners' Federation and then Industrial Relations Director at the National Coal Board, and Will Lawther, Labour MP for Barnard Castle and future President of the National Union of Mineworkers (NUM), were not ineffective backbench MPs either.

For the most part, the PLP's trade union members went a long way to support the government, despite their misgivings about its treatment of the unemployed. But there was no doubting their sullen mood as the 1931 summer parliamentary recess approached with no sign that the government was dealing with the jobless crisis effectively. Charles Dukes, NUGMW-sponsored MP for Warrington and his union's North West Regional Secretary, painted a bleak picture of how he saw the parliamentary outlook from the backbenches before the summer recess:

> The inflexibility of the parliamentary machine has never been more in evidence than during the past few days when the worn out cabinet has been faced with the responsibility of providing a schedule of parliamentary time before the end of the session. It is very difficult to convey to the outsider the actual position as it exists in the House of Commons with regard to this problem of business and time. Last week the Tories by a fluke defeated Clause 3 of the Consumers' Council Bill in committee. These tactics, which are almost childish in policy, create insuperable difficulties for the government. The government had decided in committee to continue the committee stage until 7 o'clock in the evening [which

is a very unusual procedure] but we were so pressed for time that in our attempt to get the Bill completed before the end of the session it had been decided to meet twice a day and sit also late into the evening. A few Labour members had left the Committee Room for tea. Some dozen or more of the Tories must have been in hiding awaiting this event and by a snap division defeated the clause. This means the government must now provide an additional day for the clause to be re-inserted on the committee stage when the Bill comes down to the House.[25]

Dukes' weariness with the parliamentary game was coupled with mounting concern about what was going to happen to unemployment benefit levels when the government-appointed May Committee reported its recommendations of what to do, as it did at the start of the summer parliamentary recess. Like his colleagues, he accepted the PLP would have to support the government's newly drafted measure to deal with 'anomalies' in the unemployment benefit system. After all, the Bill had been endorsed by the General Council of the TUC. The tightening of the provision of state benefits against welfare scroungers was broadly acceptable across the movement. But Dukes also recognised that support for the measure from the PLP had produced 'considerable misunderstanding' in the party and he warned, 'Under any circumstances we consider it unwise to endanger standard benefit in an attempt to defend abuses and anomalies which we feel sure cannot be defended'. Dukes added the PLP would not adopt a position on the wider benefits issue until the May report had been published. 'Our members can rest assured their representatives in the House of Commons will act with organised trade union opinion in the country in defending the workers' rightful claims when the appropriate time arrives for the matter to be dealt with.'[26]

Clearly, a limit appeared to have been reached on just how far even loyal trade union MPs like Dukes were prepared to go in supporting the government in its efforts to secure the confidence of the financial markets with action to reduce public expenditure through a cut in unemployment benefit. Whether this would have led to a serious backbench PLP revolt in the autumn was, however, uncertain. In the event, Labour MPs were not to be tested in the strength of their resolve. In fact, they were to play no direct or active role at all in the events leading to the creation of the National Government. Labour MPs were not recalled to Parliament to discuss what MacDonald had decided to do, perhaps due to the rapidity of events. It was only on 28 August 1931, when the National Government had already been formed, that the PLP met to determine their attitude to

---

25 *NUGMW Journal*, August 1931, p. 205.
26 *Ibid*.

the crisis but by then it was too late for them to make much impact. The meeting turned out to be an unusual gathering. Members of the TUC General Council, including TUC General Secretary Walter Citrine, as well as Bevin, were present; this was said to be at Henderson's request but, no doubt, their appearance helped to stiffen the backbone of many wavering or bewildered Labour MPs. The meeting was asked to endorse a defiant joint manifesto against the National Government – signed on the previous day by the party's National Executive Committee, the General Council of the TUC and the PLP's Consultative Committee.

MacDonald made a strategic error in not attending the PLP meeting to explain why he had decided to form a National Government without first discussing it with Labour backbenchers. There was a dispute over whether he had been given sufficient notice of the meeting. It was said the written request for his attendance had been delayed in delivery. By the time of the meeting the exhausted MacDonald was back in his Highland home at Lossiemouth, recuperating from the previous week's events. It was by no means certain the majority of the PLP would have repudiated the Prime Minister if he had gone to the meeting on 28 August. MacDonald himself believed if he had done so he might have carried as many as half the Labour MPs with him. After all, the PLP gave a courteous enough hearing to the Lord Chancellor, Lord Sankey, and MacDonald's son, Malcolm, when they both defended his decision at the gathering.

Some of the more poignant letters to MacDonald in the days that immediately followed his formation of the National Government came from loyal trade union-sponsored MPs, who might have been expected to regard his decision as a betrayal of both their party and the unemployed. Jack Lawson, Labour MP for Chester le Street, wrote to MacDonald:

> No words of mine can ever express my gratitude to you for all your kindness and for the privilege of your friendship. And the honour of having been associated with you for the whole of my adult life – in ever such a small way in the great work you have done. Though the political tides seem to carry us in different directions I trust it is but for the moment. The events of these days have but stirred up memories of your gallant life and I have discovered that deep respect is rooted in an undying affection. Excuse this intimate note for it is with great difficulty that I refrain myself. I have addressed you as PM but I think of you and always as Ramsay my friend.[27]

Gordon MacDonald, Labour MP for Ince and Lancashire miners' agent, believed the Prime Minister had been 'activated on this occasion by the

---

27 J. Lawson to J. R. MacDonald, 29 August 1931, Lawson Papers, Durham University Library, box 5.

same noble motives that had activated' him in his earlier opposition to British participation in the Great War. He added he would have been 'delighted to have supported the formation of the National government'. However, he disagreed with the proposed unemployment benefit cuts because they 'imposed an additional burden on the exceedingly heavily burdened shoulders of the unemployed'. 'I have come in constant contact with lifelong friends among the unemployed, knowing the tremendous sacrifice that prolonged unemployment has demanded from them and seeing their lean lives they are compelled to live and when I see at the same time a full display of immense wealth in every direction'.[28]

The decision facing Labour MPs in August 1931 on how to respond to MacDonald's decision was well described by Susan Lawrence, Labour MP for Sunderland:

> Every Socialist party in every country comes some day to this final difficulty. It must either accept or challenge the domination of orthodox capitalist finance. I am glad the Labour party is accepting the challenge and only sorry that in taking it you will be one of those whom we must fight. I hope it will be possible to do what we feel to be necessary to protect the homes of the poorest of our people without bitterness and harsh personal criticism. I have to confess that I cannot face without being deeply moved a proposal to balance a budget or maintain the value of sterling which includes an item taken directly from the unemployed. In the transactions of international finance the total sum is small. For my people in Sunderland some of them out of work for 5, 6 or even 8 years, so courageous, so poor and so generous it means so definitely less food and less clothing, the loss of such meagre comforts as they may have had that I cannot bear to hear the words 'equality of sacrifice' without a furious anger boiling up within me.[29]

Few Labour backbenchers, outside the unforgiving ILP core, were in any mood to speak of treachery in their public utterances in August 1931. But their feelings of regret and sorrow towards MacDonald and the small band of his followers who defected from the PLP hardened when, mainly under pressure from the Conservatives, he agreed to call a snap general election the following month. Through the sound and fury of the ensuing campaign it was Snowden who set the tone, with venomous attacks on his former parliamentary colleagues. The PLP's confusions and doubts of August were replaced by bitterness and recrimination.

---

28 G. MacDonald to J. R. MacDonald, 29 August 1931, MacDonald Papers, TNA/PRO, 30/69/1315.
29 S. Lawrence to J. R. MacDonald, 26 August 1931, MacDonald Papers, TNA/PRO, 30/69/316.

Those feelings were well expressed by Dukes, the defeated Labour MP in Warrington, in his NUGMW journal:

> At least forty Labour members chose to go into the wilderness and accept poverty rather than sacrifice principle. Seven million electors refused to be stampeded by the scaremongering of Mr Snowden, who goes to the peers. Some of his old comrades may have to face the Public Assistance Committee. Leaders who had been revered by a movement with which they had been associated for a lifetime, went over to the enemy. They transferred this allegiance not as ordinary recruits to a new political faith; they led the enemy against old comrades and they did this whilst covering their new allies behind stolen banners. They still professed socialistic principles whilst serving the cause of reaction.[30]

A clutch of heartbreaking letters, written to the party's General Secretary, Jim Middleton, confirmed the tragic position of many Labour MPs: 'It was a joy to greet so many old and new friends when Parliament met in 1929', wrote Middleton in the circular letter he sent out to many Labour MPs who lost their seats.

> It has been a constant pleasure to mingle with them during the intervening years. It is a real personal sorrow that so few of them will return to the House of Commons. Nothing in the history of the party has been so heartrending to me as the happenings of the last few weeks. Yet I feel that were the opportunity given them to live again the vital decision would remain. None of us would agree to our being the party to penalise the unemployed for the benefit of the well to do. We have fought a clean fight and have no cause for regret or for reproach nor for remorse.[31]

Labour's landslide defeat in the September 1931 general election brought the extinction of MacDonald's PLP, built up so patiently since the end of the Great War as a broad progressive national alliance for government. Out of its ruins a new PLP was eventually to arise, although it did so only slowly and fitfully during the 1930s. It was to take 14 years before Labour MPs returned in triumph to the Palace of Westminster to support the first majority Labour government. For the time being, divided Labour loyalties between party and class, between loyalty to government and to the needs of the unemployed, which had tested the PLP to distraction, were cruelly resolved. Labour's resulting tragedy at the polls was to resonate down the years.

---

30 *NUGMW Journal*, December 1931, p. 616.
31 J. S. Middleton to defeated Labour MPs, not dated (probably late October 1931), Middleton Papers, Labour History Archive and Study Centre, People's History Museum, Manchester, MID/28/1.

6

The Independent Labour Party and the second Labour government *c.* 1929–31: the move towards revolutionary change

KEITH LAYBOURN

It is generally accepted that the Independent Labour Party (ILP) disaffiliated from the Labour Party in July 1932 because of its reluctance to accept the 1929 revised Standing Orders of the Labour Party which forbade all Labour MPs from voting against the government and committed them to voting as directed by the Labour whips, except on grounds of conscience.[1] However, what is less agreed is what led to this state of play. Indeed, why was there so much feeling over the new Standing Orders that disaffiliation could be considered the only course of action by the majority of ILP delegates who attended the special meeting at Bradford in July 1932? Why were the new Standing Orders the reason, or pretext, for disaffiliation? In answer to these questions, R. E. Dowse, in his book *Left in the Centre*, suggests that there was a clash of personalities and policies within the context of the revolutionary fervour of ILP leaders such as Fenner Brockway and James Maxton and that this led to disaffiliation.[2] It is a view endorsed by Alan McKinlay and James J. Smyth, who suggest that

---

1 Gidon Cohen, *The Failure of a Dream: The Independent Labour Party from Disaffiliation to World War II* (London: Tauris, 2007), pp. 11–12, 18–28; Gidon Cohen, 'The Independent Labour Party, disaffiliation, revolution and Standing Orders', *History*, 86:282 (April 2001), pp. 180–99; F. Brockway, *Socialism Over Sixty Years: The Life of Jowett of Bradford* (London: Allen and Unwin, 1946); Keith Laybourn, '"Suicide during a fit of insanity" or the defence of socialism? The secession of the Independent Labour Party at the special conference at Bradford, July 1931', *Bradford Antiquary*, 3 (1991), pp. 41–53.
2 R. E. Dowse, *Left in the Centre: The Independent Labour Party 1893–1940* (London: Longman, 1966), pp. 181–2.

The ILP and the Labour government

the tensions had begun at the time of the 1926 General Strike and the 'Socialism in Our Time' campaign, which attempted to raise the pace of change to socialism but which also succeeded in dividing regional bodies such as the Scottish ILP.[3] R. K. Middlemas, in his book *The Clydesiders*, concluded that disaffiliation was a 'suicide during a fit of insanity'.[4] More recently, Gidon Cohen has suggested that there was reasoned debate in the move towards disaffiliation.[5] All three interpretations raise questions about the nature of the decision to disaffiliate. The first implies long-term decisions, the second a more immediate decision following the collapse of the second Labour government, while the third suggests that a hard-fought and reasoned debate led to disaffiliation. Ironically, these are not exclusive of each other, although they clearly vary in emphasis. The fact is that there had been tensions between the ILP and the Labour Party before the formation of the second Labour government, during its period of administration, and afterwards. The second Labour government merely heightened the potential for conflict and division. But, as David Howell has reflected, there may be no clearly defined explanation based upon the Labour Party's gradualism and the battle over the Standing Orders, for neither issue would have gained a majority for disaffiliation. Indeed, as Howell writes, 'The trajectory of the ILP in the decade after 1922 cannot be captured adequately in the narrative of socialist disenchantment with the compromises of gradualism.'[6] Nevertheless, nuanced or not, the narrative of the second Labour government provided the context and the final reason for disaffiliation.

The ILP famously voted to leave the Labour Party at a special conference of the ILP held at Jowett Hall, Bradford, in July and August 1932, almost a year after the end of the second Labour government. The fact that there was a period of a year between the end of the Labour government and disaffiliation has meant that considerable emphasis has been placed upon the events of that year, most markedly the famous negotiations over Standing Orders between the ILP and the Labour Party in May and June 1932.[7] Labour's general election defeat of 27 October 1931, when

---

3 A. McKinlay and James J. Smyth, 'The end of the "agitator workman": 1926–1932', in A. McKinlay and R. J. Morris (eds), *The ILP on Clydeside 1893–1932: From Foundation to Disintegration* (Manchester: Manchester University Press, 1991), pp. 177, 200.
4 R. K. Middlemas, *The Clydesiders: A Left Wing Struggle for Parliamentary Power* (London: Hutchinson, 1965), pp. 259–71.
5 Cohen, *The Failure of a Dream*, pp. 14–28.
6 David Howell, *MacDonald's Party: Labour Identities and Crisis 1922–1931* (Oxford: Oxford University Press, 2002), p. 308.
7 *New Leader*, 5 August 1931, indicates that the Parliamentary Labour Party (PLP) considered the revised Standing Orders on 24 May 1932 but that the Labour Party National

Labour's parliamentary representation fell from 287 to 52, had certainly pressured the Parliamentary Labour Party (PLP) to tighten ranks and to seek the full application of the new Standing Orders of 1929. Yet one should not forget that throughout the term of the second Labour government the reformed ILP group under Jimmy Maxton had simply ignored the new Standing Orders, as did a total of 126 Labour MPs throughout the lifetime of the second Labour administration.[8] Indeed, the fight over the revised Standing Orders was as fervently played out in more than two years of the second Labour government as it was in the year after its fall. Indeed, the ILP MPs became intense critics of the 'gradualist' Labour government and Labour Party, and some of them began to advocate a 'new revolutionary policy' *en route* to disaffiliation. The period of the second Labour government was thus crucial in, and central to, the process of political change within the ILP. It ensured that the disaffiliationists, probably a minority at the time of the second Labour government, were able to secure the majority of support they needed for their policy of disaffiliation and revolutionary change.

This tension between the ILP, on the one hand, and the PLP and second Labour government, on the other, was hardly unexpected given the protean nature of the Labour Party. The fact is that the ILP had always exercised its political independence of the PLP. Indeed, Fenner Brockway, sometime chairman of the ILP and long-time editor of its paper the *New Leader*, summarised this long-standing policy and practice in the *New Leader* in July 1931, stressing that the ILP MPs had always accepted the policies of the Labour Party conference except on the issue of armaments: 'The Labour Party believing in decision by international agreement, the ILP by national example.'[9] In June 1932 he added that the ILP had always honoured its 'conditions of affiliation' to the Labour Party but at the same time had 'maintained its right to advocate Socialist policies beyond the Labour programme. That right has never been and should not be

---

Executive Committee decided not to revise them on 26 May. On 1 June 1932 the PLP decided not to revise them but on 5 June 1932 the ILP offered to meet the Labour Party on the issue of revision of Standing Orders. On 23 June the Labour Party Executive informed the ILP that there would be no revision of the Standing Orders. On 8 July the National Administrative Committee of the ILP announced its intention to submit a resolution in favour of disaffiliation at the special conference in Bradford at the end of July 1932.

8 Brockway, *Socialism Over Sixty Years*, p. 300, indicates that 126 out of the 287 MPs (291 according to most indications) voted against the second Labour government during its existence. The *New Leader*, 12 June 1931, suggested that the figure was 126 out of 280 in the article 'Relation between the Independent Labour Party and the Labour Party'.

9 A. F. Brockway, 'The crisis before the ILP', *New Leader*, 10 July 1931.

challenged.'[10] In order to defend that position, the ILP had in fact taken a decision at its 1930 Easter conference (held at Birmingham) to reconstruct its parliamentary group on a resolution on the 'basis of acceptance of the policy of the ILP' as agreed at its annual conferences and the National Administrative Committee.[11] It was carried by a vote of seven to one, after a vigorous debate in which the minority expressed the view that such an action would fragment socialism and halt the socialist advance.[12] This effectively meant that the ILP was intending to act as a party within a party, but discussions took place and appeared to resolve the differences between the ILP and the Labour Party on 25 July 1930. However, on 30 July 1930 the ILP, without warning the Labour Party, reissued its request for ILP MPs to pledge themselves to the policies of the ILP. This led to a spate of meetings and correspondence between the ILP and the Labour Party in July and August 1930. The discussions went into November and December, when the ILP attempted to force ILP-sponsored MPs to commit themselves to a pledge of loyalty to the ILP.[13] Alongside this was the demand of the National Executive Committee (NEC) of the Labour Party and the PLP that the revised Standing Orders of 1929 be accepted. The ILP's failure to meet this demand led to Tom Irwin's parliamentary campaign in East Renfrew in November 1930 being supported only by the ILP. The fact is that these types of conflicts – between the ILP's demand for the loyalty of its members and the Labour Party's or the PLP's demand for the loyalty of the ILP MPs – rumbled on throughout the entire period of the second Labour government. The debate over Standing Orders might have heated up in the summer months of 1932 but it was an ever-present issue in 1930 and 1931.

Crucial to the decision of the ILP not to compromise on its assumed right of independence of action was the political record of the second Labour government, which offered proof positive of the failure of socialist 'gradualism' to some sections of the ILP and spurred them along the route to more revolutionary policies. As Fenner Brockway stated at the Easter conference of the ILP in March 1932:

---

10 *New Leader*, 12 June 1932. Elements of this also appear on 1 April 1932 in the *New Leader* report on A. Fenner Brockway's address 'On the coming revolution' to the ILP Easter conference.
11 The Labour Party, *Report of the 32nd Annual Conference* (London, 1932), appendix VIII, p. 293 (citing the 1930 ILP conference). The resolution was put forward by Hilda Jennings, an ILP delegate from London.
12 Howell, *MacDonald's Party*, pp. 292–3, indicates that the main opposition came from Patrick Dollan (the leading figure in the Glasgow ILP and strong rival to Jimmy Maxton) and Tom Stamford.
13 See Labour Party, *Report of the 31st Annual Conference* (London, 1931), pp. 295–6.

> If the experience of a Labour Government had filled the minds of only the working class section of the electorate with a positive faith and a positive sense of achievement they would be immune to all the power and scorn of the Capitalist Parties. It was the failure of the Labour Government during these months of office which made the minds of the working class in a negative condition which easily responded to the negative phrases and fears during the three weeks of the election.[14]

To some sections of the ILP the second Labour government was a missed opportunity and the introduction of socialism now required a new direction.

Early tensions

Despite this frustration with the second Labour government one should not forget that there were tensions developing between the ILP and the Labour Party long before 1929. The ILP, formed as a national socialist party at Bradford in 1893, had seen itself as the intellectual godparent of the Labour Representation Committee and the Labour Party in the early twentieth century. However, it had had to reassess its position in 1918 when the Labour Party committed itself to socialism. Eventually resolving to remain in existence and affiliated to the Labour Party in the early 1920s, it sought to influence the Labour Party through its growing influence in Clydeside. It exercised some significant parliamentary power and was largely responsible for the PLP electing James Ramsay MacDonald as Labour leader in 1922. However, its relations with MacDonald and the first Labour government, of 1924, went sour, even though John Wheatley, Fred Jowett and other ILP activists did gain office in that government. Indeed, there is the infamous remark of MacDonald, at 10 Downing Street, when presented with a resolution from the ILP parliamentary group: 'Well, Brockway, what commands have you brought me today?'[15]

Nevertheless, relations between the ILP and the Labour Party had been relatively good up to that point in the 1920s, Clifford Allen, the ILP chairman, maintaining a close personal friendship with MacDonald. However, once Fred Jowett took over from Allen as chairman in 1925 and James Maxton replaced him in 1926, relations grew much worse. The 'Socialism in Our Time' programme that the ILP mounted in the mid-1920s divided members of the ILP and worsened relations with the Labour

---

14 *New Leader*, 1 April 1932.
15 F. Brockway, *Inside the Left: Thirty Years of Platform, Press, Prison and Parliament* (London: George Allen and Unwin, 1942), p. 152; also quoted in D. Marquand, *Ramsay MacDonald* (London: Jonathan Cape, 1977), p. 409.

Party, whose leader was willing to point to the contradictions in the programme. Indeed, drawn up by Allen and friends, and advocating gradual ameliorative policies such as the 'living wage', the campaign stressed the need to redistribute income to mass consumers in order to create the home demand that would reduce unemployment. However, once Allen was removed by the Clydesiders, the preamble to the ILP's *Living Wage* pamphlet was amended to indicate that there was a need to bring about the collapse of capitalism, when it was evident that the majority of the policy was designed to make capitalism work more efficiently in the interest of the workers.[16] Several months before the new policy was approved by the ILP conference in April 1926 its advocates stated that 'They believed that "the old order was breaking down"' and that resolute socialist policies would be needed to 'carry us through the period of transition from the old to the new civilisation'.[17]

MacDonald and the Labour Party pointed to these contradictions and largely dismissed the campaign, much to the annoyance of the Clydeside section of the ILP.[18] MacDonald feared that the 'living wage' policy, with its effective advocacy of a national minimum wage, would be a 'millstone' around the neck of the Labour Party and that socialism would arise out of the healthy aspects of society and not its failing sections.[19] It was condemned further by MacDonald at the Labour Party conference in 1927 as 'a programme of flashy futilities'.[20] In addition, there was some local disquiet among ILP members. The Bradford ILP discussed the 'living wage' policy in February 1926 and voted in favour, although there was criticism from Councillor Brooke, who was 'anxious lest trade union power should be undermined', and from others who felt that 'Socialism in Our Time' would 'bolster up the capitalist system'.[21] Some felt that the proposal was 'fathered by Impatience and mothered in Piety'.[22]

This rising conflict between the ILP and the Labour Party was markedly evident at the latter's conference held at Birmingham in 1928, when Labour's policy document *Labour and the Nation* was debated over three days. MacDonald emphasised the need for gradual change to state action to deal with unemployment, the assumption being that unemployment

---

16 *Bradford Pioneer*, 1 January 1926.
17 *Ibid.*
18 *Ibid.*
19 Quoted in Marquand, *Ramsay MacDonald*, pp. 452–6, from *Socialist Review*, March 1926.
20 Quoted *ibid.*, p. 454
21 *Bradford Pioneer*, 5 February 1926.
22 *Bradford Pioneer*, 9 April 1926. The quote is taken from H. N. Brailsford's speech at the ILP conference of 1926.

was a failure of capitalism and that socialism would ultimately deal with it. MacDonald's critics talked of class conflict and the need for faster moves towards socialism. However, Jimmy Maxton did admit that socialism could no longer be approached by a 'long, slow process of gradualist, peaceful, Parliamentary change' and declared that once the 'Socialism in Our Time' programme was implemented socialism would be still as far away as ever, ending with the cry 'let your slogan be: "Socialism is the only remedy"'.[23]

Tensions were clearly running high even before the second Labour government came to power in June 1929 and even before MacDonald consigned most of the ILP's 37 (of 287 Labour) MPs to the backbenches, but still confined by the new Standing Orders that aimed to prevent them raising amendments to government legislation or voting against it. The ILP was not about to be muzzled.

Gradualism and disaffiliation

Shortly after the ILP disaffiliated from the Labour Party in July 1932, Brockway wrote an article entitled 'Why the ILP left the Labour Party'. In it he stressed emphatically that 'We have heard much of loyalty. It was not the ILP which was guilty of disloyalty. It was the Labour government.'[24] He reiterated that the ILP had always maintained its freedom of action in the House of Commons, while remaining loyal to the socialist decisions of Labour Party conferences, but explained how it had become disenchanted by the 'gradualism' of the Labour Party and the policies of the second Labour government. To him, and many other members of the ILP, the Labour government had abandoned its responsibility to introduce socialism. To Brockway it was the 'gradualism' of the Labour Party and the capitalism of the Labour government that had led to the ILP's disaffiliation and he anticipated a new, more revolutionary approach to socialism, while reminding his readers that it was going to be one developed by the ILP in a British context, not the one adopted by the Communist Party: 'The rigidity of mind and method of the British Communist Party makes it incapable of appealing to the mass British working class or of adopting policies applicable to the British situation.'[25]

Brockway had previously listed the failures of the Labour government at the Easter conference of the ILP in 1932, when, as chairman, he had

---

23 Labour Party, *Report of the 28th Annual Conference* (London, 1928), quoted in W. Knox, *James Maxton* (Manchester: Manchester University Press, 1987), pp. 79–80.
24 *New Leader*, 5 August 1932.
25 *Ibid*.

discussed 'The coming revolution'.[26] His argument was that the Labour government had failed because it did not press forward with socialist policies. He dismissed the view that it could not act because it was a minority government by stressing that, in that case, it should not have taken office. But he argued that even as a minority government it could have pressed ahead with socialist measures and forced the other political parties to reject them and form a coalition government, or that it could have ignored parliamentary defeats and hung on to power as long as it could in an attempt to highlight the need for socialist measures. Instead it flirted with capitalism: 'It meant going from compromise to compromise. It meant that a Government which called itself Labour actually became the instrument of making the condition of the working class worse....'[27] Brockway then outlined some of the policies of the Labour government, and particularly the Anomalies Act, which deprived many out of work married women of their right to unemployment insurance. In the final analysis, Brockway's explanation of the failure of the second Labour government and disaffiliation was that gradualism would not achieve socialism and that the minority Labour government simply failed to carry out socialist policies. The failure of the second Labour government was to be the platform for a flexible and more revolutionary policy that would be fought out within the ILP throughout the 1930s.

The ILP and Labour in power

The second Labour government quite simply intensified the perpetual conflict of political independence between the ILP and the Labour Party. Reflecting upon the second Labour government in January 1932, almost equidistant between the resignation of the second Labour government and disaffiliation, Brockway asserted that, apart from the tensions between the ILP and the Labour Party in the 1920s, 'There was the further shock which followed the futility of the Labour Government of 1929 to 1931.'[28]

From the formation of the second Labour government in June 1929 the ILP MPs were opposed to many of its policies. For instance, Maxton and most sections of the ILP disagreed with the Labour government's unemployment insurance proposals in the autumn of 1929, advocating amendments which they considered to be in line with the more generous approach

---

26 *New Leader*, 1 April 1932.
27 *Ibid*.
28 *New Leader*, 15 January 1932.

agreed at Labour Party conferences and the Trades Union Congress.[29] The complaints of Fred Jowett, Jimmy Maxton and John Wheatley were: that only an extra £12 million per year was being made available for the unemployed and that a higher level of expenditure was required; that they could not agree with the 'not genuinely seeking work' clause, which would have denied benefits to some of the unemployed; and that they objected to the clause preventing payments to the newly unemployed for the first six days.[30] In the end, the government proposals were amended and 'dole', or transitional payments for those without automatic benefits who had made contributions to the Unemployment Fund, was made easier to obtain. However, this opposition to the unemployment policies signalled both the difficulties that were to emerge between the ILP and the second Labour government and the serious tensions within the ILP between its factions within its parliamentary group and throughout the country.[31]

While Maxton, Jowett and Wheatley criticised the second Labour government, Patrick Dollan and a large number of Scottish ILP members remained loyal to it. Indeed, one ILP loyalist reflected that 'Wheatley will stop at nothing in his frenzy to bring Mac down.'[32] Evidently, not all ILP members saw the second Labour government as already being a failure.

Initially there was a willingness among some of the ILP rank and file in the regions to accept that dealing with unemployment and the dole was a teething problem faced by a minority government. A Huddersfield ILP member wrote that:

> Prevented from carrying out a real Socialist programme, through the lack of a Parliamentary majority, the Government has nevertheless made every effort to put some new spirit into capitalist enterprise. A new overseas Trade Development Council has been created and the Trade Mission are to go, or have gone, to South America....[33]

This particular passage, indeed, hints at acceptance of MacDonald's general assumption that socialism would arise out of the success of capitalism. Such optimism was not to last.

Within a few months of the conflict over unemployment insurance the ILP felt obliged to reiterate its long-held belief that it had a duty to

---

29 *New Leader*, 12 June 1931.
30 Referred to in the *Bradford Pioneer*, 22 November 1930.
31 Howell, *MacDonald's Party*, pp. 289–91, indicates the extent of the division within the ILP ranks over the action in the House of Commons and the nature of four meetings by the parliamentary group of the ILP.
32 *Ibid.*, p. 291.
33 *Huddersfield Citizen*, September 1930.

The ILP and the Labour government

act as the socialist conscience of Labour. Its long-assumed political and tactical independence was asserted further by the National Administrative Committee's statement to the ILP conference of Easter 1930:

> But the I.L.P. has always been an independent Socialist organisation making its distinctive contribution to Labour Party policy and having its distinctive function within the Party. Whilst the I.L.P. has worked with loyalty to the Labour Party principles, its liberty of action when fundamental Socialist issues are involved has not been questioned. Throughout the period of the war, and on many occasions before and since, I.L.P. members in Parliament, including several members of the present Government, have felt it necessary to vote according to their convictions, even though the majority of the Party took another view.
>
> The suggestion is now made that all Labour members of Parliament and all Labour candidates should undertake never to vote against the Government. It is unreasonable to ask members of the Party to accept without question all the proposals of the Government when those proposals are not themselves subject to the decisions of the Parliamentary Party, and in many instances do not comply with the programme authorised by the Labour Conference.[34]

The ILP was prepared to reprimand the Labour Party – the recalcitrant child it had helped to produce – as it fledged into the party of government. Indeed, James Maxton, the chairman at the 1930 ILP conference, informed his audience that despite the Labour Party declaring itself to be socialist in 1918 the ILP, after a lengthy debate, had concluded in the early 1920s that 'our work was not nearly finished and that we should apply our minds to bringing Socialism into the political and social affairs of this nation as an objective of speedy realisation'.[35] To Maxton and the ILP, the Labour government was far too gradualist and ineffective, and they believed that a more revolutionary approach to socialism was required. Maxton's speech on this was subsequently published in a 15-page pamphlet entitled *Where the I.L.P. Stands*.[36]

Thus, the ILP was frequently opposed to the legislation of the Labour government. As already seen, it was particularly concerned about unemployment and poverty at the end of 1929, and sought to amend the Unemployment Insurance Bill of 1929. It also tried to amend the Coal Mines Bill of 1930, in order to introduce a minimum wage. It made amendments to the attempt to form a Public Loans Board. In October

---

34 J. Maxton, *Where the I.L.P. Stands: Presidential Address of J. Maxton* (London: ILP Publications, 1930), p. 14.
35 *Ibid.*, p. 4.
36 *Ibid.*

1930 Fred Jowett, the ILP MP for Bradford East, moved an amendment to the King's Speech, because 'Socialism is the official policy of the Labour Party and it was not recognised in the King's Speech.'[37] The ILP also opposed local interference in maintenance allowances in the Education Bill and also sought the extension of rights during the discussion of the legislation on National Health Insurance between December 1930 and January 1931, stressed the need for extended membership on the Committee of Privileges, opposed all army, navy and air force estimates as a matter of principle, and demanded an alternative vote in the Representation of the People Bill.[38] There was also a general criticism of the Labour government's failure to put into place a trial for the Meerut prisoners in India.

At the Labour Party annual conference held at Llandudno in October 1930, famous more for the debate and vote on Mosley's policy than anything else, MacDonald, by popular acclaim, made a brilliant speech defending the government's performance on public works for the unemployed. Nevertheless, Maxton moved what was effectively a vote of censure on the Labour government but it was defeated by 1,800,000 votes to 330,000.[39] In the wake of this the ILP parliamentary group discussed the Mosley Memorandum economic policies for Britain and rejected them, although five ILP MPs did support Mosley's radical policies. But that was merely an interim distraction, and more serious conflict was to come.

Subsequently, the ILP's disagreement on the policy for the unemployed led to a speech by Brockway in the House of Commons, made at the time of the Conservative motion of censure of 1 April 1931, to be published under the title *A Socialist Plan for Unemployment*. The Conservative vote of censure was based upon the failure of Labour's unemployment policy but the ILP amendment to this outlined a socialist policy for unemployment based upon the 'Socialism in Our Time' programme of establishing a living wage, raising the school-leaving age, reducing the hours of the working week, increasing old-age pensions, unemployment allowances and widows' pensions, developing a national housing scheme, and extending credits to the Soviet Union in the areas of shipbuilding and engineering. On this occasion the ILP voted against the Conservative motion of censure because it felt that 'the Conservative Party are more the political enemies of the unemployed than any other section'.[40] Brockway dismissed

---

37 Brockway, *Socialism Over Sixty Years*, p. 270.
38 *New Leader*, 12 June 1931.
39 Labour Party, *Report of the 30th Annual Conference* (London, 1931), p. 40, and referred to in Sir Oswald Mosley, *My Life* (London: Nelson, 1968), p. 261.
40 A. Fenner Brockway, *A Socialist Plan for Unemployment: Speech by A. Fenner Brockway* (London: ILP, 1931), p. 3.

The ILP and the Labour government

the Conservative policies on unemployment as attempts to worsen the condition of the unemployed by reducing 'dole' and as attempts to drive the long-term unemployed to despair by separating those unemployed for more than a year from the rest of those without work. Brockway attacked their penchant for tariffs, which he saw as equally unsatisfactory as free trade. Reflecting the ILP position, he criticised the failure of the Labour government to tackle unemployment through socialist measures, regretted its acceptance of the need to increase productivity before unemployment could be properly tackled, and reminded the government that, while the ILP group would vote against the Conservative censure, 'if the Government are to secure our support, their unemployment policy must be based upon Socialist principles'.[41] Ultimately, that meant to the ILP a minimum standard of living, nationalisation and national planning, and the setting up of import and export boards to control imports and exports.

The second Labour government did not heed the warning from, what was by then, the fragmented ranks of the ILP parliamentary group, which was divided and losing some ILP MPs to Mosley's New Party. Most famously the ILP rebels opposed the second Labour government's Anomalies Bill, debated in Parliament in June and July 1931. When enacted, it eventually deprived about 220,000 insured married women of the right to unemployment benefits simply because they were unemployed but married to employed husbands and working in areas where there was no work and where they were deemed as not 'genuinely seeking work'.[42] This was blatantly discriminatory, for it did not relate to men (married or single) or single women who had paid their contributions but were seeking work in similar areas where there was no work to be had. The Bill was introduced by Margaret Bondfield, the Minister of Labour, and supported by Dr Marion Phillips, MP for Sunderland and Secretary and Chief Woman Organiser of the Women's Section of the Labour Party.[43] Although the second reading was carried overwhelmingly, by 231 votes to 19, with about 60 per cent of MPs not voting, it was a mixture of ILP MPs and Conservatives who opposed this measure, which was designed to save a mere £5 million for the Treasury.

George Buchanan, Jimmy Maxton and Fenner Brockway headed a small group of about a dozen ILP 'rebel' MPs, including Fred Jowett, Jennie Lee and J. F. Horrabin, who opposed the Bill. Brockway asked,

---

41 *Ibid.*, p. 8.
42 Keith Laybourn, *Unemployment and Employment Policies Concerning Women in Britain, 1900–1951* (Lampeter: Edwin Mellen Press, 2002), pp. 122–32.
43 Marian Goronwy Phillips, *A Woman of Vision: A Life of Marion Phillips* (London: Bridge Books, 2000).

'Why do women who claim their legal rights become spongers?', adding that 'The working woman who is married if she has a legal right to benefit has the right to get it without being blackballed and libelled.'[44] He also complained of the 'grave abuses that the unemployed suffer'.[45] As a result, the ILP 'rebel' MPs forced an all-night session which produced 32 divisions on the Bill. However, it was Duff Cooper, a Conservative MP, who probably did the government most damage when he accurately reflected that:

> There had been only two whole-hearted and effective speeches made on behalf of the Bill, the speech of the right hon. Lady who introduced the Bill and the speech of the hon. Lady the Member for Sunderland. It is remarkable, perhaps regrettable, that a Bill that is going to affect so seriously the position of so many married women could find only two sound supporters in the house, and both should be ladies and both should be single.[46]

Indeed, the Anomalies Bill was considered by Brockway to be the overwhelming justification for the ILP's willingness to flout Labour's new Standing Orders.[47] At the subsequent ILP Easter conference of 1932, he reflected that this Bill was one of the worst examples of the failure of the second Labour government:

> The Labour Government became responsible for this cruel measure as a result of one of the meanest capitalist agitations this country has ever witnessed. It was in literal truth an agitation to rob the pittance of the unemployed in order to safeguard the luxury incomes of the rich from increased taxation. The same agitation compelled the representatives of the Labour government to accept the principles of the Means Test on the Parliamentary Committee and to agree the May Committee which resulted in the cut in unemployment benefit rates, the wages of public workers, the social services – which the National Government has since imposed.[48]

Throughout the period of the second Labour government, then, the ILP had been critical of many of Labour's policies. Indeed, even when it supported the government against a motion of no confidence on 1 April 1931, Fenner Brockway made it clear that the ILP did so only because it feared the opposition parties had no better plans than Labour for the unemployed, although Brockway added that he also hoped that the government would introduce an unemployment policy based upon

---

44 *House of Commons Debates*, fifth series, 8 July 1931, 254, col. 2129.
45 *Ibid.*, col. 2189.
46 *Ibid.*, col. 2210.
47 *New Leader*, 1 April 1932.
48 *Ibid.*

The ILP and the Labour government

'Socialist principles' and that that would gain the support of the backbenchers.[49] The ILP's political support was conditional.

The political defection of Ramsay MacDonald in August 1931, his formation of a National Government and the calling of a general election in October 1931 brought matters to a head. The Labour Party demanded that all its parliamentary candidates sign a document accepting its revised Standing Orders. Nineteen ILP candidates refused to sign and were thus not endorsed by the Labour Party. Three of them were among the five ILP MPs who were elected in the 1931 general election – Jimmy Maxton, R. C. Wallhead and John McGovern, joined by two successful ILP trade unionists, David Kirkwood and George Buchanan, who also declined to accept Standing Orders. These five ILP MPs formed the ILP group in the new Parliament and were not admitted to the meetings of the PLP.

Matters were not helped by the fact that the Labour Party conference of October 1931 did not accept that the ILP could act as the organised socialist conscience of the party. Negotiations between the ILP and the Labour Party faltered and the issue of disaffiliation was seriously raised at the ILP's Easter conference of 1932, where, by a narrow majority (188 votes to 144), the delegates rejected disaffiliation and voted in favour (by 250 to 53) of the Scottish amendment for conditional affiliation. A similar motion at the Easter conference of 1931 had been defeated by 173 votes to 37. Nevertheless, as a result of the 1932 vote, negotiations were reopened between J. S. Middleton, Assistant Secretary of the Labour Party, and John Paton, of the ILP, in the hope that a compromise might be arranged. In the end, this was not to be, for, as indicated above, the negotiations of May–June 1932 failed to achieve a compromise.

Disaffiliation

Even though the vote in favour of disaffiliation was carried in July 1932, one must not assume that the majority members of the ILP were opposed to working with the Labour Party. As indicated above, the resolution to disaffiliate from the Labour Party had not been carried. The fact is that many ILP supporters, former ILP and Labour MPs, had voted against various pieces of legislation put forward by the second Labour government from time to time without wishing to disaffiliate or leave the Labour Party. Estimates offered by Brockway, Jowett and others suggest that 126 Labour MPs, from all sides of the party, voted against legislation put forward by

---

49 Brockway, *A Socialist Plan for Unemployment*, p. 8.

the second Labour government.[50] While some of those were ILP MPs who became committed to both disaffiliation and the new revolutionary policy, others were not. William Leach, an ILP MP for Bradford Central and Under-Secretary in the Treasury of the first Labour government, was strongly opposed to disaffiliation and campaigned against it fervently in the *Bradford Pioneer,* an ILP and Labour paper. A close friend, and one-time employer, of Fred Jowett, the MP for Bradford East, he wrote numerous articles in the *Pioneer* during the 1920s and early 1930s, at that time edited by Frank Betts, the father of Barbara Castle. In 1930 and 1931 Leach complained, contentiously, that the ILP was weakening the whole movement, as it had the second Labour government, 'by its continuous assertion of Labour untrustworthiness, and yapping at the heals of the present leaders'.[51] In July 1932 he suggested that there were disappointed vanities at work within some sections of the ILP and 'that MacDonald and Co. have gone East, the disaffiliationists would go West. All the fruits of ill will, antagonism and open war are bound to follow in both cases.'[52]

At the 1932 Bradford special conference itself, E. F. Wise, one of the intellectuals in the party who had been attracted into it by Clifford Allen, opposed disaffiliation, stating that while 'he made no attempt to defend the actions of the last Labour Government, nor did he reject a simple vote against them. But he saw nothing in Standing Orders to prevent members saying what they pleased inside and outside the Parliamentary Labour Party.'[53] Others agreed with this sentiment, and many members were to leave the ILP between 1932 and 1933, unable and unwilling to leave Labour or to accept the new revolutionary policy. Before the decision was taken to disaffiliate, John Arnott called for the Labour Party to prevent the ILP's defection.[54] The *Leeds Citizen* concurred and stressed that 'If the ILP is dissatisfied with the Labour Party it will not improve it by committing suicide in a passion of indignation.'[55] In the wake of disaffiliation, only one of the 32 members of the Labour group on Bradford Council left the Labour Party and the Bramley ILP agreed to remain with the Labour Party. On 24 September 1932 a Yorkshire conference of affiliated ILP members was held.[56] Patrick Dollan, in control of a substantial proportion

---

50 McKinlay and Smyth, 'The end of the "agitator workman"'.
51 Brockway, *Inside the Left,* p. 238.
52 *Bradford Pioneer,* 8 July 1932.
53 *New Leader,* 5 August 1932.
54 *Leeds Citizen,* 11 December 1931.
55 *Leeds Citizen,* 29 January and 1 April 1932.
56 *Bradford Pioneer,* 5 and 12 August, 9 and 30 September 1932; *Leeds Citizen,* 19 August 1932; City of Leeds Labour Party, Minutes, 13 October 1932, West Yorkshire Archives, Leeds Branch, Sheepscar Library.

of the Glasgow ILP, formed the Scottish Socialist Party, which claimed 107 ILP branches and about 50 per cent of the Glasgow ILP membership, in an attempt to remain loyal to the Labour Party.[57] Others agreed with the sentiments and many others were to leave in 1934 and 1935, unable to accept the new revolutionary policy of the ILP nor convinced of the need to develop Marxist policies. A rather sad editorial in the *Bradford Pioneer*, presumably written by Betts, concurred with the fears of those who felt that the ILP would now go into political oblivion:

> The Independent Labour Party now joins the numerous small groups engaged in useless and obscure warfare against the organised Labour army. Along with the Communist Party, the Socialist Party of Great Britain and other eccentric groups quite unknown to the general public, the total sterility of a once great and influential party seems assured.[58]

In the end, the ILP determined on disaffiliation, a course of action which a substantial part of its membership could not accept. It was only the furore caused by the second Labour government, and the constant pressure by Maxton, Brockway and the other leading figures, that seems to have given them and others of a disaffiliationist mind the support they sought.

Conclusion

The ILP was clearly at odds with the Labour Party throughout the 1920s and early 1930s. Yet once it had determined to continue as an independent socialist party affiliated to the Labour Party it had re-emphasised its continued commitment the introduction of socialism. It felt free to express its concern at the failure of the 1924 minority Labour government to press forward with socialist measures. Anxious to speed up the process of introducing socialism, it developed the 'Socialism in Our Time' campaign in the mid 1920s, which brought it into conflict with Ramsay MacDonald and the Labour Party. The final straw was the second Labour government, which Brockway suggested had failed to realise the 'futility' of its policies.[59] Despite attempts to muzzle internal opposition through the revised Standing Orders of the PLP, the ILP MPs regularly voted against the second Labour government, particularly on the issue of unemployment. The failure of that government to deliver socialism, indeed its commitment

---

57 *Forward*, 27 August, 3 September 1932, quoted in McKinlay and Smyth, 'The end of the "agitator workmen"', p. 198.
58 *Bradford Pioneer*, 5 August 1932.
59 F. Brockway, *Socialism at the Cross-Roads: Why the Labour Party Left the Labour Party* (London: ILP, 1932), p. 6.

to operating capitalism, convinced the ILP that it should pursue revolutionary rather than gradualist policies in establishing socialism. In the end, that meant that some members of the ILP felt it necessary to disaffiliate from the Labour Party. The problems with the second Labour government made the ILP's disaffiliation inevitable, given the Labour Party's insistence upon imposing the new Standing Orders to prevent ILP MPs from voting according to their own wishes. The record of the second Labour government ensured that the ILP would flee the Labour Party nest. The timescale of the ILP's disaffiliation arises largely from what is perceived to be the failure and futility of the second Labour government.

The ILP abandoned its own gradualist policy of 'Socialism in Our Time' when, at its 1933 conference, held in Derby, it accepted a 'new revolutionary policy'. This was based upon a type of syndicalist workers' council programme, although it meant different things to different sections of the ILP. The ILP's new policy advocated the creation of a United Revolutionary Party with the Communists and favoured approaching the Comintern, the international organisation of communism, for membership. The Revolutionary Policy Committee of the ILP, powerful in London and led by Dr Carl Knight Cullen, pushed for a close association with the communists. However, it was opposed by the competing Unity Group, strong in London, East Anglia and Lancashire, which attempted to overturn the 'new revolutionary policy' and emphasise the parliamentary and ethical aspects of socialism but, failing to do so in 1934, separated from the ILP and formed the Independent Socialist Party, taking much of the ILP membership with it. Other Trotskyist elements formed the Marxist Group and also opposed the 'new revolutionary policy'. Finally, a fragmented and weakened ILP rejected any affiliation to Comintern at its York conference in 1934.

After that, the ILP's 'new revolutionary policy' grew less relevant as the party splintered further and declined rapidly. What is important to realise here, however, is that the second Labour government convinced some powerful sections of the ILP that there was a need for a change in policy and the end of gradualism. In this context, the need to disaffiliate from the Labour Party seemed logical and necessary, although the alternative policy never seemed well defined or universally understood by the various sections of the ILP. In the end, many of the leading figures who been involved in the ILP's disaffiliation later suggested that disaffiliation had been a mistake.[60] But it was a mistake engineered and galvanised partly, possibly substantially, by the failures of the second Labour government.

---

60 Fenner Brockway, *Towards Tomorrow: The Autobiography of Fenner Brockway* (London: Hart-Davis MacGibbon, 1977), p. 107; Jennie Lee, *My Life with Nye* (London: Jonathan Cape, 1980), pp. 175–84.

7

The second Labour government and the consumer

NICOLE ROBERTSON

G. D. H. Cole wrote that 'the second Labour Government floundered from mistake to mistake'. He went on to conclude that 'It is a sorry story; and there is nothing to be gained by attempting to make it out as better than it actually was.'[1] As Ross McKibbin highlighted in his article on the second Labour government, much of the research on that government has traditionally focused on, and been seen in terms of, its downfall.[2] In domestic affairs, the focus within the historiography has often been on the government's ineffective response to rising levels of unemployment and its inability to cope in the face of economic difficulties.[3] Within the

---

1 G. D. H. Cole, *A History of the Labour Party from 1914* (London: Routledge and Kegan Paul, 1969), p. 258.
2 Ross McKibbin, 'The economic policy of the second Labour government 1929–1931', *Past and Present*, 68 (1995), p. 95.
3 For example, Robert Skidelsky's work centres on the unemployment policy of the Labour Party during the years 1929–31 and what he argues to be the 'party's commitment to a Utopian socialism which incapacitated it from effectively working the parliamentary system and prevented it from coming to terms with economic reality.... It thought in terms of a total solution to the problem of poverty, when what it was offered was the limited opportunity to cure unemployment.' Robert Skidelsky, *Politicians and the Slump: The Labour Government of 1929–1931* (London: Macmillan, 1967), p. xii. Kenneth Brown's study of the years 1929–31 largely focuses on the failings of the Labour Party's unemployment policy and the party's 'inability to break out of the constraints of orthodox, budget balancing finance'. Kenneth D. Brown, *The English Labour Movement* (Dublin: Gill and Macmillan, 1982), p. 260. Henry Pelling's account of the second Labour government highlights how its 'domestic policies were proving singularly unsuccessful' and how it was ultimately crippled by its political opponents. Henry Pelling, *A Short History of the Labour Party* (London: Macmillan, 1965), p. 66.

context of a short-lived government that was overwhelmed by political and financial crisis, much has also been written analysing the life, leadership and personal failings of the Prime Minister – Ramsay MacDonald.[4] In more recent years, there has been a much-needed reassessment of the fall of this government and events leading to the crisis of 1931,[5] and an examination of the Labour government within the context of the wider labour movement.[6]

The focus taken in this chapter is on an aspect of domestic policy, but one that has received relatively little attention – that of the Labour government's relationship with the consumer. The Labour Party was primarily associated with the interests of the working class as producers and labourers. Despite being a party formed to represent the 'workers in their capacity as producers rather than as consumers',[7] the plight of the consumer was part of Labour's agenda during the 1929–31 period of government. This chapter considers the second Labour government's reaction towards the working-class consumer; how debates about consumer politics were constructed and articulated; and what, if anything, was achieved during this period to promote the interests of the consumer.

The Labour Party and the general election of 1929

In the days preceding the 1929 general election, the General Council of the Trades Union Congress (TUC) issued 'a stirring manifesto calling on the workers of the country to rally to the support of Labour at the polls';[8] it encouraged all workers to support the Labour Party, as it was the only party committed to making 'the welfare of the workers their first duty'.[9] The Labour Party's electoral manifesto included a variety measures designed to protect the worker. These included schemes to

---

4   See, for example, C. L. Mowat, 'Ramsay MacDonald and the Labour Party', in Asa Briggs and John Saville (eds), *Essays in Labour History 1886–1923* (London: Macmillan, 1971); R. Barker, 'Political myth: Ramsay MacDonald and the Labour Party', *History*, 61:1 (1976), pp. 46–56; David Marquand, *Ramsay MacDonald* (London: Jonathan Cape, 1977); Austen Morgan, *Ramsay MacDonald* (Manchester: Manchester University Press, 1987).
5   Andrew Thorpe, *The British General Election of 1931* (Oxford: Clarendon Press, 1991).
6   Neil Riddell, *Labour in Crisis: The Second Labour Government, 1929–31* (Manchester: Manchester University Press, 1999).
7   Eleanor Barton, *Women – in the Home, the Store and the State* (Manchester: Co-operative Union, c. 1929), pp. 5–6.
8   TUC, *The 1929 Elector*, 22 May 1929, p. 1.
9   *Ibid.*

establish adequate provision for unemployed workers, the ratification of the Washington Eight Hours' Convention, a minimum wage for farm labourers, and adequate pensions for aged workers.[10] These addressed a variety of issues pertinent to the working class in their capacity as workers, producers and labourers.

The Labour Party's manifesto of 1929, however, also incorporated a number of proposals to protect these workers against exploitation in their capacity as consumers. It was committed to taking measures against profiteering in food and stated that it would 'watch the operations of Trust and Combines' that enhanced prices unreasonably.[11] Labour's election manifesto was based on *Labour and the Nation* (1928).[12] Plans formulated by the party were given in greater detail in this programme, including those policies that were of importance to the consumer. Part of the party's programme for the 'Democratic Control of Industry' was explicitly devoted to how this would be of benefit to the consumer. Measures designed to protect the consumer against excessive prices included 'establishing a stringent control over monopolies and combines', 'enlarging the powers of the Food Council' and 'utilitising the experience secured during the war as to the advantages of the bulk import of foodstuffs and raw materials by a public authority'.[13] Election literature specifically addressed the issue of profiteering in the food trades at the expense of the consumer. One such pamphlet, *Ten Reasons Why a Vote Given to Labour Is a Vote Well Used*, stated that the Labour Party stood for 'the prevention of profiteering and the abolition of the taxes on food' and highlighted shortfalls of the Tory administration under Stanley Baldwin in refusing to provide the Food Council with the powers to prevent profiteering in food.[14]

Safeguarding the interests of the working-class consumer against high food prices, profiteering and monopolies did not appear just as part of a campaign the Labour Party used for the general election of 1929. Literature published by the party during the 1920s highlights its involvement in issues directly affecting the consumer and the household economy. The Labour Research Department publication *Who Keeps Prices High? Facts About Food Trusts and Other Profits* had claimed that the price of food was 'of the most vital concern to Labour' because 'food accounts for 60 per

---

10 'Labour manifesto 1929', in F. W. S. Craig, *British General Election Manifestos 1918–66* (Chichester: Political Reference Publications, 1970), pp. 55–60
11 *Ibid.*
12 Riddell, *Labour in Crisis*, p. 36.
13 Labour Party, *Labour and the Nation* (London, 1928), p. 27.
14 Labour Party, *Ten Reasons Why a Vote Given to Labour Is a Vote Well Used* (London, 1929).

cent. of working-class expenditure'.[15] This leaflet was a critique of price-fixing associations and combines among capitalist firms.[16] Christopher Addison's pamphlet *Why Food Is Dear* further condemned the 'menacing hold of a few greater corporations over the bulk of our food'.[17] Addison was also highly scathing of the nature of the Food Council established by Stanley Baldwin's government. He argued that a 'Voluntary Food Council which will issue Reports, and "watch"' would not be sufficient to protect the consumer, and expressed concern that 'the sole protection for the British consumer consists in the fact that this powerless body may instruct the Trusts to "desist from such behaviour"'.[18] Moreover, the Labour Party initiated a debate in the House of Commons, reprinted in the pamphlet *The Men Who Work Must Eat: Labour Denounces Food Profiteering* criticising the composition and proceedings of the Royal Commission on Food Prices, and George Lansbury moved a motion demanding protection of the public against profiteering in the sale of food.[19] Promoting the interests of the working class as consumers was a firm part of Labour's agenda when the party came to office in 1929.

The Consumers' Council Bill

Once in government, one of the most prominent measures to safeguard consumer interests was to be brought in under the Consumers' Council Bill.[20] The Bill was presented to Parliament as a much-needed step in consumer protection that would build on previous efforts to deal with excessive profiteering in the food trade. When discussing this Bill, William Graham (President of the Board of Trade) drew attention to the

---

15 Labour Research Department, *Who Keeps Prices High? Facts About Food Trusts and Other Profits* (London, c. 1924), p. 3.
16 *Ibid.*
17 Christopher Addison, *Why Food Is Dear* (London: Labour Party, 1925), p. 3.
18 *Ibid.*, p. 19.
19 Labour Party, *The Men Who Work Must Eat: Labour Denounces Food Profiteering* (London: Labour Publications Department, c. 1925), pp. 2–3.
20 The consumer was also given a certain degree of protection through the Agricultural Marketing Bill. The Labour Party's policy on agriculture focused primarily on the benefits that would be bought to the producer and the farm labourer. However, Leonard Tivey describes the establishment of a consumers' committee under the Agricultural Marketing Act as marking an important step in the history of legislation for consumer representation. Leonard Tivey, 'The politics of the consumer', in R. Kimber and J. J. Richardson (eds), *Pressure Groups in Britain: A Reader* (London: Dent, 1974), p. 201.

The Labour government and the consumer

investigation by the Linlithgow Committee (1922–23) and what was termed 'the quite unfair spread between the producers' prices and the price which was charged in the retail trade'.[21] He also paid tribute to the work carried out by the Royal Commission on Food Prices, which in 1925 had recommended the establishment of a Food Council. He argued that although this Food Council had carried out useful work, it was limited by the fact that it was given no powers of a statutory character.[22] Thus the aims of the Consumers' Council Bill, as defined in the words of Graham, were to 'make good what was not done by our predecessors' and to put the Consumers' Council on a statutory basis.[23] The Consumers' Council would be endowed with compulsory powers to get the information it required, and it would enable the Board of Trade to 'regulate by order the prices to be charged for certain commodities' if prices were found to be excessive.[24] Graham used the measures within the proposed Consumers' Council Bill to respond to a great number of questions that were put to him regarding the rise in prices of a variety of items or, more specifically, the differences between the wholesale and retail price of commodities. These included queries concerning the price of bread, milk, oils, fats and soaps.[25]

Ultimately, under the second Labour government, the Consumers' Council Bill did not become law. Perhaps this, and the fact that it was just one Bill on a list of many 'left "on the stocks" by the Labour government',[26] goes some way to explaining why there is relatively little mention of it within the historiography on that administration. If it is mentioned at all, it is more often than not discussed in relation to other 'failures' in domestic policy.[27] Despite the disappearance of this Bill, it was significant in a number of ways. It can be argued that it is worthy of study because of the manner in which it was framed around the working-class female

---

21 *House of Commons Debates*, fifth series, 8 May 1930, 238, col. 1166.
22 *Ibid.*, cols 1167–8.
23 *Ibid.*, col. 1173.
24 *Ibid.*, col. 1173, and 30 April 1930, col. 199.
25 *House of Commons Debates*, fifth series, 28 April 1931, 251, cols 1429–31; 20 May 1931, 252, cols 1969–70; 9 June 1931, 253, col. 790.
26 *Labour Magazine*, September 1931, p. 217.
27 G. D. H. Cole's *A History of the Labour Party* (p. 232) is an example of this. There are two pieces of work that do incorporate some discussion of the Consumers' Council Bill: a description of attempts to pass the Bill through Parliament is given by Robert A. Bayliss, 'The Consumers' Council Bills 1929–1939', *Journal of Consumer Studies and Home Economics*, 4:2 (1980), pp. 115–23; and, within his study of twentieth-century consumerism, Matthew Hilton includes a short, but perceptive, discussion of what he considers to be the unworkable inconsistencies of the Bill that contributed to its demise – Matthew Hilton, *Consumerism in 20th-Century Britain: The Search for a Historical Movement* (Cambridge: Cambridge University Press, 2004), pp. 124–8.

consumer. The Bill also provides a means of exploring the relationship between different elements of the labour movement.

The female consumer and the Labour government

'Labour, as its founders and many of their successors have stressed, was formed to represent the workers' and, as Jim Tomlinson highlights, through its campaign slogans and sources of financial support it sustained an 'emphasis on the centrality of work through the last century'.[28] One of the most interesting aspects, therefore, of the proposed Consumers' Council Bill is that it provides an opportunity to explore how Labour constructed a Bill that was designed to promote consumer interests. Within the proposals for this Bill, the consumer is very much articulated as being female. The subject of gender and consumption has been explored in a number of studies,[29] although there remains a lack of material incorporating the Consumers' Council Bill of 1929–31. From literature addressing the female consumer and the politics of consumption, a trend emerges in how the consumer is defined and promoted. It is argued that during the early part of the twentieth century, consumer politics was associated with the working-class housewife and her cause was promoted by the Labour Party. In the period after the Second World War, the consumer was no longer portrayed exclusively within the framework of the working-class housewife and consumer politics was no longer dominated by Labour.[30]

---

28 Jim Tomlinson, 'Labour and the economy', in Duncan Tanner, Pat Thane and Nick Tiratsoo (eds), *Labour's First Century* (Cambridge: Cambridge University Press, 2000), p. 73.

29 Maggie Andres and Mary M. Talbot (eds), *All the World and Her Husband* (London: Cassell, 2000); Susan Strasser, Charles McGovern and Matthias Judt (eds), *Getting and Spending: European and American Consumer Societies in the Twentieth Century* (Cambridge: Cambridge University Press, 1998); Martin Daunton and Matthew Hilton, *The Politics of Consumption* (Oxford: Berg, 2001).

30 Matthew Hilton argues that in the first part of the twentieth century the consumer was considered to be working class and female, and issues affecting the consumer were articulated by those of the political left. By the 1940s, although these gender assumptions remained, it was now middle-class women's voluntary groups defending the consumer. By the 1950s the definition of the consumer tended to a gender-neutral category promoted by consumer organisations 'concerned more with the value for money of goods regarded as luxuries or "comforts"'. Matthew Hilton, 'The female consumer and the politics of consumption in twentieth-century Britain', *Historical Journal*, 45:1 (2002), p. 107. Martin Francis, in his work on Labour and gender, similarly has identified the period after the Second World War as one during which the Labour Party placed greater emphasis on the male manual worker, and could be perceived as appearing unsympathetic to the expectations of female consumers.

The Consumers' Council Bill of the second Labour government certainly appears, in this sense, to be a product of its time. Discussions that took place during 1929–31 surrounding the issue of a Consumers' Council were very much articulated and framed in relation to the working-class housewife. This can be seen in publications associated with the labour movement. For example, the *Labour Magazine* declared, in December 1929, that 'the Government will get the thanks of every housewife in the land for their bold step in deciding to set up a powerful Consumers' Council to stop profiteering in foods and other commodities'.[31] In *Labour Woman* the Consumers' Council Bill was designated the 'Housewives' Bill', designed to 'save the housewife's money'.[32] The *Clarion* declared that housewives should welcome the proposed Bill.[33] What is more, this Bill was used by the labour press to construct a political 'battle' between the working-class female consumer (supported by the Labour Party) and the businessmen and profiteers (who had the support of the Tory Party).[34] Similarly, in the parliamentary discussions of the Bill, politicians were reminded 'how extremely serious this is to the housewife'[35] and that 'it will give a direct advantage to the millions of housewives who are struggling under very difficult circumstances'.[36]

The labour movement and the Consumers' Council Bill

The case of the Consumers' Council Bill also provides a means of examining the reactions of different elements within the labour movement to the issue of consumer protection. The second Labour government's interest in consumer affairs received much support from the co-operative movement. Providing wholesome, unadulterated food was one of the main principles upon which the co-operative movement was founded, and safeguarding the consumer remained one of the key objectives of the movement in

---

Martin Francis, 'Labour and gender', in Tanner, Thane and Tiratsoo (eds), *Labour's First Century*, p. 207.
31 *Labour Magazine*, December 1929, p. 360.
32 *Labour Woman*, July 1931, p. 98, and October 1931, p. 152. Details of the Consumers' Council Bill were given in *Labour Woman* in minute detail. Within the magazine the objects of the Bill are explained, the dates on which it was discussed in Parliament are given, and details on its obstruction in Parliament are provided. See *Labour Woman*, April 1931, p. 56; May 1931, p. 73; July 1931, p. 98; October 1931, p. 152.
33 *The Clarion*, December 1929, p. 4.
34 *Labour Magazine*, June 1930, p. 84.
35 *House of Commons Debates*, fifth series, 4 February 1930, 234, cols 1682–3.
36 *House of Commons Debates*, fifth series, 8 May 1930, 238, col. 1237.

the twentieth century.[37] The movement opposed trusts and combines. It argued that their restriction on competition and their control over prices were not in the interests of the consumer.[38] It had been highly critical of the limitations imposed by the Food Council's lack of statutory power. In 1929, the Joint Parliamentary Committee of the Co-operative Congress stated that 'the efforts of the Food Council to prevent unjustifiably high food prices could not be successful unless they had statutory powers to compel the production of accounts and the provision of information'.[39] The co-operative movement, therefore, welcomed the Labour government's plans to set up a Consumers' Council and was a strong supporter of such action.[40] It anticipated that the Council would form a valuable 'weapon in the hands of consumers'.[41] It was A. V. Alexander (Lord of the Admiralty and Co-operative/Labour MP for Sheffield) who was entrusted to get the Bill through the Commons.[42] Other Co-operative MPs were also very vocal in supporting the Labour government on this issue.[43]

A degree of support for the Consumers' Council Bill was also shown by other elements of the labour movement. The official journal of the Trade Union Congress and the Labour Party published articles that were very positive towards the idea of legislating in favour of the consumer. Within this publication, the Consumers' Council Bill was considered to be a 'sign that there is now a Government in office that is determined to put the welfare of the mass of the people before that of wealthy little groups

---

37 Nicole Robertson, *The Co-operative Movement and Communities in Britain, 1914–1960: Minding Their Own Business* (Aldershot: Ashgate, 2010), p. 133.
38 For example, in the 1920s Co-operative MPs had argued that the object of these trusts and combines was 'not as in the case of co-operation, to benefit the great mass of consumers, but to make as large a margin of profit as possible for shareholders'. A. V. Alexander, *Is Co-operation a Social Menace?* (Manchester: Co-operative Union, 1925), pp. 15–17.
39 Joint Parliamentary Committee of the Co-operative Congress, *Co-operative Congress Report* (Manchester: Co-operative Union, 1929), p. 89.
40 See, for example, Joint Parliamentary Committee of the Co-operative Congress, *Co-operative Congress Report* (Manchester: Co-operative Union, 1930), p. 71.
41 F. Hayward, *The Co-operative Boycott and Its Political Implications* (Manchester: Co-operative Union, 1930), p. 13.
42 Thomas Carbery, *Consumers in Politics: A History and General Review of the Co-operative Party* (Manchester: Manchester University Press, 1969), p. 189. Curiously, no mention of this work is made in John Tilley's biography of A. V. Alexander, *Churchill's Favourite Socialist* (Manchester: Holyoake Books, 1995).
43 For example, during the Bill's second reading S. F. Perry (Labour/Co-operative MP for Kettering) emphatically declared that the movement welcomed the establishment of the Consumers' Council with statutory power, viewing it as the 'first step in a policy of protecting the interests of the consumer'. *House of Commons Debates*, fifth series, 8 May 1930, 238, col. 1231.

of vested interest'.[44] The Bill was promoted as the first step in fulfilling Labour's election pledge to prevent profiteering in the food trade and thus offer some protection to the consumer.[45]

The apparent cohesion within the labour movement around this Bill, however, has been challenged. In fact, it was challenged during the 1929–31 administration itself. It has been argued that the concerns of the trade unions about the Consumers' Council Bill 'ensured fractures occurred in the consumerist alliance'.[46] More generally, the notion that trade unions are in a position to support a consumerist ideology of any type has been challenged by Leonard Tivey. He has stated that the idea of a trade union promoting consumer interests 'is amiable nonsense'. In his words, 'the essential purpose of trade unions is to protect their members in their working lives, not their consuming lives. The whole structure and activity of the trade union movement is focused on the employer–employee relationship, and not on the supplier–consumer relationship'.[47]

It has also been suggested that the Labour Party was not fully committed to supporting the interest of consumers either. Matthew Hilton raises the point that insufficient attention to the implications of fixed prices, together with the delaying of the initial introduction of the Bill near to the end of the 1930 parliamentary session, 'calls into question the Party's commitment to the consumer interest'. He suggests that the party's faith in 'consumerism' at this time must be doubted, a notion supported by the Liberal Party's claim that Labour 'had had its hand forced by the Co-operators, who had designed the Bill purely to attack the small shopkeeper'.[48]

Any implication that there was a degree of tension within the labour movement surrounding this issue must be seen within the context of the relationship between the Co-operative Party and the Labour Party at this time. This was a period when concern and unease had been generated within the labour movement regarding the independence, control and influence that the Co-operative Party would have within Labour Party machinery.[49] Evidence of an inability to 'co-ordinate a strategy which satisfied the whole of the labour movement' during this period is also

---

44 *Labour Magazine*, December 1929, p. 361.
45 *Labour Magazine*, June 1930, p. 83.
46 Hilton, *Consumerism in 20th-Century Britain*, pp. 125–6.
47 Tivey, 'The politics of the consumer', p. 195.
48 Hilton, *Consumerism in 20th-Century Britain*, pp. 125–7.
49 Robertson, *The Co-operative Movement*, pp. 167–71. The Cheltenham Agreement that had formalised the relationship between the Co-operative Party and the Labour Party had been passed by their respective national executives only two years before the election of the second Labour government. A degree of friction between the two parties still existed over what this meant in terms of affiliation, finance and policy.

raised by Peter Gurney, who highlights tensions that existed between the Co-operative Party and William Graham (President of the Board of Trade).[50] The Consumers' Council Bill that was introduced by the Labour government was anticipated to be of huge importance to consumer politics and there is evidence to suggest that it received support from the labour movement. But it was also a Bill that, to a certain degree, highlighted the varying priorities of different elements of the labour movement and a level of tension between them. This was not just an issue that was flagged up by their political opponents, but was also recognised within the labour movement itself.

Food policies: product descriptions, food standards and nutrition

As Jim Phillips and Michael French have stated, it is generally agreed within the historiography on food legislation that British food law of the Victorian era had succeeded in reducing the amount of dangerous adulteration (for example, lead filings in tea leaves).[51] Yet adulteration in more 'benign forms' (for example, the dilution of products) persisted into the 1930s.[52] Phillips and French identify the absence of any genuine state regulation of producers (as opposed to regulation of retailers) as an important contributing factor in any explanation of why adulteration of foodstuffs remained 'a significant commercial ploy' during the inter-war period.[53]

The second Labour government did make some attempt to address the issues of food standards and product descriptions. A number of consumer concerns relating to the composition and description of food were bought to the attention of the Minister of Health, Arthur Greenwood. These

---

50 Peter Gurney, *Co-operative Culture and the Politics of Consumption in England 1870–1930* (Manchester: Manchester University Press, 1996), pp. 229–30.
51 Jim Phillips and Michael French, 'Adulteration and food law, 1899–1939', *Twentieth Century British History*, 9:3 (1998), p. 353. Alongside the importance of legislation, John Burnett also emphasises the role of voluntary reform in the mid-nineteenth century. He argues that for some years before legislation was implemented, widespread publicity in the press, popular literature, parliamentary debates and medical journals regarding the subject of food adulteration created a climate of opinion 'which induced significant numbers of manufacturers and traders to put their own houses in order before they were compelled to do so'. This voluntary reform marked an 'important prelude to the legislative suppression of adulteration'. John Burnett, *Plenty and Want* (Harmondsworth: Penguin Books, 1968), p. 248.
52 Phillips and French, 'Adulteration and food law', p. 353.
53 *Ibid.*, pp. 350–5.

included calls for the amount of cocoa beans contained in chocolates to be stated on the wrappers,[54] queries as to the acceptable ratio of flour to water in bread,[55] and questions as to whether the low standard of fruit content in jams sold under the descriptions of 'Full Fruit Standard' and 'Lower Fruit Standard' was adequately described on each container.[56] Greenwood did appoint a Committee on Food Standards (in May 1931) under the Ministry of Health. Its remit was 'to inquire into the working of the law as to the composition and description of articles of food other than milk', and to report on 'what alterations, if any, in the law or its administration appear to be desirable'.[57] Unfortunately, the committee's first meeting, in June 1931, was also to be its last. It was suspended the following September as the 'Whitehall Heads of Division sought economies in state expenditure in the weeks following the formation of the National government'.[58] The committee was reappointed in 1933 and proceeded to examine issues relating to definitions, standards, advertisements and labelling. It has been argued that the committee's report in 1934 'led in due course to the Food and Drugs Act of 1938'.[59] Although its actions were ultimately marred by the political turmoil of 1931, the second Labour government did contribute in some way to the ongoing investigations of the inter-war period into food standards and product descriptions.

In addition to investigations into the quality of certain foods, broader issues about inadequate diets and undernourishment were also raised. Here the focus was not on improving food standards and the way products were described, but on ensuring that the poorest consumers, those in most need, had access to affordable food. One of the main concerns was that 'the excessive price charged for milk and foodstuffs generally prevents thousands of poor mothers and children from having the sufficiency essential to their

---

54 *House of Commons Debates*, fifth series, 30 June 1931, 254, col. 1081.
55 *House of Commons Debates*, fifth series, 23 April 1931, 251, cols 1146–7.
56 *House of Commons Debates*, fifth series, 11 June 1931, 253, col. 1211W.
57 *House of Commons Debates*, fifth series, 4 June 1931, 253, col. 342.
58 Michael French and Jim Phillips, *Cheated Not Poisoned? Food Regulation in the United Kingdom 1875–1938* (Manchester: Manchester University Press, 2000), p. 146. French and Phillips note, however, that there was some reluctance on the part of the Ministry of Health to undertake such an inquiry. One factor contributing to this was a concern that it would summon opposition by those in business, who would be reluctant to accept too much state intervention on this matter. Thus, although the Ministry of Health did initiate an investigation into the composition, description, standards and definitions of food on behalf of the consumer, the interests of producers remained influential.
59 G. W. Monier-Williams, 'Historical aspects of the Pure Food Laws', *Proceedings of the Nutrition Society Sixty-Sixth Scientific Meeting* (London: London School of Hygiene and Tropical Medicine, 3 March 1951), p. 366.

health requirements'.[60] Part of this problem was attributed to the amount of control certain companies wielded within the food industry and the consequent exploitation of consumers 'by those who trade in the nation's food supplies'. It was claimed that certain companies were making large sums of money at the expense of the consumer.[61] Debates about access to food were constructed with reference to Britain as a 'C3 nation', the cause of which being that 'so many women are unable to get enough food to bring up strong and healthy children'.[62] As John Burnett notes, during the inter-war period the population ate a more nutritious diet than they had in the years before 1914. However, the rising levels of unemployment, evident during the Labour Party's second administration, resulted in malnutrition being a real problem.[63] Complaints of overcharging affecting access to milk were addressed by the government, and it was planned that these would be dealt with under the proposed Consumers' Council.[64]

In addition to ensuring that consumers could afford to eat, it was also recognised that their food must be nutritious. The nutritional benefit of milk, and especially the 'importance of milk as an article of children's diet', was recognised and promoted by various groups.[65] Further investigation to demonstrate the nutritional value of milk, in order to promote greater consumption of it, was organised under the direction of the Department of Health for Scotland.[66] In 1930 the question of supplying milk to all children in schools was put to Sir Charles Trevelyan, President of the Board of Education.[67] Although he came under criticism for 'doing no

---

60 *The Clarion*, December 1929, p. 4.
61 *Ibid.*
62 *House of Commons Debates*, fifth series, 8 May 1930, 238, col. 1219. The 'C3 nation' referred to the high percentage of recruits deemed by the army medical authorities to be physically unfit for service. See John Burnett, 'The rise and decline of school meals in Britain, 1860–1990', in John Burnett and Derek J. Oddy (eds), *The Origins and Development of Food Policies in Europe* (Leicester: Leicester University Press, 1994), p. 64.
63 Burnett, 'The rise and decline of school meals', p. 64.
64 *House of Commons Debates*, fifth series, 20 May 1931, 252, cols 1969–70.
65 *Report of the National Conference of Labour Women* (London: Labour Party, 1930), p. 88.
66 *House of Commons Debates*, fifth series, 13 February 1930, 235, col. 634W. As Frank Trentmann's work shows, clean milk 'was already by the Edwardian period part of the British diet and its health benefits appreciated'. Frank Trentmann, 'Bread, milk and democracy: consumption and citizenship in twentieth-century Britain', in Martin Daunton and Matthew Hilton (eds), *The Politics of Consumption* (Oxford: Berg, 2001), p. 140. P. J. Atkins' work highlights that by the 1930s milk was associated with an image of a clean and healthy food. P. J. Atkins, 'White poison? The social consequences of milk consumption, 1850–1930', *Social History of Medicine*, 5:2 (1992), pp. 207–27.
67 *Report of the National Conference of Labour Women*, p. 20.

The Labour government and the consumer

more than has been done by the late Government',[68] there was some action taken on these issues. He did make enquiries into the provision of milk for school children, was supportive of the National Milk Publicity Council's milk service scheme, and stated that he was 'anxious to see an increase in the consumption of milk in the schools'.[69] Moreover, a representative from the Board of Education attended the National Milk Publicity Council's meetings, and the Board sought to bring the Council's scheme of providing school children with milk 'to the notice of local authorities and teachers'.[70] Measures undertaken by the previous government to help address the problem of malnourishment in school pupils were reviewed in the Board of Education's 1929 annual report, with the Board's medical officers monitoring the impact that such schemes were having on children's health.[71]

The consumer and hire purchase

Safeguarding the interests of consumers during this period was not limited to issues associated with food policy. There were also attempts to amend the law with respect to the system of hire purchase (HP). This was a very important issue for a large number of working-class families. Melanie Tebbutt states that hire purchase multiplied 20-fold between 1918 and 1938, and accounted for two-thirds of all larger purchases.[72] Many working-class consumers used hire purchase to buy the mass-produced consumer goods which became available during the inter-war years.[73] However, the consumer faced a number of pitfalls and problems arising from hire purchase agreements. Peter Scott's research on hire purchase agreements in relation to domestic furniture in inter-war Britain identifies how 'the nature of retail competition fostered opportunistic behaviour

---

68 *House of Commons Debates*, fifth series, 1 May 1930, 238, cols 358–9.
69 *House of Commons Debates*, fifth series, 27 March 1930, 237, cols 591–2; 1 May 1930, 238, cols 358–9; 31 March 1930, 237, cols 911–2W.
70 House of Commons Parliamentary Papers, *Education in 1930. The Report of the Board of Education and the Statistics of Public Education for England and Wales* (London: His Majesty's Stationery Office, 1931), Cmd 3856, pp. 72–3.
71 House of Commons Parliamentary Papers, *Education in 1929. The Report of the Board of Education and the Statistics of Public Education for England and Wales* (London: His Majesty's Stationery Office, 1930), Cmd 3545, pp. 67–8.
72 Melanie Tebbutt, *Making Ends Meet: Pawnbroking and Working-Class Credit* (Leicester: Leicester University Press, 1983), p. 193.
73 Avram Taylor, *Working Class Credit and Community since 1918* (Basingstoke: Palgrave Macmillan, 2002), pp. 31–2.

by HP multiples, who had a bad reputation for selling shoddy goods to customers at inflated prices, using various devices to disguise quality and cost'.[74] Devices that could assist retailers in suppressing price comparisons at the expense of the consumer included misleading advertising, a refusal to display manufacturers' brands and the sale of non-branded goods.[75] A number of studies relating to hire purchase agreements highlight abuses and unscrupulous practices. These included: instances where customers signed blank agreements, only to find that a price much higher than that agreed with the salesman was later added;[76] high-pressure sales techniques from the door-to-door salesmen, which made customers 'lose sight of the real price of the purchase';[77] and the notorious use of 'snatch back'.[78]

One of the greatest concerns about hire purchase schemes from the perspective of consumers was not related to the antics of specific firms or industries, but linked to the fact that the law itself offered them little protection with regard to these agreements. Consumers were at a distinct disadvantage should they no longer be able to continue payment under a hire purchase contract. The legal situation in 1930 was laid out in the House of Commons: 'if someone has paid practically the whole of the instalments on furniture – and furniture is the main item so far as the working classes are concerned – or on any other kind of goods, if the last few instalments are not kept up, the hire purchase company can come in and take the whole of the goods back, without giving to the purchaser one penny of surrender value'.[79] Changes to this aspect of the law were attempted by the second Labour government. A discussion was constructed around the need to assist consumers in the face of increasing unemployment.[80] The Hire Purchase Bill, introduced in 1930, was described as 'one which has become important because of the unemployment crisis. It has made acute the defects in the hire purchase law which have been admitted for a very long time, but now that so many people are becoming unemployed, their instalments cannot be kept up.'[81] It was introduced not as a government measure but by Ellen Wilkinson, a Labour MP (for Middleborough East) and the Private Parliamentary Secretary to Susan Lawrence (who was

---

74 Peter Scott, 'Mr Drage, Mr Everyman, and the creation of a mass market for domestic furniture in interwar Britain', *Economic History Review*, 62:4 (2009), p. 824.
75 *Ibid.*
76 *Ibid.*
77 Tebbutt, *Making Ends Meet*, p. 194.
78 Taylor, *Working Class Credit*, pp. 32–3.
79 *House of Commons Debates*, fifth series, 2 December 1930, 245, cols 1989–91.
80 *Ibid.*
81 *Ibid.*

Parliamentary Secretary to the Minister of Health).[82] The Bill was designed 'to prevent poor people having goods taken away, without compensation, for which they have nearly completed the payments'.[83] It proposed two main ways of defending the consumer against an existing hire purchase system which provided them with very little protection. The Bill proposed that where people had paid 50 per cent of their instalments they would 'be able to receive compensation in cash (or goods) if the hirer takes back the goods because they cannot complete the instalments'.[84] It was also proposed that in cases where goods were seized it would be possible for the hire purchaser to recover possession of the goods provided that 'the remainder of the instalments are tendered, and a reasonable sum is paid for the cost to the company of actually seizing the goods'.[85] The introduction of the Bill 'drew no opposition, was formally accepted, but lapsed when parliament was dissolved'.[86]

Although this Bill was not passed during the 1929–31 Labour administration, the Hire Purchase Act was passed in 1938 and was a Labour MP's triumph. This Act was credited as giving 'some much needed protection to the customer'.[87] This provides a further example of where attempts made to protect the consumer during 1929–31 failed, but some of the issues and discussions from this period were taken up in succeeding years and eventually formed an important component of legislation designed to protect the consumer.

Conclusion

Although a party traditionally closely associated with producers, during 1929–31 Labour while in government by no means neglected the needs of the consumer. In some respects the topic of the second Labour government and the consumer fits with traditional accounts of domestic policy being somewhat disappointing. None of the bills discussed in this chapter came to fruition under that government, and many of the committees were

---

82 Betty D. Vernon, *Ellen Wilkinson* (London: Croom Helm, 1982), pp. 101–2. Although Ellen Wilkinson's official appointment was in the Ministry of Health, she described helping those who were 'suffering under the present unjust Hire Purchase legislation' as 'one of the "sideshows" that was of interest'. *Labour Woman*, May 1931, p. 73.
83 *Labour Woman*, May 1931, p. 73.
84 *Ibid.*
85 *House of Commons Debates*, fifth series, 2 December 1930, 245, cols 1989–91.
86 Vernon, *Ellen Wilkinson*, p. 148.
87 Labour Party, *Fair Deal for the Shopper* (London, 1961), p. 16.

abandoned. They do, however, provide evidence of attempts to promote consumer interests, even if these attempts were ultimately swamped by the crisis of 1931. The action taken during the period is noteworthy, though, for a number of reasons.

Some of the work carried out was among the first to highlight areas of the law that needed to be changed in order to safeguard the consumer. This can be seen in relation to the hire purchase system. During the inter-war years consumers had virtually no protection under existing legislation, hence they were extremely vulnerable. Much of the historiography on working-class credit discusses the Hire Purchase Act 1938, but often very little acknowledgement is given to the initiatives in 1929–31. Another important aspect of the work of the Labour government was in relation to the description and content of food products. This was recognised to be an area where the consumer remained at a disadvantage, and investigations into food standards were initiated. This topic was to remain of key importance in future debates about consumer protection.

There were also ideas in the proposed Consumers' Council Bill that were relatively advanced for their time, and resonated with the issues of the consumer politics of a later period. Plans for the Consumers' Council attempted not only to protect consumers against monopolies and profiteering by gathering information and applying sanctions, but also to educate the consumer. During the Bill's second reading in Parliament it was promoted as a Bill 'designed to build up a body of knowledge regarding production, wholesale and other, distribution and retail prices; in other words, so far as we can do it, to educate the consumers in the country – one of the greatest tasks on which any man in existing conditions has to embark. This is our constructive purpose.'[88] A desire to 'educate' the consumer in this way was to become increasingly prominent in the discourse of consumer protection during the 1950s and 1960s.[89]

Although much has been made of the problems that plagued the second Labour government, it did make some significant attempts to promote and safeguard the interests of consumers, a number of issues pertinent to the consumer were investigated and conceptualised, and acknowledgement was given to the growing need for more protective legislation.

---

88 *House of Commons Debates*, fifth series, 8 May 1930, 238, col. 1178.
89 The 1950s and 1960s saw an increase in the number of organisations that sought to provide consumers with information and advice on the products they had purchased (or were considering buying). One of the most noticeable examples is the Consumers' Association. See Lawrence Black, '*Which?*craft in post-war Britain: the Consumers' Association and the politics of affluence', *Albion*, 36:1 (2004), pp. 52–82.

8

Making farming pay: agricultural crisis and the politics of the national interest, 1930–31

CLARE GRIFFITHS

There was an agricultural sub-plot to the story of the second Labour government. Agriculture rarely receives much attention in the context of political history, nor is it afforded much prominence in general narratives about the impact of the depression and the economic crisis in the 1920s and 1930s. Yet, in early 1930, Labour in office was faced with more than usually vociferous complaints about the state of British farming. By the spring of 1931, attempts to handle the economic problems in the arable sector had provoked deep divisions within the Cabinet and exposed the difficulties of reconciling intervention to assist the industry with ambitions for longer-term restructuring. They also revealed the Labour Party's decidedly mixed feelings about free trade, and did so in relation to the most potentially inflammatory aspect of any return to protectionism: the price of wheat.

The debates about the future of home wheat production have an additional significance for thinking about the political travails of MacDonald's second administration. Agriculture presented an important test case, raising questions about national responsibility as against the adoption of a narrow party platform, about the expedients demanded by industrial crises, and about the potential to broaden government beyond party boundaries. The peculiarities of agriculture, and the Labour Party's relationship with farming and the rural electorate more generally, complicated the response to what was already a difficult challenge in policy terms. In this context, politicians and representatives of the industry emphasised the goal of adopting a 'national' policy. The notion of reaching beyond party division and particular interests within agriculture prefigured some of the rhetoric and pragmatism that were to emerge more broadly as a response to handling the depression and finding political coalitions which could do so. The response to what was seen at the time as a 'crisis' in farming thus became a focus for strategies and debates which point to some interesting aspects of the notion of the national interest – themes which were to come to the fore in politics more generally in the summer of 1931.

This chapter discusses the problems surrounding the Labour government's attempts to address the economic difficulties in farming, notably within the arable sector, and most significantly within wheat production.[1] It explains how the depression manifested itself in the agricultural sector, how that 'crisis' was perceived, and why it mattered. The question of the reintroduction of protection found its most emotive context within discussions about potential assistance for domestic wheat production.[2] The debates within the Labour government about support for agriculture in this way offer a particularly interesting case for thinking about how some politicians responded to the prospect of moving away from free trade, or found ways of justifying short-term measures and practical expedients which were felt to keep the principle intact.

On 1 March 1930, there was a demonstration on Parker's Piece in Cambridge, drawing together representatives from different sections of the agricultural industry – farmers and farm workers appearing alongside each other on a platform – all calling for immediate action to save agriculture. The symbolism of this gathering added weight to the arguments it intended to promote, projecting an image of agriculture united. The drawing together of 'masters and men' campaigning for the same cause was in marked contrast to the more usual roles of their respective representative bodies: the National Farmers' Union (NFU) on the one hand and the trade unions on the other were generally on opposite sides of an argument rather than making common cause. Their statutory representation on agricultural wages boards, in particular, emphasised their distinct and competing interests.

The Parker's Piece demonstration was overtly non-sectional and non-party political. Its aim was to draw public attention to the plight of arable farming and to call for the government to intervene to arrest the decline in cultivation and protect employment on the land. From Labour's own

---

1 On the second Labour government's agricultural policy see David Marquand, *Ramsay MacDonald* (London: Jonathan Cape, 1977), pp. 557–64; Kenneth Morgan and Jane Morgan, *Portrait of a Progressive: The Political Career of Christopher, Viscount Addison* (Oxford: Oxford University Press, 1980), ch. 7.
2 Gerald Egerer, 'The political economy of British wheat, 1920–1960', *Agricultural History*, 40:4 (1966), pp. 295–310.

ranks, the Agricultural Labour Group of MPs, led by an East Anglian farmer, W. B. Taylor, were also calling on the government to take immediate steps to redeem the promise made at the 1929 general election, to 'make farming pay', or at least to make a 'practical gesture' to demonstrate its good faith.[3] One of the prominent figures in the Parker's Piece demonstration was another Labour MP – George Dallas – who was active within the development of the party's agricultural policy, as well as being an important figure in the organisation of agricultural workers within a section of the Transport and General Workers' Union (TGWU). Dallas' approach, and that of the TGWU, was to foster common cause with the farmers and landowners to achieve greater prosperity for the agricultural industry as a whole. But it was not an approach that received universal approval within the labour movement. The major industrial union for land-workers, the National Union of Agricultural Workers, was much less convinced of the value of such an approach. The Parker's Piece demonstration was a staging of industrial unity – making a case for the common interests of all those within agriculture, and promoting the interest of 'agriculture' itself, in a way which was in part contentious.

The demonstration also articulated a particular reading of the state of domestic agriculture, tending to suggest a national crisis of the whole sector. Agricultural historians in recent years have been increasingly interested in uncovering an alternative economic history, emphasising the varied experiences of different areas of production and indeed of different regions of the country. It is possible to look at the 1920s and 1930s as a period in which diversification could reap rewards, as could expansion in certain areas, modernisation and development.[4] However, in 1930, accounts of the fortunes of agriculture were dominated by the fate of one aspect of the industry – wheat production – and particularly its position in one area of the country – the counties of East Anglia. The interests of this region and this sector were particularly prominent in representations made by the NFU, and this was also the part of the country where agricultural trade unionism had its heartlands, especially in Norfolk. Falling grain prices were not bad news for everyone involved in agriculture: livestock producers reliant on purchasing feedstuffs benefited. Nor was wheat by any means

---

3   W. B. Taylor to Ramsay MacDonald, 25 March 1930, MacDonald Papers, The National Archives/Public Record Office, TNA/PRO, 30/69/244/437. The section on agriculture in the party's manifesto included the phrase 'Farming must be made to pay': Labour Party, *Labour's Appeal to the Nation* (London, 1929).
4   See, for example, the revisionist collection of essays edited by Paul Brassley, Jeremy Burchardt and Lynne Thompson, *The English Countryside Between the Wars: Regeneration or Decline?* (Woodbridge: Boydell, 2006).

a significant crop in many parts of Britain. But the wheat lobby shouted loudly and had powerful, emotive arguments in support of its case.

Wheat was treated as a high-status crop, of national importance as a domestic safeguard against any disruption of imports. It had been adopted as the barometer of the industry's fortunes. The amount of ploughed acreage lost each year was taken as an index of agricultural decline, and the reduction of the area devoted to arable was commonly equated with the problems of British wheat farming. Farmers who found it uneconomic to continue with the labour- and capital-intensive cultivation of grain crops found the easiest response was to put their land down to grass, or simply let it go into disuse. The resulting economies in labour costs had an obvious knock-on effect on unemployment in agriculture. And, in addition to these factors, wheat was directly connected to the running-sore in the social memory within British agriculture in the inter-war years: the 'great betrayal' of 1921, when Lloyd George's administration reneged on the agreement to continue the guaranteed-price regime introduced during the First World War with the aim of encouraging wheat production in wartime. This history had created a sense of political expectation among farmers – about the possibility of financial support as something which had existed within recent memory – and a sense of grievance about government's perfidy towards agriculture.[5] Wheat was central to those narratives.

This, then, was the 'crisis' as it was perceived at the beginning of 1930. Imports of high-quality 'hard' wheat from North America had made much British production uneconomic, and the situation was worsened further by the impact of the 'dumping' of wheat from Germany and later from the Soviet Union. In a market in which many of Britain's competitors were protecting and subsidising food production, arguments grew among agriculturists for Britain to do likewise. By the time of the Parker's Piece demonstration, the Labour government was already wrestling with its own worries about what to do about agriculture; the publicity accruing to the wheat lobby's case only made Labour's indecisiveness and inactivity the more obvious. MacDonald commented to his Minister of Agriculture, Noel Buxton, in December 1929, 'We have been talking so many generalities and have been producing such grandiloquent promises, none of which

---

5   On the 'great betrayal', see Edith Whetham, 'The Agriculture Act, 1920 and its repeal – the "great betrayal"', *Agricultural History Review*, 23 (1974), pp. 36–49. E. C. Penning-Rowsell points out the complexities of the NFU's role: 'Who "betrayed" whom? Power and politics in the 1920/1 agricultural crisis', *Agricultural History Review*, 45 (1997), pp. 176–94; also Jonathan Brown, 'Agricultural policy and the National Farmers' Union', in J. R. Wordie (ed.), *Agriculture and Politics in England, 1815–1939* (Basingstoke: Macmillan, 2000), pp. 178–98.

have really been worked out in detail.'[6] Labour had drawn up a substantial policy document on agriculture in 1926, but the practical expedients required in government still raised questions about how to proceed. Some of its commitments, notably over land ownership and control of production, were not in the realm of realistic politics in 1929 – not least under a minority administration. The government promised to issue a White Paper, and by April 1930 there was a text in place, but it was never published. Buxton feared that it might present 'an unpalatable sermon' to farmers, while the agricultural expert Daniel Hall observed that it could destroy the last remnants of hope for those struggling to continue in arable farming.[7]

As this criticism suggests, one of the dominant instincts within Labour at the time was to reconstruct the industry, to shift production into areas where Britain enjoyed natural advantages and which could address the needs of domestic consumers, notably milk, fruit and vegetables. These products could more readily hold their own against foreign imports, while dairying and horticulture were also sectors which offered considerable potential for expanded employment. It is notable that the Chancellor of the Exchequer, Philip Snowden, approved of what he regarded as the 'accurate diagnosis' of agriculture's problems contained in the draft White Paper. Even as the calls for support became ever more shrill, Snowden remained immune to the pleas of the arable lobby, and consistently unsympathetic to its requests for help in propping up forms of production which he considered inherently uneconomic.

A further context for the Labour government's approach to the subject was a persistent interest in the potential for agricultural development to alleviate unemployment.[8] Christopher Addison, Parliamentary Secretary and later Minister of Agriculture, argued that agricultural policy should 'dovetail' with unemployment policy, and identified three aspects to an agricultural programme: to improve standards of farming, to maintain the arable area, and to settle more people on the land.[9] 'The outstanding fact', Addison told the party conference in 1930, 'is that we ought, if we can, to make agriculture render its contribution towards the amelioration of the conditions of unemployment.'[10] Labour's employment schemes ranged

---

6 Ramsay MacDonald to Noel Buxton, 19 December 1929, MacDonald Papers, TNA/PRO, 30/69/672/III/199–200.
7 Noel Buxton to Ramsay MacDonald, 29 April 1930, MacDonald Papers, TNA/PRO, 30/69/243/42.
8 Labour Party, *How to Conquer Unemployment – Labour's Reply to Lloyd George* (London, 1929).
9 Notes on discussion at Ministry of Agriculture, 5 June 1930, Addison Papers, Bodleian Library, Oxford, box 35.
10 Labour Party, *Report of the 30th Annual Conference* (London, 1930), p. 205.

from major programmes of land drainage and afforestation to ambitious visions for thousands of new smallholdings. Meanwhile, threats to the future of arable cultivation offered the prospect of the loss of jobs, rather than their creation, in the countryside.

Against this background of uncertainty about what the government should be doing, Ramsay MacDonald began to canvass ideas for a consensual policy, involving groups from within agriculture itself. A series of confidential conferences was convened from January 1930, with representatives drawn from the organisations of land-workers, farmers and landowners – a similar coalition, in fact, to the one which stood up publicly at Parker's Piece to make open representations to the government. The mood of the conferences began relatively positively, but by March most of that goodwill seemed to have dispersed, prompted by frustration at the government's unwillingness or inability to give any indication of its intentions.[11] The one thing that Buxton made clear to those involved was that Labour would not entertain the possibility of subsidies.[12] Unfortunately, the farmers had come to the discussions with that as their main priority. This was the mechanism they understood as the most effective and immediate way to make farming an economic proposition.

Existing Labour Party policy had identified restructuring, reforms of land holding, capital investment and the more effective organisation of the marketing of produce as the ways to return agriculture to prosperity without offending free trade principles – or, as a more immediate concern, upsetting a working-class electorate which had benefited from the availability of cheaper food. Buxton's deputy at Agriculture, Christopher Addison – who was to take over the senior position in June 1930 – spent the first months in government preparing measures to address some of these concerns, with notable emphasis on marketing, and the formulation of what became the marketing legislation of 1931, establishing the practice of producer marketing boards, which became an important feature of the industry during the later 1930s and after. The interest in marketing reflected a more positive reading of the industry's prospects, suggesting that there was money to be made in farming, but that this was currently being dissipated between producer and consumer, through the malevolent intervention of the middleman. Although Labour's marketing schemes were about compelling producers to co-operate in grading and selling, they were essentially a form of self-help for the industry.

---

11 Correspondence and papers, MacDonald Papers, TNA/PRO, 30/69/244 and PRO, 30/69/676/191–2.
12 Letter of invitation, 25 October 1929, MacDonald Papers, TNA/PRO, 30/69/244/219–22.

Labour's policies, then, focused on two areas: firstly, restructuring production, in terms of what kind of farming was going on, the units in which it was being conducted, the controls over how people farmed and the ownership of the land itself; and secondly, reorganising the operation of the markets for agricultural produce, both internally and in relation to imports. Both of these areas of policy were concerned with fundamental adjustments in agricultural and food policy. However, the developing crisis in agriculture placed the emphasis more firmly on the need for action which would have an immediate effect. The temptation in any crisis is to pursue short-term policies, and MacDonald's government was aware of the dangers of confusing emergency measures with longer-term agricultural policy.[13] But, if the voices raised at Parker's Piece were to be believed, then agriculture was in imminent danger. Moreover – from a politically pragmatic point of view – a failure to offer any palliative to arable farming in the short term was also judged to have potential electoral consequences.

This may seem in some ways an uncompelling deduction for the Labour Party in government. Yet Buxton in particular was always conscious of the potential impact of the government's actions (or lack of them) on the rural electorate. In April 1930, he observed to MacDonald that the political implications of their handling of the arable crisis should not be ignored: if Labour was to stand any chance of winning sufficient seats in the countryside to form a parliamentary majority at some point, he argued, the party must have 'an *active* policy and not passively look on while economic forces have full play'.[14] MacDonald himself expressed concerns about Labour's vulnerability in the few rural seats it held following the 1929 general election. As Buxton's poor health prompted him to consider retiring from the Commons in the summer of 1930, MacDonald hesitated, unwilling to provoke a by-election in North Norfolk, which he feared the party might lose.[15]

W. B. Taylor also emphasised the importance of positive action in support of agriculture, writing to MacDonald in October 1930 that 'it is imperative alike for *arable* industry and [the] future of our Party in Eastern Rural England that some gesture is made *by the Government* to

---

13 See statement to the Prime Minister, 10 March 1930, MacDonald Papers, TNA/PRO, 30/69/244/139–44.
14 Memorandum by Buxton, 17 April 1930, MacDonald Papers, TNA/PRO, 30/69/243. Original emphasis.
15 Correspondence between Noel Buxton and Ramsay MacDonald, 28 and 30 May 1930, MacDonald Papers, TNA/PRO, 30/69/676/210–12 and TNA/PRO, 30/69/1753/4. Labour held the seat, with Buxton's wife as the successful candidate, though the party lost North Norfolk at the 1931 general election.

the growing demand for an economic price for home grown food stuffs. To do this, *without Food Taxes*, would spike their [Labour's opponents'] guns. What is good enough for coal, is not too good for cereals, meat, and fruit.'[16] Following the 1929 general election, the Labour Party held 40 seats which could be regarded as rural in character, on the basis of employment patterns or of more impressionistic contemporary identifications, including their inclusion in agricultural or rural campaigns organised by the party. It was a share of the rural vote that Labour hoped to build on, regarding this as key to its future prospects and the chance of forming a majority government. The general election had been preceded by two years of campaigning on an agricultural platform, in an attempt to build Labour's credentials as a party which could represent the countryside. Its handling of the agricultural crisis offered an opportunity to demonstrate that it was not only able to handle this area of policy, but could show itself responsive to the needs and wishes of the rural voters in the process.

One of the problems about finding remedies to address the concerns of the agricultural electorate was that the same remedies did not necessarily suit all types of farming. MacDonald observed ruefully that the policies which would suit Norfolk were liable to be opposed by the whole of Scotland.[17] Getting agriculturists to agree on what the industry needed was no easy task. Even while he had so recently set the conferences of agricultural representatives to work, MacDonald began to explore expedients outside that forum, always with the aim of finding a way to alleviate the problems in arable without resorting to direct subsidy or tariffs. In February 1930 he was canvassing opinion about imposing a registration fee on imported grain as a temporary measure to generate income for some form of subsidy for home production, though this soon gave way to the more favoured idea of a 'quota': a legal requirement for millers to include a certain proportion of home-grown wheat in British-milled flour. A committee of the Cabinet (chaired by the Secretary of State for War, Tom Shaw) was looking at these options in March, including the possibility of a state monopoly on the purchase of grain.[18] There was some precedent for this in the proposals for import boards which had been developed, by the Independent Labour Party (ILP) in particular, and had been included in Labour's agricultural programme in 1926 – though evidently not in a sufficiently worked-up

---

16 W. B. Taylor to Ramsay MacDonald, 16 October 1930, MacDonald Papers, TNA/PRO, 30/69/244/429. Original emphasis.
17 Ramsay MacDonald to George Dallas, 4 June 1930, MacDonald Papers, TNA/PRO, 30/69/1175/74–5.
18 Letter from chairman of Committee on Agricultural Policy to Prime Minister, 17 March 1930, Cabinet Papers, TNA/CAB 24/210, C.P.99 (30).

form to lend themselves to automatic implementation. Import boards were an anti-middleman policy, but some Labour members were also enthusiastic about their potential to satisfy rural producer and urban consumer alike: securing markets for home produce, stabilising prices and providing a reasonable return for the farmer, while actually lowering the cost of food to consumers as a benefit of the state's power to bulk purchase and store staple goods. Buxton described import boards as the 'best measure available, of a spectacular character, calculated to assist the agricultural industry'.[19]

Addison thought that the status of import boards as part of Labour's agreed programme should have established the principle of 'the deliberate and purposeful regulation and development of home industries', allowing, as he saw it, some interference 'with the system of buying in the cheapest market wherever the goods come from and whatever their effect on the producer and worker at home'.[20] But the idea of a quota for home-produced wheat raised anxieties among some of his colleagues. Buxton admitted to his own misgivings: 'The scheme jars upon Free Trade traditions and it has taken me some time to become a convert to it, but I am strongly in its favour as the only plan which gives a solid advantage to the farmer, and which also meets the bounty-fed wheat trouble, without either protection or subsidy.'[21] A quota would not technically guarantee a price for farmers, but it would guarantee a market. Buxton came round to the idea as the only practical option to prevent a severe rise in unemployment in arable areas. Given Buxton's own concerns that the quota could infringe against free trade, it is interesting that he believed most Liberals would support the policy, viewing it as a way to prevent rural unemployment which fell short of invoking protection or subsidies.[22] Addison was also convinced by its potential to 'give us a non-party atmosphere in the House of Commons'.[23]

Of the scheme's opponents within Labour ranks, Philip Snowden was the most significant – not least because of his position as Chancellor. When the proposal was laid out in the draft White Paper in April 1930, he

---

19 Noel Buxton to Ramsay MacDonald, 3 March 1930, MacDonald Papers, TNA/PRO, 30/69/44/149–51.
20 Memorandum on the wheat quota, n.d. [1930], Addison Papers, 129/165, Bodleian Library, Oxford.
21 Noel Buxton to Ramsay MacDonald, 5 April 1930, MacDonald Papers, TNA/PRO, 30/69/243/179–179B.
22 Noel Buxton to Ramsay MacDonald, 17 April 1930, MacDonald Papers, TNA/PRO, 30/69/244/89–90.
23 Christopher Addison to Ramsay MacDonald, 17 April 1930, MacDonald Papers, TNA/PRO, 30/69/676/6–9.

declared himself opposed to it as objectionable in principle and unlikely to work in any case. For Snowden it was incompatible with the 'free breakfast table' of free trade: he believed it would raise the price of bread. Addison, though, by late 1930 was presenting the quota as if it were agreed policy.[24] However, the argument in favour of the policy – namely that it was a good thing to maintain a significant acreage under wheat – was being undermined by discussions in a committee of the Economic Advisory Council. The case here was that – however compelling the need for short-term, emergency measures – the quota would serve only to prop up artificially forms of production which could not be justified on economic grounds in the long term: agriculture, like other industries, should rationalise itself to develop more efficient and profitable forms of production, and it had no greater claim on the state's generosity than the country's other depressed industries.[25] Only one member of the committee – who was from the agricultural section of the TGWU – argued against this critique, insisting that the arable sector required immediate relief, even if this entailed 'a departure from our traditional economic policy'.[26] A government committee on agricultural development, set up in late 1930, was also divided on the virtues of the quota, though its majority report came out in favour of the policy, accepting that the consumer would have to make a 'sacrifice' to bridge the gap between domestic and world prices.[27] Two members of the committee signed a reservation: the co-operator A. V. Alexander, and F. W. Pethick-Lawrence, who had been put on the committee at the behest of Snowden. Pethick-Lawrence's role was specifically to keep the Chancellor informed about discussion of the quota, which involved, as Snowden saw it, 'very heavy financial commitments which are quite new'.[28]

MacDonald had taken an active interest in the question of how to solve the problems of the grain market, but by the beginning of the following year he was clearly increasingly frustrated at his government's inability to act decisively on agriculture. He confided to his diary in February 1931 that the ministers charged with producing a statement on agriculture 'have been

---

24 MacDonald was concerned in November 1930 that Addison and Will Graham (then at the Board of Trade, and himself a free trader) had given the impression to the Imperial Conference that the government had decided to adopt the quota. Diary entry, 12 November 1930, MacDonald Papers, TNA/PRO, 30/69/1753/1.
25 Cabinet Papers, CAB 24/213, C.P.244 (30).
26 Cabinet Papers, CAB 24/213, C.P.244 (30) and CAB 24/214, C.P.272 (30). The dissenter was John Beard, a former agricultural labourer who had become a leading union official, first in the agricultural section of the Workers' Union, and later in the TGWU.
27 Cabinet Papers, CAB 24/220, C.P.52 (31).
28 Philip Snowden to Ramsay MacDonald, 19 December 1930, MacDonald Papers, TNA/PRO, 30/69/244/404–6.

unable to propose anything. That will put me in a tight corner, for I cannot go on unless Ministers can produce policies.'[29] The problem, in fact, was not so much the absence of policies, as the weakness of a consensus within the government's ranks. The quota scheme was recognised as infringing on the principle of free trade, though its supporters argued that this was justified as a short-term measure, and the consumer could be expected to make a minor sacrifice to prevent a catastrophic collapse in wheat farming. Opponents, however, objected to singling agriculture out for special treatment at a time when many industries were depressed. They also pointed out that such intervention would make it more difficult to bring about the necessary shifts in production to create a sustainable agricultural industry in the long term. As Snowden put it in a note to MacDonald:

> Sooner or later these farmers will have to turn their land to other uses … and the sooner the better. A little wheat growing will remain, where as at present, owing to special circumstances it can be done profitably. The encouragement of dairy farming, flowers and bulbs in the Eastern Counties is the right policy.[30]

The topic of the quota came before the Cabinet in March 1931, and returned weekly as the predictable substance of the agenda item 'Agricultural Policy'. During this period, Snowden was absent, convalescing after surgery. He attacked the scheme from his sickbed in a memorandum describing the quota as 'the crudest of all possible subsidies…. Protection without the one benefit of Protection, in that it brings no revenue to the Exchequer.' Snowden characterised it as a scheme which would 'put millions in the pockets of the wheat trade at the expense of consumers', identify Labour with the Conservative programme (since the Conservatives had already been promoting their own ideas for a quota) and represent 'political suicide'.[31] When the Cabinet finally got to discuss the issue on 15 April the debate took up much of the day but was inconclusive.[32] Further soundings were taken, from millers and from MPs for agricultural constituencies, neither of which groups was able to offer a ringing endorsement. The millers disliked the proposal but admitted that they could work with it if they had to. The rural MPs were divided. Some (including George Dallas and W. B. Taylor) were enthusiastic, calling for the introduction of the quota without delay. Others (J. H. Alpass and Fred

---

29 Diary entry, 16 February 1931, MacDonald Papers, TNA/PRO, 30/69/1753/1.
30 Note to MacDonald, n.d. [c. 7 May 1931], MacDonald Papers, TNA/PRO, 30/69/244/317–18.
31 Cabinet Papers, CAB 24/220, C.P.89(31).
32 Cabinet Papers, CAB 23/66, 15 April 1931.

Gould) produced a memorandum expressing dismay at the suggestion of taxing food.[33] There was press speculation that Addison was going to resign.[34] In Cabinet on 4 June, it was concluded that the Cabinet and the government's supporters in the House of Commons were too divided on the subject for it to go ahead.[35] There was no 'plan B' in place, and the prospect of agreeing any form of assistance for arable farmers at that point seemed remote, despite continued pressure from the industry to introduce a quota in time for that year's harvest.[36]

Part of the controversy surrounding the quota was connected to divergent attitudes to the place of agriculture in Britain's economy. At the same time, what lay at the heart of much of the discussion about the future of British agriculture came down to questions about the relevance and sustainability of a commitment to free trade.[37] Most advocates of the scheme admitted that it compromised free trade. However, for some Labour politicians, the attraction of a quota scheme and of the party's wider policy on import boards was that these mechanisms suggested a way to outflank Conservative calls for protection. Principle and electoral pragmatism were often difficult to disentangle. Labour's prospective candidate in the agricultural constituency of King's Lynn welcomed the establishment of an import board as something which 'would sweep all the ground from the Protectionists' feet and ensure a victory ... at the next Election'.[38]

The National Government did indeed introduce measures to protect wheat growers by guaranteeing them a market in milled grain and stabilising prices through the Wheat Act 1932.[39] By this point, tariffs had already been introduced in a number of areas, including for some foodstuffs. The wheat subsidy in 1932 was met from a charge on flour, rather than paid from general taxation as had been the case in 1920. The Labour

---

33 Memorandum circulated to Cabinet, 1 May 1931, Cabinet Papers, CAB 24/221, C.P.112 (31).
34 Ramsay MacDonald to Christopher Addison, 23 May 1931, MacDonald Papers, TNA/PRO, 30/69/1176/1.
35 Cabinet Papers, 4 June 1931, CAB 23/67.
36 W. Hill Foster, Secretary to the Central Chamber of Agriculture, to Ramsay MacDonald, 30 June 1931, MacDonald Papers, TNA/PRO, 30/69/562.
37 On Labour's position on free trade in this period, see Philip Williamson, *National Crisis and National Government: British Politics, the Economy and Empire, 1926–1932* (Cambridge: Cambridge University Press, 1992), p. 97; Anthony Howe, *Free Trade and Liberal England, 1846–1946* (Oxford: Clarendon Press, 1997), pp. 284–6.
38 David Freeman to Arthur Henderson, 15 May 1930, TNA/PRO, 30/69/243/403;
39 For a discussion of the Act, see J. A. Mollett, 'The Wheat Act of 1932. A forerunner of modern farm price support programmes', *Agricultural History Review*, 8 (1960), pp. 20–35.

Party in opposition was able and willing to voice its concerns about this development, particularly over the absence of safeguards for consumers in the legislation, but also over its interference in necessary economic development. Alfred Salter, in a Labour Party pamphlet entitled *The Bread Tax*, complained that English farmers should stop trying to compete with prairie farming and concentrate on aspects of agriculture 'for which our country and our soil are admirably adapted and specially favourable, such as poultry farming, stock breeding, meat production, pig rearing and so on.'[40] However, there was already a more nuanced acceptance of protectionist measures. The bulk of the criticism over the Wheat Act focused on the dangers to consumer interests because of the way in which the scheme would operate, while Clement Attlee acknowledged in the House of Commons the special circumstances which had made it necessary for the government to take some transitional action.[41]

Labour politicians had long acknowledged that a straightforward adherence to free trade could compromise other desirable policies. In 1931 Addison defended the continuation of the subsidy for home-grown sugar beet production (first introduced, by a Labour government, in 1924), arguing that the central issue was not free trade: 'The point was whether the farmers were going to plough the fields for beet or not ... I had to do the best I could in the interests of agriculture in those desperate circumstances.'[42] Addison acknowledged that his critics might be better free traders than he was: 'all the same I am not so bad'.[43] There were tensions with Labour's attempts to offer itself as a supporter of British farming, but also with its evolving ideas about consumption and the encouragement of domestic production in many spheres. E. F. Wise, who had had an important role in developing the policy on import boards in the 1920s, warned the Labour Party conference in 1932 of the need to rethink the emphasis on cheapness at any cost which had lain at the heart of the free trade philosophy.[44]

Nonetheless, opposition to protection marked a tempting ground for differentiating Labour from the position adopted by the National Government. The spectre of 'dear bread' – perhaps more than any other form of protection – was likely to raise hackles, on grounds of principle and also of electoral pragmatism. 'As far as the working class of Great Britain is concerned', observed the Labour Research Department, 'cheap

---

40 Alfred Salter, *The Bread Tax* (London: Labour Party, 1932), p. 11.
41 *House of Commons Debates*, fifth series, 2 March 1932, 262, cols 1134–9.
42 *House of Commons Debates*, fifth series, 31 July 1931, 255, col. 2676.
43 *Ibid.*
44 Labour Party, *Report of the 32nd Annual Conference* (London, 1932), p. 230.

grain is of unqualified benefit', while small farmers also had the advantage of more affordable feed for their livestock: wheat producers were only a minority interest group, even within British agriculture.[45] But the symbolic importance of home-grown wheat, and the power of the agitation which could be raised from the arable sector, undoubtedly influenced the positions adopted by many Labour politicians during 1930 and 1931. Wheat was accepted – realistically or not – as the index of the health of domestic agriculture, and carried with it associations with self-sufficiency in times of national emergency and an ideal of productive, prosperous and labour-intensive farming. To go against the plaintive cries about land falling derelict and people being driven out of work was a brave thing to do in those circumstances, though Snowden was not alone in calling for the subject to be considered more objectively in terms of longer-term economic development. MacDonald and Addison's attitude, on the other hand, says something about concerns within Labour ranks over the desirability of appearing to be a friend and supporter of the agricultural sector, and also about a rhetoric which was already becoming well established in relation to agriculture, about addressing the issues of the industry in a non-political and non-sectional way.

A non-party, 'national' approach emphasised the involvement of the different groups within agriculture to make best use of expertise; this was an area of policy in which many politicians tended to assume that the industry itself knew best. From the early 1920s, the NFU was already talking up the idea of an agreed, non-party-political agricultural programme,[46] even though its own political sympathies seemed to tend in particular directions and be antipathetic to Labour. The Labour Party too – partly in acknowledgement of its own limited competence in the area – was keen to voice its preference for a 'national' policy for agriculture. Its statement on rural policy in 1921 claimed: 'What the Labour Party stands for, in the first place, is the deliberate adoption and the persistent application of a National Policy for Agriculture. It is not any sectional interest or local advantage that should determine the policy of the nation.'[47] The notion of a 'national policy' as expressed here was partly about producing policies for Britain as a whole, rather than for particular local interest groups. But the reference to abjuring 'sectional interest' also implied that Labour was committed to not taking sides in agriculture:

---

45 *Labour Research*, November 1930.
46 For example, the commitment 'to lift our industry out of the rut of Party politics, so that there may be fair prospects of a settled and enduring national agricultural policy': *NFU Year Book, 1923* (London, 1923), p. 108.
47 Labour Party, *The Labour Party and the Countryside* (London, 1921).

most obviously, and in many ways surprisingly, by not favouring the interests of organised labour over those of farmers. At around the same time, however, the identification of a 'national' interest in agriculture acquired associations which rendered it potentially toxic for the labour movement. The creation of the National Agricultural Party in the early 1920s, with related attempts to enrol agricultural labourers into a non-Labour union, suggested the potential for this terminology to camouflage political positions which were distinctly hostile to the articulation of any specifically working-class interest within the countryside.[48]

The NFU would have disclaimed any such political positioning in its own adoption of this vocabulary. For the NFU, a 'national' policy for agriculture was about freeing the sector from the vacillations of party politics. This diagnosis of agriculture's current ills placed much of the blame with faithless politicians and with the impossibility of planning on the farm without some assurance about future prices and demand for produce. No single event had demonstrated agriculture's political vulnerability more dramatically than the 'great betrayal' of 1921: the coalition's *volte face*, when savage cuts made it impossible to underwrite pledges of financial support for arable cultivation. It served as a reminder that there were risks for farmers in planning their business on the basis of politicians' promises, even when it was tempting to do so. Agriculturists needed stability to plan ahead, and yet the policies affecting them were in some ways peculiarly vulnerable to changes in political power and public opinion. While agricultural organisations were trying to gain assurances from the government in spring 1930, the *Manchester Guardian* warned farmers against putting their faith in Labour politicians; if farmers chose political over economic solutions to their problems, this would always would leave them at the mercy of a predominantly urban electorate.[49]

The best way to insulate agriculture against such political fortunes was to establish a consensus on agricultural policy. The goal of taking agriculture outside political wrangling was a prominent theme during the second Labour government. In late 1929, Lloyd George buttonholed Noel Buxton for a chat in his room about agriculture, when he told Buxton that he wanted to get things done 'regardless of party interests'.[50]

---

48 Alun Howkins, *Poor Labouring Men: Rural Radicalism in Norfolk 1872–1923* (London: Routledge, 1985). On an earlier attempt to create a national union, see Paul Readman, 'Conservatives and the politics of land: Lord Winchilsea's National Agricultural Union, 1893–1901', *English Historical Review*, 121:490 (2006), pp. 25–69.
49 'The government and the farmers', *Manchester Guardian*, 17 April 1930.
50 Noel Buxton to Ramsay MacDonald, 6 December 1929, MacDonald Papers, TNA/PRO, 30/69/672/III/184–5.

Addison, despite becoming a prominent exponent of a 'socialist' policy for agriculture, seems to have been attracted by the possibility of finding solutions outside normal party politics. In July 1931 he complained that 'party controversies have stood in the way of a constructive agricultural policy for many years'.[51] In many respects, the role of the Ministry of Agriculture already lent itself to a practical reformist and administrative approach, where positive work, which made a real impact on the industry, could often be achieved outside the realm of ideological division and political debate, responding to expert advice and promoting better farming. The second Labour government's main legacies in this area were in improved schemes to promote drainage and land improvement, and in the more novel, but essentially apolitical, introduction of domestic marketing boards for producers.[52] More far-reaching reconstruction of the industry, meanwhile, fell into a different category altogether. On paper, the Labour Party in this period was committed to land nationalisation and state interventions in the way in which land was cultivated. In practice, the former was beyond the scope of practical politics in this period, while the government's attempts to open up experiments in state farming fell victim to the administration's minority position in the Commons as its Land Utilisation Bill was filleted by the opposition.

The pursuit of a 'national' policy for agriculture in 1930 and 1931, then, could be linked to practical political considerations, as well as more altruistic ambitions for the well-being of the farming industry. Discussions about agricultural policy seemed to offer the potential to find common ground with the Liberals and ease the day-to-day business of running a minority government, although such contact with the Liberals attracted some suspicion within the Labour Party. In July 1931, after reading in *The Times* that Addison, a former Liberal Cabinet minister, was pursuing a dialogue with the Liberals, Snowden complained to MacDonald that he was 'up to his tricks again'.[53] Yet a 'national' approach to agriculture was never simply about brokering arrangements between parties. The aim of the conferences which MacDonald convened at the beginning of 1930 was to arrive at 'the main features of an agreed and *stable* policy for

---

51 Notes of meeting with deputation from Central Chamber of Agriculture, 29 July 1931, TNA/PRO, 30/69/562.
52 Most historical accounts of the second Labour government's agricultural policy focus on the introduction in 1931 of legislation on agricultural marketing. See for example Edith H. Whetham, *Agrarian History of England and Wales, Volume 8: 1914–39* (Cambridge: Cambridge University Press, 1978), pp. 241–3.
53 Philip Snowden to Ramsay MacDonald, 15 July 1931, MacDonald Papers, TNA/PRO, 30/69/673/I/60.

agriculture'.⁵⁴ This vision of stability included ambitions to marry together the various interests within agriculture. W. B. Taylor talked in October 1930 about the desirability of a movement towards 'classless justice' for the whole agricultural industry – an appropriate sentiment for a Labour MP who was a branch secretary and one-time parliamentary nominee of the NFU, and who had supported the demonstration of industrial unity at Parker's Piece.⁵⁵ Assistance for farmers could be defended in this context, against some trade unionists' feelings that the farmers should be able to look after themselves, and that Labour's role should be to bolster the position of employees in the industry rather than the employers.

The search for a 'national' policy in agriculture reflected a number of elements in Labour's complex relationship with the countryside, as well as the party's concerns about its status in the nation more broadly. It grew out of Labour's anxieties about legislating for an industry in which it still felt underrepresented and in which agriculturists themselves were deemed to have levels of expertise which made it difficult for the layperson to speak with any authority. It was also about attempting to broker solutions to a perceived crisis, solutions which might otherwise be deemed ideologically inappropriate or as offending against Labour's traditional interests, but which appeared to be justified by the urgency of the depression. And it was about aiming for a stable policy, the lack of which was deemed to have been detrimental to agriculture's fortunes in the past. In some ways, too, Labour's susceptibility to the complaints of a 'united' industry was perhaps a reflection of ambitions to govern 'the nation' rather than a class-based section of it: to represent interests regardless of class or political affiliation, even when this trespassed against the interests of Labour's core support.

---

54 Letter of invitation, 25 October 1929, MacDonald Papers, TNA/PRO, 30/69/244/219–22. Emphasis added.
55 *House of Commons Debates*, fifth series, 28 October 1930, 244, col. 12.

9

Labour and the Kremlin

JONATHAN DAVIS

As Labour formed its second government at the end of the 1920s, the principle that most guided its understanding of how to bring about change was gradualism. While the nature of the party's ideology was constantly open to debate, the way to force change was not. It would be brought about gradually, through reforms fought for and won in Parliament, and, according to Ramsay MacDonald, it would be achieved only when capitalism was successful (an assumption which was thrown into confusion when Wall Street crashed within six months of Labour taking power). It was the belief in gentle reformism that made Labour's desire to work with the Soviet Union so interesting. Here was a party that believed in reform, not revolution, and in parliamentary, not workers', democracy. Change was to come about peacefully, as Labour was 'opposed to force, violence and confiscation as means of establishing the New Social Order'. Labour believed in 'ordered progress and in democratic methods'.[1]

Yet the party was broadly united in its desire to work with the USSR, despite the fact that its system of government was alien to British political traditions, as the ruling Communist Party had been brought to power by revolution and had then created a one-party state. By the time Labour returned to power in 1929, the Soviet Union was at the start of a 'revolution from above' which would radically transform every aspect of the country. Labour had wanted closer ties with Russia since both revolutions in 1917, as it saw hope of a left-liberal future for Russia should the Provisional Government succeed. Russia's turn to Bolshevism in October

---

1   Labour Party, *Labour and the Nation* (London, 1928), p. 49.

saw a more hostile mood take hold of the Labour Party. Arthur Henderson had denounced Lenin's party before the Bolshevik revolution and others urged support for the western powers' intervention during the Russian Civil War (having been swayed by Aleksandr Kerensky's call to aid Russia's 'democratic forces').[2] However, many Labourites came round to the idea that Russia should be left to sort out its own problems, and this, combined with an assumption that 'socialism' in one form or another was being constructed there, led to the adoption of a pro-Soviet policy which was pursued unwaveringly by MacDonald when he was Prime Minister, as he had when Foreign Secretary in 1924.

Although it was only a partial success when Labour was in power the first time, the party achieved what it set out to do in 1929 – it re-established diplomatic and commercial relations with the USSR. This chapter does not therefore seek to question the view that foreign affairs gave Labour its main successes during its second period in government (or its 'least unsuccessful feature', as David Carlton called it).[3] Instead, it will reappraise Labour's dealings with the Soviet Union and show that, to accomplish its aims where the Kremlin was concerned, the party was forced to question, and at times sacrifice, certain values. It overlooked the oppressive nature of the Stalinist system, which eroded the personal freedoms of many Soviet citizens in ways that challenged Labour's own beliefs and values. It will therefore be argued here that Labour's successes came at a price, as the party's idealism was superseded by its pragmatism.

However, because it was the Soviet Union with which Labour was dealing, that idealism could not be cast aside and ignored. Left-wingers hoped for and expected normal relations to be resumed as soon as Labour returned to power, not only because it seemed to make sense politically and economically, but also because there was a sense that both were

---

2 See C. Wrigley, *Arthur Henderson* (Cardiff: University of Wales Press, 1990), pp. 113–17, and C. Wrigley, *Lloyd George and the Challenge of Labour: The Post-War Coalition 1918–1922* (Hemel Hempstead: Harvester Wheatsheaf, 1990), pp. 211–14.

3 D. Carlton, *MacDonald Versus Henderson: The Foreign Office of the Second Labour Government* (London: Macmillan, 1970), p. 15. For Labour's specific dealings with the Soviet Union, see J. Davis, 'Labour's political thought: the Soviet influence in the interwar years', in P. Corthorn and J. Davis (eds), *The Labour Party and the Wider World: Domestic Politics, Internationalism and Foreign Policy* (London: Tauris, 2008); K. Morgan, *Labour Legends and Russian Gold* (London: Lawrence and Wishart, 2006); A. Williams, *Labour and Russia: The Attitude of the Labour Party to the USSR, 1924–1934* (Manchester: Manchester University Press, 1989); B. Jones, *The Russia Complex: The British Labour Party and the Soviet Union* (Manchester: Manchester University Press, 1977); D. N. Lammers, 'The second Labour government and the restoration of relations with Soviet Russia (1929)', *Historical Research*, 37: 95 (May 1964), pp. 60–72.

travelling a socialist path. It was this shared belief in socialism that tied some Labourites to the USSR, despite the obvious differences in how Labour and the Soviet Communist Party interpreted the ideology.

No other country had such an impact on Labour's activities. Where domestic issues were concerned, Labour was influenced by the apparent construction of socialism in the USSR[4] but this meant that it was often forced to deal with Soviet-inspired problems. On the left there was the troublesome presence of the Moscow-backed Communist Party of Great Britain, which sought to replace Labour as the party of the working class, through affiliation (which Labour constantly rejected) or infiltration (of the overall labour movement), or by standing on its own, offering a revolutionary alternative. From the right, Labour was constantly forced to reject accusations that it was nothing more than a British Bolshevik party doing the Kremlin's work, and the party's 1929 general election manifesto warned voters that 'misrepresentation of Socialism and the aims and Policy of the Labour Party … are already pouring from our opponents'.[5]

Foreign affairs were no less complicated. Ramsay MacDonald mixed ideology and pragmatism as he made it clear that including the Kremlin in international affairs was necessary for European disarmament, peace and stability. MacDonald linked a pro-Soviet foreign policy with his wider aims where Britain and Europe were concerned, and sought to use the USSR to fulfil generally progressive politics. There were, however, still questions over the nature and purpose of Labour's foreign policy, as some on the left wanted to see genuinely socialist aims in international affairs declared. This is one reason why the Soviet Union had such appeal. Recent histories of Labour's foreign policy have debated its socialist nature, focusing on how socialist it was or whether it was socialist at all.[6]

It is arguable that while a general socialism defined both Labour's political thought and the mood of the party, its foreign policy under

---

4   See Jonathan Davis, 'Labour's political thought', in Corthorn and Davis (eds), *The Labour Party and the Wider World*, ch. 3.

5   I. Dale, *Labour Party General Election Manifestos, 1900–1997* (London: Routledge, 2000), p. 33.

6   For example, see J. Shepherd, 'A gentleman at the Foreign Office: influences shaping Ramsay MacDonald's internationalism in 1924', in Corthorn and Davis (eds), *The Labour Party and the Wider World*, ch. 1; J. Callaghan, *The Labour Party and Foreign Policy: A History* (London: Routledge, 2007); H. R. Winkler, *British Labour Seeks a Foreign Policy, 1900–1914* (New Brunswick, NJ: Transaction, 2005); R. Vickers, *The Labour Party and the World. Volume 1: The Evolution of Labour's Foreign Policy, 1900–51* (Manchester: Manchester University Press, 2003); and S. Howe, 'Labour and international affairs', in D. Tanner, P. Thane and N. Tiratsoo (eds), *Labour's First Century* (Cambridge: Cambridge University Press, 2000).

MacDonald was guided more by the 'set of ethical stances', whose roots were in 'Victorian radical Liberalism', that Stephen Howe speaks of, than by any explicitly socialist values.[7] This is unsurprising given the co-operation that existed between radical Liberals and some members (MacDonald included) of the Independent Labour Party during the First World War. MacDonald became chairman of a new organisation – the Union of Democratic Control (UDC) – which brought socialist and liberal critics of British foreign policy together. Liberal UDC members like E. D. Morel and Arthur Ponsonby, who later became Labour MPs, contributed to the party's debates on international matters.

This infusion of radical liberalism into Labour's ideas perhaps made it less likely that the party would develop a distinctly socialist view of world affairs. Rhiannon Vickers has argued that where foreign policy was concerned, 'it is not clear that the Labour Party ever had any socialist ideology as such'; rather, it adopted an internationalist position 'which stressed co-operation and interdependence, and a concern with the international as well as the national interest'.[8] Egon Wertheimer correctly claimed that Labour's foreign policy choices, together with its economic and social ideas, stemmed from 'an ethical postulate, the repudiation of war'.[9]

Henry R. Winkler notes, however, that there *was* an 'attempt to relate socialist theory to the changing realities of the international scene' but this led to complex arguments 'against capitalism and imperialism' and 'commitments to religious and secular pacifism' while attempting to 'promote broad-based rather than limited international organization'.[10] This did not lead to a clearly defined socialist foreign policy, but rather to a desire to work more closely with other governments to ensure peace and stability through a 'League of Nations policy'.[11] In some ways, this makes Labour's pro-Soviet approach in 1929 quite remarkable, as the USSR was not a member of the League of Nations and it had embarked on a radical path of domestic change which was supposedly laying the foundations for the transition to socialism. In other ways, though, it was entirely consistent with MacDonald's view, which, according to Andrew Williams, echoed Lloyd George, 'who had stated that trade would civilise these Russians'.[12] Democracy and peace, rather than a general notion of socialism, were

---

7 S. Howe, 'Labour and international affairs', in Tanner, Thane and Tiratsoo (eds), *Labour's First Century*, p. 120.
8 Vickers, *The Labour Party and the World*, p. 5.
9 E. Wertheimer, *Portrait of the Labour Party* (London: Putnams, 1929), p. 158.
10 Winkler, *British Labour Seeks a Foreign Policy*, p. xii.
11 *Ibid.*, p. xiii.
12 Williams, *Labour and Russia*, p. 33.

the important aspects of MacDonald's overall foreign policy. Where the communists in the Kremlin were concerned, normalising relations and 'civilising' them would come about through trade, which would also bring jobs and money into Britain.

Prior to Labour's victory in 1929, advocates of a renewal of Anglo-Soviet relations after the 1927 Arcos raid and the subsequent diplomatic break between the two countries[13] were heartened by domestic changes in the USSR and by a favourable report from British capitalists concerning trade with the Soviet Union. It seemed, in the 1920s, as though Soviet personnel and policies were becoming less extreme. Lenin's New Economic Policy (NEP) had allowed market forces to play a part in the economic affairs of the country, thus helping to create a mixed economy, and a British trade union delegation visiting the Soviet Union in 1924 was impressed with this change. Delegates saw the NEP as the first and most fundamental compromise of the Soviet regime, and they commented that it was 'not only viable, but has real vitality and stimulates the economic recovery that peace has now made possible'.[14]

The second noticeable change was the victory of so-called 'moderates' in the power struggle which occurred after Lenin died in 1924. MacDonald had an early understanding of the nature of the post-Leninist Communist Party from a despatch from R. M. Hodgson, the British chargé d'affaires in Moscow. He described the post-Leninist party as 'sick physically and morally' and said that it 'cuts a sorry figure'. Lenin was 'gone, never to return as a serious factor in politics; Trotski is an invalid'.[15] He described the other old Bolsheviks in similarly unfavourable terms, stating that Zinoviev was a 'poor creature at the best' and Kamenev a 'depressing personality'. Stalin was a 'narrow-minded obstinate Georgian, entangled in the intricacies of Party doctrine' and Bukharin was 'a fanatic, popular with the working man, but without the makings of a leader'.[16]

By the time that MacDonald was again Prime Minister, the 'obstinate Georgian' was first among equals in the Communist Party, which comforted the Labour leader, as Stalin advocated 'socialism in one country' rather than Trotsky's international revolution. MacDonald and his comrades in the

---

13 For details of the raid see W. P. Coates and Z. Coates, *A History of Anglo-Soviet Relations* (London: Lawrence and Wishart, 1943), pp. 267–90; and L. Fischer, *The Soviets in World Affairs* (New York: Vintage Books, 1960), pp. 504–7. For the Soviet response, see *Dokumenti vneshney politiki SSSR*, 10 (Moscow, 1965), pp. 245–88.
14 *The Official Report of the British Trade Union Delegation to Russia in November and December 1924* (London: Trades Union Congress General Council, 1925), p. 59.
15 Despatch from R. M. Hodgson, 28 January 1924, The National Archives/Public Record Office, TNA/PRO, 30/69/104.
16 *Ibid*.

party leadership saw this as power shifting away from those he considered extremists to the supposedly more moderate elements in the Kremlin. After the first Russian revolution of 1917, Stalin's comrades in Narkomindel (the Soviet Foreign Ministry) were Georgy Chicherin until 1930, and then Maksim Litvinov, the 'self-styled "Plenipotentiary Representative of the Russian Federation of Socialist Republics of Soviets" in London'.[17] After the second Labour government fell, Litvinov became known for his determined calls for a collective security campaign between the USSR, Britain and France to stop Nazism.

The final sign that things might be moving towards a more welcoming attitude towards the west was the positive response given to the British industrialists who visited Moscow in March 1929. *Pravda* duly published articles about Anglo-Soviet relations,[18] while in Britain the *Daily Herald* covered the visit and stated that 'important negotiations were to be entered into'.[19] This was certainly true, and the basis was being laid for future negotiations. Ernest Remnant, a member of the trade delegation, said that they were 'naturally hopeful of success'.[20]

While the chairman of the Soviet State Bank, Georgy Pyatakov, commented that trade between the USSR and Britain would be impossible without the restoration of normal diplomatic relations, he also said that relations should improve as a result of the delegation's visit. He stated that an agreement between the two countries could lead to Anglo-Soviet trade being worth £150 million, possibly rising to £200 million.[21] The delegates reported that Pyatakov was prepared to discuss with the government 'all questions, including private British claims'. This was 'an important achievement', and delegates were 'confident his statement will be welcomed in all serious circles as evidence that with goodwill on both sides the negotiations should lead to an economic settlement of mutual advantage'.[22]

---

17 J. Smele, '"*Mania Grandiosa*" and "the turning point in world history": Kerensky in London in 1918', *Revolutionary Russia*, 20:1 (2007), p. 1. Litvinov was also sometimes referred to as the Soviet ambassador to London. For example see the *New York Times*, 5 January 1918.

18 For example, see *Pravda*, March and April 1929, 'Zayavlenie makdonal'da ob anglo-sovetskikh otnosheniyakh' and 'Angliyskie otkliki na zayavlenie tov Pyatikova'. Interested parties had continued to visit Soviet Russia in the 1920s. For example, a delegation of teachers went in August 1926, as did George Lansbury. See *Izvestiya*, 28 August 1926 and 29 August 1926, respectively.

19 *Daily Herald*, 3 April 1929.

20 *Ibid*.

21 For details of Pyatakov's speech to the delegation, 7 May 1929, see TNA/PRO, FO 371/14029.

22 *Ibid*., 24 April 1929.

The need for a quick resumption of diplomatic relations was also highlighted in *Pravda*, which hoped that the British delegates would come to the same conclusion.[23] Just over a month before the election which returned Labour to power, MacDonald made it clear that he agreed with this position, noting that it was Labour's contention 'that the fullest and most complete diplomatic intercourse should be resumed at once'[24] as this was the only way to have any concerns over Anglo-Soviet trade dealt with satisfactorily. As for obtaining Soviet orders for British engineering and manufacturing, he said that businesses were anxious to get these deals done.

Labour's rapprochement with the Soviet Union can therefore be portrayed as being pragmatic in both economic and political terms. Michael Jabara Carley notes that as 'Anglo-Soviet trade increased in the 1920s, so did the pressure for pragmatism in relations with the USSR. Anti-Bolshevism was one thing; the purse quite another.'[25] It was seen as a necessity which would allow the party to undo the damage it said the Tories had done after the cancellation of the 1921 trade agreement and the suspension of diplomatic relations. Labour remained convinced that the two countries had 'everything to gain by trading with each other'[26] and it criticised the Conservatives for the way they handled Anglo-Soviet affairs. The party claimed that Stanley Baldwin's government had been eager to 'snatch a fleeting political advantage by exploiting the bogy of revolution' and this had led to the tearing up of the 1924 Anglo-Soviet trade agreement, 'with the result that orders for machinery and manufactures, which would have found employment for thousands of British workers, have been lost to this country'.[27] In words perhaps designed to make Labour again seem credible as a party of government, 'gestures of this kind' were denounced as 'neither common sense nor good business'.[28]

Labour went into the 1929 election with its policy towards the Soviet Union unchanged since 1924. While still opposing Soviet interference in other nations' domestic policies, it was made clear that Labour would move immediately to 'establish diplomatic and commercial relations' with the USSR, that any outstanding differences would be settled 'by treaty or otherwise' and that a Labour government 'would make every effort to

---

23 *Pravda*, 10 April 1929.
24 *Daily Herald*, 9 April 1929.
25 M. Jabara Carley, '"A fearful concatenation of circumstances": the Anglo-Soviet rapprochement, 1934–36', *Contemporary European History*, 5:1 (1996), p. 31.
26 Labour Party, *Labour and the Nation*, p. 49.
27 *Ibid*.
28 *Ibid*.

encourage a revival of trade with Soviet Russia'.[29] The *Daily Herald* had already nailed its red colours to the pro-Soviet mast, and the *New Leader* called for a quick renewal of relations with the Kremlin, stating that 'We hope that the earliest possible step will be taken in this direction – first, because it is a simple act of justice and common sense; second because the development of Russian trade is urgently needed; and third because normal relations with Russia are so essential to peace.'[30] As MacDonald's party believed that the USSR was important for European peace and economic stability, these promises were pursued once Labour was returned to power on 30 May.

Perhaps the most significant difference between the first and second Labour Cabinets was the inclusion of Arthur Henderson as Foreign Secretary. Henderson had personal experience of Russian affairs, having been sent to Petrograd by Lloyd George to convince the Provisional Government to stay in the war in 1917. Unlike MacDonald, he had faith in the League of Nations as a means for international change and progress, a fact which saw him make Lord Robert Cecil advisor on questions about the League of Nations. Other important individuals Henderson took to the Foreign Office were Hugh Dalton as Parliamentary Under-Secretary and Philip Noel-Baker as Parliamentary Private Secretary. David Carlton notes that while these three held positions of 'no great nominal importance', they were significant members of the team, as 'their influence on Henderson was indeed considerable, since they were an *avant-garde*, much more sympathetic to the Labour Party's distinctive foreign policies'[31] than the permanent Foreign Office staff. Yet despite surrounding himself with these able men, Henderson knew that MacDonald 'lacked full confidence in him and that he could not expect unquestioning support if he ran into difficulties'.[32]

Although there were clear problems in the relationship between the Prime Minister and his Foreign Secretary, the two agreed that the USSR was needed to help ensure European peace and British economic stability. Henderson maintained that 'Russia, with its vast population, cannot be permanently ignored; only by diplomatic and other intercourse with her will it be possible to bring her once more into the family of nations.'[33] This pro-Soviet policy continued the pragmatic line of MacDonald and

---

29 Ibid.
30 *New Leader*, 21 June 1929.
31 Carlton, *MacDonald Versus Henderson*, p. 20.
32 *Ibid.*, p. 16.
33 Cited in F. M. Leventhal, *Arthur Henderson* (Manchester: Manchester University Press, 1989), pp. 155–6.

neither he nor Henderson thought they were pursuing a policy that would lead to socialism soon. Labour's foreign policy was not a means by which a socialist world would be created. For Labour's pragmatists, the Soviet Union was simply another government with which to work as they tried to ensure that the post-war stability continued.

Once he set to work, Henderson found that dealing with the USSR would force him and his party to make certain compromises which challenged the traditional left-liberal beliefs evident within the Labour Party. An early test to such values came in the form of Leon Trotsky, although not because of earlier concerns about international socialism. Instead, Trotsky became a domestic political issue in the summer of 1929 after Stalin expelled him from his party and country and he applied to Britain for political asylum. Labour was now in a very difficult position. Allowing Stalin's most detested rival the right to asylum would be viewed as a hostile act and thus greatly complicate negotiations with the Kremlin. It would simply not be possible to negotiate seriously with the USSR while simultaneously taking in Stalin's greatest political opponent. The Home Secretary, J. R. Clynes, told the Cabinet that Trotsky's admission might be regarded as an 'unfriendly act by the Soviet government, and they might allege that the British Government has given hospitality to Trotsky for political reasons and was using him as a means of weakening the existing government in Russia'.[34] Added to that was the fact that, just a few years earlier, Trotsky had been one of the fiercest critics of the British labour movement and its leaders.[35] It is therefore understandable that they approached this issue with a wary caution.

However, Trotsky's application would not be dismissed without arguments and discussion, as denying him refuge in Britain challenged the traditional view that Britain was a safe haven to those who needed it most. According to Kenneth Miller, Henderson thought that 'the Cabinet should consider Trotsky's application for residence in England since there was, after all, "a right to asylum"'.[36] Henderson and Dalton both felt that a rejection of Trotsky's plea would question Britain's historic image as a haven for the internationally oppressed. Henderson was not alone in disagreeing with the Home Office, as left-wingers also supported Trotsky. Fenner Brockway and John Strachey rejected the suggestion that allowing him in would lead to problems in the Anglo-Soviet negotiations. George

---

34 Memorandum by the Home Secretary on the application by Leon Trotsky for permission to reside in England, 24 June 1929, Cabinet Papers, CAB 24/204.
35 R. Segal, *The Tragedy of Leon Trotsky* (Harmondsworth: Penguin Books, 1983), p. 322.
36 K. E. Miller, *Socialism and Foreign Policy: Theory and Practice in Britain to 1931* (The Hague: Martinus Nijhoff, 1931), p. 200.

Bernard Shaw, like Brockway and Strachey, saw the history of asylum under attack. All three distanced themselves from Trotsky's ideas but still felt that he should be allowed to find refuge in Britain.

In the end, it is highly unlikely that Trotsky stood any real chance of being granted political asylum by a party he had denounced and a country which was dealing with his political enemy. After much debate, Clynes refused Trotsky's request because 'the right to asylum did not mean the right of an exile to demand asylum, but only the right of the state to refuse it'.[37] Labour's rejection of Trotsky's application for asylum demonstrates the importance the party placed upon reconciliation with the Soviet Union. Getting orders for British businesses, which would ensure jobs and money for the country, took precedence over long-held values which had once allowed other left-wing revolutionaries such as Karl Marx and Vladimir Lenin to settle in Britain. The case of Leon Trotsky highlights the influence that the USSR had on Labour's domestic and foreign policies, even without exerting specific pressure.

Henderson also had to deal with less philosophical constraints, such as MacDonald's declaration that the government would exchange ambassadors only after parliamentary approval. The problem with this approach was that it meant that official relations could not be resumed until October, when Parliament next sat. Although the Foreign Secretary disagreed, he realised that he had to pursue this course as to do otherwise would have suggested that there were splits in the party. Hugh Dalton noted in his diary that Henderson believed he could not go back on MacDonald's statement 'wrong though it was. We should have all the Press against us and the danger of 1924 all over again. Russia has brought us down once. We can't afford to let it happen twice.'[38] In July 1929, Henderson met Valeryan Dovgalevsky, the Soviet ambassador in Paris sent to London to represent the USSR during the negotiations, and reluctantly informed him of this development.

Part of the problem was the unresolved issues from the last time Labour dealt with the USSR. Article 16 of the 1924 trade agreement pledged that both sides would refrain from acts that could endanger the stability of either nation. This was the 'propaganda' article which linked Narkomindel to the Comintern's actions, something which Narkomindel officially rejected. Dovgalevsky stated that he had not expected that the resumption of Anglo-Soviet relations would be dependent on resolving questions of Comintern propaganda and tsarist debts. With the Soviet point of view made clear, he left Britain.

---

37 Segal, *The Tragedy of Leon Trotsky*, pp. 292–3.
38 Cited in Wrigley, *Arthur Henderson*, p. 169.

On the British side, it was hoped that the parliamentary interval would allow time to work on these problems and thus allow a smoother process in October. However, Henderson had to decide what to do about further obstacles to a resumption of relations. On 3 June, the Foreign Office received a note from the Department of Overseas Trade on the 'Financial and economic deterioration in the Soviet Union'. It reported a conversation between the British vice-consul in Łódź, Poland, and a member of Eitigon and Company, a Łódź firm which traded with the USSR. The note pointed out that 'Mr Eitigon considers the financial situation is becoming precarious and that the position is worsening steadily'.[39] The hand-written response underneath states that 'This is extremely interesting, as coming from a firm infinitely better fitted than any British firm to estimate the situation accurately, and which after [a] second years' trading with the Soviet Government now resolves to grant no further credits.'[40] Underneath this reply was a note agreeing that this was indeed interesting, and that, at a time when reliable information was needed to help decide whether credits should be offered to the USSR, it showed fairly conclusively that 'such trading is not possible on any scale appreciably larger than at present'.[41]

There was also a warning against believing the figures given to the 1929 trade delegation by Pyatakov, as his 'daring' would 'not bear close analysis'.[42] The Anglo-Russian Committee stated that it was 'quite inconceivable that the whole of [the] increased foreign trade will be awarded to Great Britain, since some of the main requirements of Soviet industry are raw materials which neither Great Britain nor the Dominions could possibly furnish'.[43] It also ruled out any hope that British banks, at a time when British industry was suffering from 'the prevailing tightness of money',[44] would be 'in a position to give such huge credits to a country which has steadfastly refused to honour its old debts'.[45] It is information such as this that led the Chancellor of the Exchequer, Philip Snowden, to deny credit loans to the Soviet Union, although advocates of closer ties with the USSR could find encouragement in the Soviet Union's employment of 'American experts' who were helping to 'reconstruct the Soviet

---

39 Note from the Department of Overseas Trade, 'Financial and economic deterioration in the Soviet Union', 3 June 1929, TNA/PRO, FO 371/14029.
40 Ibid.
41 Ibid.
42 From Prime Minister's Private Secretary, Statement by chairman of Anglo-Russian Committee on British delegation's visit to the Soviet Union, 5 July 1929, TNA/PRO, FO 371/14030.
43 Ibid.
44 Ibid.
45 Ibid.

economy'. These 'experts' apparently 'whetted the appetite of American finance and industry'.[46]

This interest in the United States raised concerns that renewed relations with Britain were merely a cover which the Soviets were using in order to get closer to American products. In September, S. Walton, a member of the delegation of businessmen who had gone to the USSR earlier in the year, wrote to Henderson expressing similar fears to those of his fellow delegate and Committee member Ernest Remnant. Both suggested that the Soviets wanted a quick recognition 'with vague pledges' but would then give 'trade to America and nothing to Britain'.[47] Simon Harcourt-Smith agreed that there was a 'certain amount of truth in Mr Walton's contentions' and claimed that it was probable that the Soviets would use the resumption of relations with London 'as a lever to obtain favourable terms from America. The Bolsheviks are obsessed with ideas of American efficiency, and do not hesitate to say that they infinitely prefer American machinery to English.'[48]

It was not only the economic arrangements which were raising questions, as there was still some confusion about the propaganda issue. Maksim Litvinov had given Ernest Remnant 'a vague assurance that the Third International was an organisation entirely separate from the Russian Government'.[49] On the strength of this assurance, the Anglo-Russia Committee was convinced that 'an effective guarantee for the cessation of hostile propaganda can be obtained'.[50] However, earlier in the year Remnant, Harcourt-Smith and Lawrence Collier discussed this point with Dovgalevsky, who 'evaded the point about Komintern activities', 'took refuge in a general complaint of the "vagueness" of our accusations' and did not deny 'the connection between the Soviet government and the Komintern'.[51] Remnant subsequently resigned from the Committee, believing that the Soviets had fooled the delegates when they were in Moscow, and he was anxious that they should not fool anyone else in the same way.[52]

On top of questions raised over financial assistance and communist propaganda, the Foreign Secretary also had to contend with royal disapproval of closer links with the Kremlin. On 27 September 1929, he received a letter explaining that the King was not happy with Henderson

---

46 TNA/PRO, FO 371/14032.
47 *Ibid.*
48 *Ibid.*
49 Statement from Prime Minister's Private Secretary concerning British delegation to the USSR in March 1929, TNA/PRO, FO 371/14030.
50 *Ibid.*
51 *Ibid.*
52 TNA/PRO, FO 371/14032.

and Dovgalevsky referring to one another as 'Ambassador' when they met. The King believed that friendly courtesies given to 'real' ambassadors should not be given to ministers from the USSR, who, 'if they did not actually plan, certainly approved of the brutal murder of the King's first cousins, the late Emperor and Empress of Russia'.[53] After discussing the issue with Ramsay MacDonald, the King had understood that government policy was to 'insist on a satisfactory settlement of the points at issue between our two countries, such as propaganda and debts, before resuming relations'.[54]

The Foreign Office reply reminded the King that the majority returned to the House of Commons represented the importance of ending Soviet isolation. Labour and Liberal MPs were 'committed by declarations made at the time of the elections to the resumption of relations with the Soviet Government' and, further,

> if this was to be achieved an essential condition would be the exchange of Ambassadors, as the Soviet Government representing as it does at the moment, a country with which we have for decades past maintained relations through the medium of representatives of the highest diplomatic rank, would be satisfied with nothing less.[55]

Henderson's Cabinet colleagues supported his approach, agreeing that the intricate nature of re-establishing relations meant that 'if a settlement of the question of debts is to be reached there is more likelihood of such a settlement once normal diplomatic relations are re-established rather than if relations remain suspended as at present'.[56]

It probably never crossed Arthur Henderson's mind that seeking closer ties with the USSR would raise problems that ranged from Leon Trotsky to King George V. But despite all of the difficulties thrown up in the early months of Labour's return to power, Henderson was still determined in his pursuit of policies which he hoped would achieve some of Labour's foreign policy aims. At the 1929 party conference in Brighton in September, he reminded delegates that at the general election 'we made it unmistakably plain that if we formed a government one of the first things we would do would be to bring about a resumption of diplomatic relations with Russia'.[57]

When Dovgalevsky returned to Britain, he met with Henderson in the White Hart Hotel in Lewes, where Henderson informed him that 'the

---

53 Henderson Papers, 27 September 1929, TNA/PRO, FO 800/280.
54 *Ibid.*
55 *Ibid.*
56 *Ibid.*
57 Cited in Wrigley, *Arthur Henderson*, p. 169.

Government inferred that any guarantees regarding propaganda would extend to the Third International'.[58] For Labour, this issue was still fundamentally important and was therefore 'embodied in a protocol signed on October 3rd between the Secretary of State for Foreign Affairs and the Soviet Ambassador to Paris'. It 'provided for the renewal of the pledge contained in Article 16 of the General Treaty of August 8th 1924'.[59] In December, the two countries exchanged notes pledging that they would 'live in peace and amity' with each other and 'respect the right of the other to live its own life in its own way within its jurisdiction'.[60] However, the links between the Comintern and Moscow still caused problems. The 'conflict of opinion between the two Governments as to the relations existing between the Soviet Government and the Third International' was made clear: 'His Majesty's Government have always maintained that to all intents and purposes they were the same. The Soviet Government, on the other hand, contended that they have no control whatsoever over the activities of the Third International'.[61]

F. M. Leventhal argues that by 'papering over their difficulties the Foreign Office could appear to snatch a modest victory without the Soviet authorities agreeing to specific references in the formal protocol that admitted their responsibility for the actions of the Comintern'.[62] On 5 October the House of Commons approved the restoration of diplomatic relations with the Soviet Union, and a month later the government won the vote by 324 to 199 that would allow the exchanging of ambassadors.

The Soviet Union's envoy to London was Grigory Sokolnikov, and Henderson observed that Sokolnikov was 'in many respects more acceptable as Ambassador than Monsieur Kamenev'.[63] Henderson's choice of ambassador in Moscow was Sir Esmond Ovey, an experienced diplomat, rather than an ideologically sound Labour man. Leventhal notes that Ovey 'spoke Russian' and was 'in the traditional ambassadorial mold' (*sic*).[64] His appointment is another reminder that Henderson was more concerned with pragmatism than socialism where Anglo-Soviet relations

---

58 Leventhal, *Arthur Henderson*, p. 157.
59 TNA/PRO, FO 371/14846 (1).
60 *Ibid.*
61 *Ibid.*
62 Leventhal, *Arthur Henderson*, pp. 157–8.
63 Henderson Papers, 27 August 1929, TNA/PRO, FO 800/280. Kamenev was briefly envoy to Italy and Henderson believed he was being considered for the post in Britain. The reason for the turn away from Kamenev can be found in the internal politics of the Soviet Communist Party, as he was a victim of Stalin's victory in the power struggle after Lenin's death.
64 Leventhal, *Arthur Henderson*, p. 158.

were concerned. It is possible, of course, that he may also have been swayed by his surroundings, as the Foreign Office was conservative by nature. David Carlton observes that the background and training of Foreign Office officials 'stressed prudence, continuity and especially the defence of the national interest in foreign policy'.[65] Henderson's Cabinet colleagues had similar traits, as MacDonald believed in gradual change and Snowden was fiscally conservative.

Andrew Williams emphasises how important Ovey was in shaping Labour's attitudes towards the USSR while the party was in power, and he was certainly crucial in keeping Henderson well informed about what was happening inside the country and the Communist Party.[66] He also made clear the differences between the rhetoric and reality of Soviet foreign policy, reporting in February 1930 that he was convinced that the Soviets would go 'as far as possible in vituperation of all foreign countries and Governments, without actually causing a breach of relations. In this the Communist Party, who are directors of the policy are at least logical and consistent.'[67]

Henderson quickly realised that dealing with the Kremlin would never be an easy task and it is to his credit that he achieved what he did. But he had to tread a fine line where the USSR was concerned. As he became increasingly aware of the type of system with which he was dealing, he had to ensure that he did not let down supporters of the government's pro-Soviet policy. The latter included the socialist journalist H. N. Brailsford, who attacked Labour's opponents who criticised the government for apparently giving too many concessions to the Soviets. He said that the Tory tactic of baiting the Russian bear by challenging the Labour government over its business with the USSR was not just 'the usual effort of an Opposition to embarrass the Government of the day',[68] and that the Tories had 'something much more important in mind'.[69] He then claimed that they were 'bent on a final breach with Russia' and that the only way of attaining this was to 'manoeuvre a Labour Government into doing it'. He said that any 'rupture for which a Tory Ministry alone were responsible would be temporary. But if any subtlety could tempt Labour into a quarrel that ended in the expulsion of the Russian Ambassador from London, a generation might pass before another took

---

65 Carlton, *MacDonald Versus Henderson*, p. 20.
66 Williams, *Labour and Russia*, p. 128.
67 28 February 1930, TNA/PRO, FO 371/14846 (1).
68 *New Leader*, 7 February 1930.
69 *Ibid*.

his place.'⁷⁰ Brailsford feared that this would lead to a long-term break in relations or possibly worse. Not only would the 'oil magnates ... again allow their imaginations to stray toward the pipe-line that crosses Georgia' but an 'occasion for an intervention would soon present itself, and even if a Labour Government had pronounced the Russians impossible, the resistance to warlike adventure might be weak'.[71] He also questioned why, even though Henderson had already exchanged ambassadors, the right wing did not realise 'that an expansion of trade in Russia is one of the hopeful issues from our tribulations of unemployment'.[72]

Brailsford's advocacy of Anglo-Soviet trade became an even more urgent demand as unemployment grew at an alarming rate once the Great Depression took hold of the capitalist world. In Britain it rose from 1.1 million in May 1929 to 1.5 million in January 1930, and continued to rise month by month for the rest of the year, until it reached 2.7 million. A successful trade agreement in this climate was now an economic necessity, and it finally came on 16 April 1930. It was agreed that the Soviet Union would take up to £7 million worth of British engineering, chemical and electrical goods, while Britain would take £34 million worth of Soviet goods. This agreement led to a flourishing of trade between the two countries and the USSR 'became for a time the most important market outside the United States for British machine tools' as a 'number of important technical assistance agreements were concluded between the Soviets and British firms'.[73] These firms included Imperial Chemical Industries Ltd and Metropolitan-Vickers, an electrical company which became embroiled in the famous 'wrecking' trial in 1933. Orders also came to other firms for steel works equipment and marine diesel engines. British manufacturers 'supplied £15 million worth of goods for the first Soviet five-year plan', which, as F. S. Northedge and Audrey Wells correctly noted, was 'by no means a massive contribution to the unemployment problem, but achieved at a time when almost any business of this kind was welcome'.[74]

But while Labour pursued closer links with the USSR in order to facilitate trade, Henderson became more and more aware of the price the party would have to pay, as he received numerous reports about the distasteful nature of the Soviet regime, which challenged the party's ethics,

---

70 *Ibid.*
71 *Ibid.*
72 *Ibid.*
73 F. S. Northedge and A. Wells, *Britain and Soviet Communism: The Impact of a Revolution* (London: Macmillan, 1982), p. 216.
74 *Ibid.*, pp. 216–17.

morals and beliefs. In December 1929 he received a copy of a despatch to the Norwegian Foreign Minister from Andreas Urbye, the Norwegian representative in Moscow. This gave a detailed account of what he called the 'New Period of Terror'.[75] It stated that hardships resulting from the lack of food in the towns and provinces, which Soviets feared would only get worse as winter was approaching, had led to the return of unrest and revolt to the regions. Urbye's note commented on rumours regarding dissensions within the party, which 'remain persistent.... Cleansing of the party constantly takes place, and there are many who do not feel safe.'[76] It referred to the 'threat of danger from below', which would be met by the Communist Party with 'the old method ... namely terror'.[77]

Noting that certain groups were targeted (tsarist generals who were shot by the State Political Directorate 'for contra-revolutionary sabotage', 21 Ukrainians 'condemned to death for contra-revolutionary conspiracies') Urbye makes it clear that there were 'accounts of capital punishment either with or without trial' with 'a very large number' recently being arrested in Moscow. He concludes that the victims came from all classes and included 'old and infirm ladies, of whom it is not possible to conceive how they could be dangerous to anyone'.[78] Ovey wrote of similar attacks, although his coverage of the *chistka* (purge) was more concerned with the thousands of party workers and state employees who lost their jobs.[79]

These letters are evidence that Henderson and his Cabinet colleagues not only knew about Soviet persecution and the rise in the use of terror tactics in the USSR, but also that they were willing to ignore such matters to ensure that relations with the Kremlin remained as cordial as possible. This could be seen as a desperate pragmatism, which forced long-standing Labour members to overlook attacks on the vulnerable, the weak and the voiceless – just the type of people the Labour Party hoped to protect and represent. It is little wonder that Henderson commented on how unhappy he was at the progress being made with the Soviets. Although he had successfully overseen the exchanging of ambassadors and a trade agreement, the MacDonaldite desire to 'civilise' the Russians had failed. He was also mindful of the fact that the USSR was still a stick with which the Tories could beat Labour. He complained to Ovey that he was 'bitterly disappointed at the results of one year's experience of renewed relations with

---

75 Despatch from Urbye to Norwegian Minister for Foreign Affairs, 29 October 1929, TNA/PRO, FO 418/71.
76 *Ibid.*
77 *Ibid.*
78 *Ibid.*
79 Ovey writing about the purges, 21 July 1930, TNA/PRO, FO 418/73.

the Soviet government whose actions seem designed deliberately to play into the hands of the opponents of continued Anglo-Russian relations'.[80]

Henderson's Christian conscience was also put under stress as stories emerged about Soviet persecution of the Russian Orthodox Church, which led to fears for the freedom of religion in the USSR. Given the Labour Party's Christian origins, these stories were deeply concerning. Andrew Williams claims that many members 'felt the need to define their faith in quasi-religious terms. The ghost of "christian socialism" still haunted the party and at times it remained a part of its distinctive style.'[81] Yet while accounts of how the Russian Orthodox Church was being harassed by the Soviet authorities touched numerous consciences, there was also a stubborn refusal to accept these stories.

When the Soviet ambassador arrived in London, he told Sidney Webb and Philip Noel-Baker that 'he had left Russia in the middle of December unaware that there was any such thing as Religious Persecution … he arrived in England to find the question becoming to be one of burning political importance' (sic).[82] Pro-Soviet Labourites dismissed the stories as nothing more than a campaign by the Conservative Party and Christian right-wingers.[83] The *Daily Herald* carried a declaration from the Russian Holy Synod – 'There is no religious persecution by the Soviet Union and there never was' – and it stated that stories in the Tory press were 'absolutely untrue'.[84] The *Daily Herald* correspondent wrote that the 'Soviet Press prints a signed interview with the leading orthodox churchmen, denying religious persecution by the Soviet Union, and sharply taking the Pope and the Archbishop of Canterbury to task over recent anti-Bolshevik declarations'.[85]

Ramsay MacDonald failed to make his position totally clear. This may have been a consequence of the fact that he was still receiving information about this issue and was still discussing it in Cabinet meetings.[86] He therefore may not have wanted to make any rash statements that could have harmed Anglo-Soviet relations. He said that the history of religion in Russia was 'unfortunately full of the records of persecution' but also

---

80 Cited in Wrigley, *Arthur Henderson*, p. 170.
81 Williams, *Labour and Russia*, p. 103.
82 Cited in Williams, *Labour and Russia*, pp. 104–5.
83 For a pro-Soviet account of the 'alleged' religious persecution, see Coates and Coates, *A History of Anglo-Soviet Relations*, ch. 14. For a more balanced account, see Williams, *Labour and Russia*, pp. 102–10.
84 *Daily Herald*, 17 February 1930.
85 *Ibid*.
86 Cabinet discussion on religious persecution in Russia, 12 February 1930, Cabinet Papers, CAB 23/63.

claimed that 'a good part of the statements which have done duty from time to time have been proved to be false'.[87] He would wait until the news had been corroborated, as the government did not have the full facts.

Some facts had come through in the previous month. On 18 January 1930, Ovey sent a letter to the Foreign Office in which he replied to a memo about religious persecution. He said that there was 'no doubt whatsoever as to the determination of the Soviet Government eventually to substitute Marxian atheism for belief in the tenets of the Orthodox Church'.[88] Propaganda and 'other means' were being employed to train 'not only the new but the present generation to disbelief in Christianity'.[89] He did add, however, that the government was not 'proceeding with any undue haste and services are permitted in some places'. It was Ovey's view that the Soviet government ultimately intended to 'abolish religious belief entirely'.[90] Interestingly, he proved to be correct about the nature of the Stalinist purges later in the decade, and he was also right about this. By that time, though, the Labour government had long since fallen and the successes and failures of this administration were a distant memory as Nazism gripped Europe as tightly as the effects of capitalism's failures had done during the Great Depression.

How should Labour's attempts to deal with the USSR be considered in a reappraisal of the party's second period in office? Henry R. Winkler offers a somewhat critical assessment:

> neither the economic nor the political advantages of the Russian rapprochement were realized. Communist propaganda continued unabated and the increase in trade in a troubled world was modest at very best. As Hugh Dalton later put it, the best that could be said was that Labour's policy made Anglo-Russian relations less unsatisfactory than might otherwise have been the case.[91]

While this is an accurate description of what happened, it does not consider seriously the difficulties Labour faced when negotiating with the Kremlin. Nor does it allow for MacDonald's pragmatism, which mixed a 'wait and see' approach with a casual dismissal that implied that little else could be expected when dealing with the Soviets. But, seen within the context of what Henderson and MacDonald knew and overlooked, Labour's foreign

---

87 *Daily Herald*, 25 February 1930.
88 Memo from Ovey on religious persecution in the Soviet Union, 18 January 1930, TNA/PRO, FO 371/14840.
89 *Ibid.*
90 *Ibid.*
91 Winkler, *British Labour Seeks a Foreign Policy*, p. 86.

policy demonstrated the party's pragmatic thinking on Anglo-Soviet matters. The party was not in power to lead the world to socialism, but rather to lead Britain out of economic depression and towards stability.

Labour's international hopes of ensuring peace and democracy rested upon traditional methods of negotiation, trade agreements and cordial relations with other powers, irrespective of who those powers were. Where the Kremlin was concerned, Labour was certainly frustrated and Henderson became less positive about dealing with the USSR. But, given the great constraints which were laid upon the government after the Wall Street Crash and the start of the Great Depression, David Carlton's assessment of Henderson as being 'generally acknowledged as one of the successes of the second Labour government'[92] is still true.

Labour's dealings with the USSR demonstrated a mixture of pragmatism and principle. MacDonald's Labour hoped that Anglo-Soviet trade would help bring vital money into the British economy and ultimately bring the Soviet Union into the League of Nations, thus extending the possibilities of a continued peace in Europe. This pragmatism therefore had a principled purpose – it was not simply to ensure British stability, but to ensure capitalist stability, as, according to MacDonald, socialism could follow only if capitalism was successful. However, it is questionable whether socialism was the long-term aim of MacDonald's government. Perhaps an ethical stability was the most that was possible from a government that favoured such a pragmatic approach to Anglo-Soviet relations.

---

92 Carlton, *MacDonald Versus Henderson*, p. 16.

10

'Bolshevism run mad': Labour and socialism

JOHN CALLAGHAN

We take it for granted that most socialists in Britain were to be found in the Labour Party at the end of the First World War, even though Labour had responded patriotically to the crisis of August 1914 and had supported the war effort until the end. It really is a very good indicator of how weak socialism had always been in Britain. There had been no schism of the labour movement and though a Communist Party was founded in the summer of 1920 it consisted only of the fusion of pre-existing socialist groups. The Labour Party and trade unions escaped the damage inflicted upon their counterparts in France, Italy and Germany by the twin impact of the war and the Bolshevik revolution. Labour emerged with no serious electoral rival to its left and – with the exception of the 2,000 who formed the Communist Party – such socialists as there were found themselves trapped in an organisation more dominated by the non-socialist trade unions than ever before. Thus Labour – unique among the parties of the Second International in this respect – emerged from the war with its Edwardian leadership more, not less, securely in the saddle. The party constitution drafted by Arthur Henderson with help from Sidney Webb in 1918 institutionalised this dominance. While it conceded a 'socialist' statement of aims for the first time – the famous Clause 4 – it also strengthened the organisational power of the affiliated unions, upon which the party's finances depended, by fixing their dominance of both the National Executive Committee and the annual conference of the party.

Since the formation of the Independent Labour Party (ILP) at Bradford in 1893, most British socialists had realised that the future of their ideals depended upon the trade unions. Since 1910, and until the economic crash of 1920, there were grounds for hope on this score. The rapid expansion of trade union membership had begun in 1910 in circumstances of rising militancy, when syndicalist ideas and scepticism about the value of the Labour Members of Parliament were both evident on the left. Marxist ideas had been taken into the unions through the activities of the Socialist Labour Party, based chiefly on Clydeside, and by socialists active in South Wales who formed the Unofficial Reform Committee among the miners. Embittered industrial relations and wage militancy were no guarantee of socialist advance, however, as the war emergency illustrated. Trade union membership massively increased during the war in conditions of full employment. The coal industry continued to generate strikes, and a shop stewards movement emerged in centres of heavy industry such as the Clyde, Sheffield and Manchester, but the unions remained solidly behind the war effort. This began to falter only in 1917, when discontent with the official explanation of the war and demands for a Labour voice in any peace settlement found expression in a *Memorandum of War Aims*, adopted by a special conference of the Trades Union Congress (TUC) and the Labour Party on 28 December.[1] Though the general election of December 1918 returned the Lloyd George coalition to power, a widespread perception of insurgency afflicted the middle classes in the course of 1919 and until the middle of 1920 it could not be dismissed as a mere illusion. Trade union membership was reaching its peak of 8.25 million.[2]

But with the onset of economic slump it began to fall. The shop stewards movement – identified by a hopeful Lenin as the core of a British revolutionary party in the unions – fell apart. Governments pursued deflationary policies, and unemployment, concentrated in the old centres of heavy industry, never fell below 10 per cent of the insured workforce for the rest of the inter-war period. Much of the creative thinking of British socialists in the period after 1910 seemed redundant under these circumstances. Schemes for industrial democracy and guild socialism depended on the perception of strong trade unions with active and politically ambitious rank-and-file militants capable of dislodging conservative and bureaucratic leaderships. The Communist Party launched the National Minority Movement in August 1924 to create such an alternative leadership within the unions and prepared for industrial confrontations which they intended to politicise. Though that party did its best during the nine-day General Strike of May 1926, and even claimed that the working class was racing ahead towards revolutionary consciousness after the defeat of the strike, it grew to only 10,000 members and then shrank rapidly in the course of

---

1 J. Callaghan, *The Labour Party and Foreign Policy: A History* (London: Routledge, 2007), pp. 48–55.
2 J. Saville, *The Labour Movement in Britain* (London: Faber and Faber, 1988), pp. 42–3.

1927. Indeed, as the rhetoric and posture of the Communist Party became increasingly intransigent, its membership continued to fall until the eve of the second minority Labour government, when it stood at little more than the 2,000 recorded at its foundation.[3] What the General Strike's defeat really signified was the end of any syndicalist or communist plans for building a socialist movement in Britain via the rank and file of the unions. The pre-strike left on the TUC General Council was weakened and the moderation associated with Walter Citrine and Ernest Bevin came to prevail; the moderates' chief ambition was to turn the trade union leadership into a trusted partner of government and employers, securely based on its capacity to bargain effectively on wages and conditions of employment.

The Parliamentary Labour Party, meanwhile, steered its way through the 1920s charting its own course of moderation designed to displace the Liberal Party permanently as the alternative to the Conservatives. This meant it needed to prove its fitness to govern. Ramsay MacDonald, Britain's most famous socialist, had arguably taken this road since at least 1903, when he negotiated an electoral pact with Herbert Gladstone, the Liberal Chief Whip. He returned to Parliament at the general election of 1922, now popular on the left because of his reputation as an opponent of the Great War, to manage this strategy as the formal leader of the party. There was no question of any collaboration with the diminutive Communist Party, while every effort was made to exclude individual Communists from the Labour Party, especially from 1924. MacDonald formed his first minority government in January of that year in the conventional way, taking advice, certainly, but ultimately choosing his own Cabinet and making clear his intention to govern in the interests of the nation as a whole. The first Labour Cabinet contained four former Liberals, two Conservatives and one former Conservative, and at least two more Conservatives had been invited to join but failed to do so. MacDonald's intention had been to fashion Labour as 'a responsible instrument of Radical thinking' while excluding the socialist left in the party from any major influence (though John Wheatley was included as Housing Minister).[4] The government lasted only nine months. Contemporary opinion deemed its greatest success to have been in foreign policy, which MacDonald himself conducted, rather than the party's foreign policy experts, most of whom were recruits from the Liberal Party and rather more radical than MacDonald.

---

3 J. Callaghan, *The Far Left in British Politics* (Oxford: Blackwell, 1987), pp. 27–54.
4 M. Cowling, *The Impact of Labour* (Cambridge: Cambridge University Press, 1971), p. 360.

Socialists did not hide their disappointment and almost from the beginning of Labour's first minority government, in January 1924, George Lansbury's *Daily Herald* and H. N. Brailsford's *New Leader*, the ILP weekly, aroused MacDonald's disdain with their criticisms of his administration. By the end of this experiment a compelling argument took hold of the Labour left, not for the last time, that socialists needed to construct a practical programme so that a future Labour government could move Britain in the desired direction. This mood, which also produced talk of imperial protection and a more co-operative Commonwealth to deal with chronic unemployment in Britain, eventually led the ILP to publish *Socialism in Our Time* in 1926. It amounted to a plan for income redistribution to boost aggregate demand, based on an under-consumptionist analysis of the causes of unemployment inspired by J. A. Hobson. MacDonald showed no interest in the scheme and the gulf between his policies and those of the ILP only widened in the late 1920s. The unions backed MacDonald, mistrusting radicalism and placing their hopes in another Labour government under MacDonald.[5] Though the ILP could count as many as 142 MPs in its membership, only a handful worked with those left-wingers, such as Fenner Brockway and James Maxton, who ran the organisation by 1929. This group was already alienated from MacDonald's moderation but, as John Saville says, 'its internal dynamic was weakening' and it was heading for political irrelevance.[6] The mood of the Labour Party annual conferences of 1927 and 1928 was hostile to any form of radicalism and loyal to MacDonald. Unemployment was widely acknowledged as the dominating issue of the 1929 general election and yet it was the Liberal Party, rather than Labour, that put forward the more novel and radical programme for tackling it. None of the Labour leaders saw merit in Lloyd George's *We Can Conquer Unemployment*, with its Keynes-inspired proposals for large-scale public works, and MacDonald and Philip Snowden in particular dismissed such 'flashy futilities', preferring instead to stress Labour's moderation and caution.

There was no pretence in Labour's manifesto, *Labour's Appeal to the Nation*, that the answer to unemployment was 'socialism' and in the campaign itself the Conservative Party was much more likely to use the term than Labour – both leaderships calculating that it would lose the left votes to be associated with socialism.[7] Though Labour was nearing the end

---

5 D. Howell, *MacDonald's Party: Labour Identities and Crisis 1922–1931* (Oxford: Oxford University Press, 2002), pp. 271–3.
6 Saville, *The Labour Movement*, p. 52.
7 W. Knox, *James Maxton* (Manchester: Manchester University Press, 1987), p. 83.

of its third decade, it was still thought necessary to explain to the voters that the party was 'neither Bolshevik nor Communist. It is opposed to force, revolution and confiscation as means of establishing the New Social Order. It believes in ordered progress and in democratic methods.'[8]

C. L. Mowat observed that 'Few governments have entered office with higher hopes and wider goodwill, few have fallen less lamented by friends as well as foes'.[9] There was optimism at the outset, but disappointment with the government's failure to make any impression on unemployment was already present by the end of 1929. Ordered progress, of the sort referred to in the manifesto, was conspicuously absent. By mid 1930 the world economy was in a state of free fall. In March the last Social Democrat-led Weimar coalition fell when the Social Democratic Party's Reichstag group refused to support demands for tax cuts and cuts in social spending and unemployment benefits to deal with the German economic crisis. By this time MacDonald had already rejected the Mosley Memorandum. Mosley also failed to persuade the annual conference of the party later in the year and only 17 Labour MPs supported the Mosley Manifesto when that was produced in December (see chapter 4). It left the ILP – which officially rejected the Manifesto – as sole representative of the Parliamentary Labour Party's left wing, but it had few supporters. Evidence was accumulating that the crisis was global and resolutions to the 1930 annual conference even called for a socialist solution.[10] But there was little idea what that would look like. In both Germany and Britain, orthodox economic logic dictated that, when faced with growing mass unemployment, business bankruptcies and worsening trade, the sensible response was to balance the budget to protect the value of the currency, even if this meant further deflationary measures and growing unemployment. Lacking a partisan policy of his own and trusting in the political neutrality of the advice he was given, MacDonald drifted, free of serious checks from within his own party, until Labour was ousted from office in the worst possible circumstances for political recovery.[11]

MacDonald told Labour's 1930 annual conference that the government could not be blamed for the worsening economic outlook: 'It is the system under which we live. It has broken down, not only in this little

---

8 Labour Party, *Labour's Appeal to the Nation* (London, 1929).
9 C. L. Mowat, *Britain Between the Wars, 1918–1940* (London: Methuen, 1955), p. 536.
10 Labour Party, *Report of the 30th Annual Conference* (London, 1930), pp. 186–7.
11 R. McKibbin, *Parties and People: England 1914–1951* (Oxford: Oxford University Press, 2010), pp. 69–105.

island; it has broken down everywhere, as it was bound to break down.'[12] Susan Lawrence, who was chairing the proceedings, advised the conference that 'it is not within the power of any single country to deal with the roots of these evils by any purely national policy'.[13] J. A. Hobson detected a 'spirit of bewilderment and despair' among the public, based upon a 'widespread realization that governments were hopelessly incompetent to manage decaying capitalism'.[14] The left-wing press in Britain, including the recently relaunched *Daily Herald*, provided a steady flow of news of worsening economic conditions from around the globe. 'Knowledge of what happened in other countries was widespread', as Richard Overy observes, 'so that recession was viewed not just as a national disaster but as a possibly terminal crisis of world capitalism'.[15] The perception of global crisis strengthened in 1931, especially when the collapse of the Credit Anstalt bank in May triggered the withdrawal of foreign funds from Germany. The Brüning government, having implemented the budget cuts which the Social Democrats were unable to stomach, was now required to find new economies. Another round of unemployment benefit cuts in Germany was announced in June, together with emergency orders for further reductions in public sector salaries. By July British unemployment had reached 2,783,000. But the situation was worse on the continent. Stanley Hirst, chairman of Labour's National Executive Committee (NEC), returned from a meeting of the Labour and Socialist International in Vienna in August to warn that 'the economic crisis ... threatens to destroy democracy in Central Europe'.[16] In September this moved a step closer when the Nazi vote in the Reichstag elections shot up to 18.3 per cent from the 2.6 per cent recorded in 1928. But it was not the march of authoritarianism that caught the attention of the *Daily Herald* so much as the power of international finance to 'dictate' to national governments, whether in Germany, Austria or Britain.[17]

A few days after the formation of the National Government on 24 August, the executives of the TUC, the Parliamentary Labour Party and the wider Labour Party issued a manifesto which continued this theme.

---

12 Quoted in R. Skidlesky, *Politicians and the Slump* (Harmondsworth: Penguin Books, 1971), p. 270.
13 Quoted in T. Cliff and D. Gluckstein, *The Labour Party: A Marxist Analysis* (London: Bookmarks, 1988), p. 153.
14 Quoted in R. Overy, *The Morbid Age: Britain and the Crisis of Civilization, 1919–1939* (Harmondsworth: Penguin Books, 2010), p. 63.
15 Overy, *The Morbid Age*, pp. 68–9.
16 Quoted in the *Daily Herald*, 8 August 1931.
17 *Daily Herald*, 25 August and 12 September 1931.

It stressed the role of 'international and national financial interests' that had brought about 'a process of world-wide degradation'. These forces of 'finance and politics' were determined 'to attack the standard of living of the workers'.[18] A 'bankers' ramp' theory – already adumbrated on 16 August by Christopher Addison, the former Minister for Agriculture – was further elaborated at the Bristol TUC of 1931 when the President, Arthur Hayday, in his address referred to 'political and financial influences of a sinister character, working behind the scenes' with an 'irresponsible and uncontrolled' power capable of bringing 'even a country like ours ... to its knees and to threaten it with financial ruin'.[19] It was 'not merely the freedom of action of a People's Government' that was at stake, it was 'the very existence of such a Government [which] is seen to be impossible until the financial organisation of the country has been brought under control'. What Hayday called 'the fundamental facts of world economic disorder' had already claimed at least 15 million unemployed workers in the USA, Britain and Germany combined.

The annual conference of the Labour Party debated the nationalisation of the banks soon after the Bristol TUC, with contributors stressing the same problem: 'it is not only a national problem; it is an international problem. Today eight or ten men, the Governors of the central banks can meet in secret ... and ... take decisions ... which may mean bankruptcy for hundreds of businesses'.[20] The chairman's address set the tone by emphasising that 'the deep-seated causes are to be found, not in our national situation, but in our international situation'.[21] But Labour activists were already familiar with this trope. Ever since the war, speakers at trade union and Labour Party meetings had bemoaned the loss of international markets, and had petitioned for the implementation of policies designed to recover them. The 'intractable million' was largely laid at this door. Even now, in the throes of a world crisis, the old problems of the Great War, with its legacy of political–economic dislocation, international debts and reparations burdens, were still thought to be relevant and Labour speakers continued to express faith in the old nostrums such as free trade, disarmament and international conferences at which agreements between nations could be negotiated. But even leaders of the party were now much more inclined to stress the systemic nature of the crisis too, sometimes alongside the more familiar rhetoric. Thus Herbert Morrison, one of those

---

18 Labour Party, *Report of the 31st Annual Conference* (London, 1931), p. 5.
19 Arthur Hayday, in TUC, *TUC Annual Report* (London, 1931).
20 Labour Party, *Report of the 31st Annual Conference*, contribution of J. M. Kenworthy, p. 193.
21 *Ibid.*, p. 156.

who had seriously considered joining MacDonald in the National Government, told the conference that 'the capitalist system, not only in our own country, but in the world generally has led to chaos.... Capitalism cannot last if reasonable security is to be given to the masses of the workers of the world.'[22] In the absence of any evidence that Morrison had been suddenly converted to a more intransigent socialist perspective, we must conclude that the real significance of this and other statements of the same sort were calculated to appeal to the sentiments of Labour's assembled activists.

They also covered up the fact that the leadership associated with MacDonald's government had actually agreed to most of the economies which the National Government was formed to carry out. That leadership was still bereft of an alternative approach that could be called socialist. The manifesto of 27 August had argued that 'we could overcome the immediate difficulty by mobilising the country's foreign investments by a temporary suspension of the Sinking Fund, by taxing fixed interest-bearing securities and other unearned income ... and by measures to reduce the burden of War Debts'.[23] Since then, a policy free-for-all had developed, signifying an absence of new thinking and a lack of belief in any of the measures on offer, which ranged from disarmament, to tariff reductions and 'a new system of finance'. Henderson made a speech at Burnley on 25 September insisting that emergency powers were needed to deal with the financial crisis and to 'control' the financial system and the main industries. Four days earlier the National Government had done what Henderson and his colleagues had never dreamed of and took Britain off the gold standard. By the time of the general election of 27 October, Labour was still defending free trade and balanced budgets while talking about taking steps towards a planned economy. 'We must plan or perish', Labour sloganised, but no one knew what planning entailed or could explain how public ownership answered the immediate needs of the crisis.

This is hardly surprising. Labour and the trade unions had developed no alternatives to the regnant economic orthodoxies since 1920, apart from the ILP's under-consumptionist analysis, which MacDonald rejected. Britain had been subjected to deflationary policies for most of the period, unemployment was permanently high and the power of organised labour had shrunk. Nowhere in Europe was there a social democratic alternative economic programme, or any evidence of social democratic achievements in office, that could inspire confidence that a socialist alternative was possible. By Labour's own reasoning, 1931 was the worst possible moment

---

22 *Ibid.*, p. 177.
23 *Ibid.*, p. 5.

for experimentation if Frederick Pethick-Lawrence, the former Financial Secretary to the Treasury under MacDonald, was right and 'the keystone of the arch has fallen out and Capitalism is breaking to pieces before our eyes'.[24] Certainly the socialism of Snowden and MacDonald – and even after the formation of the National Government MacDonald continued to regard himself as a socialist – was utterly useless.[25] MacDonald's socialist writings had always presented a vague evolutionary perspective and both men had imagined socialism emerging seamlessly from an expanding capitalist system, not a system in crisis. Their critics within the Labour Party were not much better equipped to cope with a system 'breaking to pieces'. The ILP's redistributionary policies were not designed to cope with a crisis on this scale, as many in the organisation realised when they turned to self-styled 'revolutionary' politics and seceded from the Labour Party in 1932.

But if the Communist Party was anything to go by – and this was an organisation in a mood of intransigence, convinced since 1926 that revolution was in the offing – the revolutionary path was also sterile. The party had never been weaker, with just 2,724 members in June 1931. The crisis was all that it could have wished for, except that there was no evidence of 'the masses' turning to communism for solutions. Other variants of socialism, some of them home grown, were in no better shape. Chronic unemployment and falling trade union membership had undermined the brief, but theoretically innovative, guild socialism that developed over 1910–20, a remarkable period of trade union growth. Syndicalist ideas which had paralleled the guild socialists' belief in the need for workers' encroachments on managerial prerogatives had been finished off by the defeat of the General Strike. The Fabian conviction in the 'inevitability of gradualness' was no more convincing; even the Webbs had turned their backs on it after the experience of the second Labour government. The sort of 'ethical socialism' associated with R. H. Tawney's critique of 'the acquisitive society' had always been devoid of practical policies, embarrassingly so in the context of 1929–31. G. D. H. Cole spoke for most socialists in 1929 when he recognised that the social and economic agenda accumulated since the war called for measures that inevitably demanded an extension of state powers.[26] It was acknowledgement, too, that the extraparliamentary left-wing movements were in any case moribund by then.

---

24 *Ibid.*, p. 188.
25 *Daily Herald*, 3 October 1931.
26 G. D. H. Cole, *The Next Ten Years in British Social and Economic Policy* (London: Macmillan, 1929).

But Cole also recognised that socialists in 1929 seemed frightened, rather than encouraged, by 'the growing difficulties of capitalism'.[27] What was the use of nationalising sick industries? What did the right to work mean in the face of chronic unemployment (which, as Cole said, was 'of a different kind' to that of the 1880s, when the 'right to work' slogan had been first coined)? The left had constructed utopias of the mind, but had no solutions, Cole complained. It was no answer to the needs of the hour 'to urge the useless employment of redundant labour'.[28] Cole in this mood would not have believed that only two years later the Labour Party would fight an election claiming that socialism was the only answer to the crisis.

'The only complete cure for the industrial and economic evils of our time is to be found in the establishment of a Socialist state of life.' So said party loyalist and former Home Secretary J. R. Clynes at the Labour annual conference in September 1931.[29] In the same speech he said he was quite sure that socialism was 'an ordered plan for social well-being', contrasting sharply with the 'disordered state of social life' of capitalism – the 'accident' of capitalism, as he put it. Clynes claimed that the party 'was no longer frightened of the term Socialism' and was prepared to 'affirm it more than ever in [the] coming election'. Other leaders of the party had made the same conversion as Clynes. Morrison 'begged' the party conference 'to make Socialism itself the big, the fundamental and the most acute issue' of the coming general election.[30] Henderson told it that 'the nation must make a decisive choice ... on the one hand capitalism ... all the world over it has broken down.... On the other hand Socialism ... the only alternative to the present chaos'.[31] Pethick-Lawrence explained that while capitalism was incapable of dealing with humankind's growing power over nature, 'our socialist system *is* capable and has got to be made to deal with plenty'.[32] Even when it was acknowledged that expert and detailed policies for socialism were yet to be developed, speakers were quite clear that the capitalist breakdown was an opportunity to introduce what one of them called 'the Socialist state'.[33]

Even if we assume that these were rather desperate pleas intended to manage a potentially fatal moment in the history of the Labour Party, when morale might have collapsed entirely, and when there was an

---

27 *Ibid.*, p. 7.
28 *Ibid.*, p. 16.
29 Labour Party, *Report of the 31st Annual Conference*, p. 176.
30 *Ibid.*, p. 177.
31 *Ibid.*, p. 244.
32 *Ibid.*, p. 190.
33 *Ibid.*, p. 178.

overriding need to give the membership something to believe in and mark out the party anew from its rivals, there is still something curious about this language.[34] What was this 'Socialist state'? Where was 'our Socialist system', in Pethick-Lawrence's words? How could Henderson say 'on the one hand capitalist disorder.... On the other hand Socialism ... the only alternative to the present chaos'? To what did 'the other hand' refer? Why did rhetoric about socialism carry any weight at all? The Labour Party had had no answers to mass unemployment for the previous 10 years. Its best-known socialists – MacDonald and Snowden – had formed a National Government with the Conservative Party to inflict necessary economies. According to informed opinion, including that of the previous Labour government, the only credible emergency measures were the ones favoured by the banks. The pragmatists in the party might have concluded, reasonably enough, that talk of socialism was just empty rhetoric. Instead, leaders who were not known for their immoderate socialist ambitions calculated that this was the right moment, as Henderson put it, to announce that 'the decaying fabric of Capitalism cannot be patched up'.[35] Labour's election manifesto carried the same message and, as R. M. Bassett acknowledges, did its best to make socialism 'the great election issue' – something that the Tories had been more likely to do in the 1920s.[36] Snowden famously denounced it all as 'Bolshevism run mad' in a BBC broadcast of 17 October. Churchill was not alone in seeing the general election as an opportunity to smash socialism once and for all – and simultaneously restore the confidence of the money markets. By-election evidence had been pointing to a Labour defeat for many months before the crisis of August 1931.[37] Indeed, defeat was viewed with something like foreboding by those – like the *Daily Herald* – who suspected an authoritarian outcome if a National Government was formed.[38]

So how have historians explained Labour's lurch to the left? A. J. P. Taylor suggests that it was 'a natural reaction to the experiences of the second

---

34 Maurice Cowling stressed Labour's need to survive with its identity intact and the leaders' need to persuade the membership that the movement had a future. See his *The Impact of Hitler* (Cambridge: Cambridge University Press, 1975), p. 23.
35 Labour Party, *Report of the 31st Annual Conference*, p. 244.
36 R. M. Bassett, *Nineteen Thirty-One: Political Crisis* (London: Macmillan, 1958), p. 293.
37 *Ibid.*, pp. 217–18 for Churchill's comments; see also A. Thorpe, *The General Election of 1931* (Oxford: Clarendon Press, 1991), pp. 8–9, 46, for by-election evidence.
38 The chairman's address to the Labour annual conference referred to the danger of a dictatorship if a National Government were to be formed, while the *Daily Herald* believed 'the whole fundamental system of democracy is at issue' and accused the National campaign of being 'fascist in conception'. See Labour Party, *Report of the 31st Annual Conference*, p. 158, and *Daily Herald*, editorial of 26 October 1931.

Labour government'.[39] His logic is that 'Labour had tried to make capitalism work and had paid a bitter penalty' – therefore it turned to socialism. Philip Williamson refers to 'soothing socialist images' and 'the new freedom to enunciate simple socialist "truths"'.[40] But what was socialism and why was it soothing now, in 1931? The crisis had exposed the variants of Labour or British socialism as redundant and shown that its champions – MacDonald, Snowden and Webb – were helpless in the face of it. Why assert one's faith in socialism in this context? Part of the answer, it has been suggested, is generational: a new breed of socialist had emerged since the war. Indeed, S. H. Beer talks of a 'socialist generation'.[41] Ben Pimlott also sees the emergence of a 'second generation' in 1931, which took control of the party for the next 20 years.[42] Margaret Cole's memoirs even referred to a generation *Growing Up Into Revolution* (1949). There is some truth in all of this – it goes some way in explaining the enthusiastic reception which references to the socialist state received at the TUC and Labour conferences and suggests that, for all Labour's official shyness with regard to socialism in the 1920s, sympathy for socialism had grown significantly within the party. George Orwell argued in 1940 that the generational conflict that 'always occurs' was 'exceptionally bitter' after the First World War – 'partly due to the war itself, and partly … an indirect result of the Russian Revolution', though 'an intellectual struggle was in any case due about that date'.[43] This inter-generational approach at least alerts us to the broad sweep of change and positions the Russian Revolution within it. But one must emphasise that these socialists had precious little evidence of socialist construction to point to outside of the Soviet case. Partial exceptions to this generalisation emerged only later, such as 'Keynesian' Sweden and Léon Blum's short-lived Popular Front government in France, even Roosevelt's New Deal in the United States. None of these was available in 1931 and none possessed the ideological

---

39 A. J. P. Taylor, *English History 1914–45* (Oxford: Oxford University Press, 1965), pp. 429–30.
40 P. Williamson, *National Crisis and National Government: British Politics, the Economy and Empire, 1926–1932* (Cambridge: Cambridge University Press, 1992), pp. 378–9 and 380.
41 S. H. Beer, *Modern British Politics* (London: Faber and Faber, 1965), ch. 5, pp. 126–53 and his 'The comparative method and British politics', *Comparative Politics*, 1:1 (October 1968), pp. 19–36.
42 B. Pimlott, *Labour and the Left in the 1930s* (Cambridge: Cambridge University Press, 1977), p. 17.
43 G. Orwell, 'Inside the whale' (1940), in *Collected Essays, Journalism and Letters* (Harmondsworth: Penguin Books, 1970), vol. i, p. 553.

clarity of the Soviet successes.[44] In 1931 even Keynes privately thought only communism could cure unemployment.[45]

Taylor (and others) in any case shifts the focus of explanation away from the question of cohorts to one of individuals:

> The new line had ... a ... specific cause. It was, in large part, the creation of a new element in the Labour party: the left-wing intellectual.... The new development was basically a revolt of conscience by intellectual members of the educated class, ashamed of 'poverty in the midst of plenty'.[46]

Bassett adds that, for a few years, Labour fell under the influence of 'antiparliamentary tendencies'.[47] Both ignore the possibility that what really needs to be emphasised is not the conversion of intellectuals to Marxism or quasi-Marxism but the representative nature of such intellectuals – intellectuals such as Harold Laski, who were immensely popular among the Labour activists of the 1930s.[48] The Left Book Club is another indicator of this after 1936, with its 57,000 members. It was not simply dominated by those figures sympathetic to Marxism and the Soviet Union who chose the books; those of its titles which shared their bias were promoted more vigorously and read more widely than those (like Clement Attlee's *Labour Party in Perspective* [1937]) which did not, reaching an average estimated readership of a quarter of a million.[49] Certainly there was more impatience with Parliament, doubts as to its efficacy and an attraction for extraparliamentary agitation in some circles. But none of this explains why socialism was thought relevant in 1931 by people like Henderson and Bevin, the pillars of party moderation and scourges of the intellectual and extraparliamentary left. This leadership was conscious, if any section of the party was, that 'opinion in the Labour movement was in fact genuinely

---

44 On the export-led Swedish economic recovery see: H. W. Arndt, *Economic Lessons of the 1930s* (London: Oxford University Press, 1944); D. Winch, 'Labour politics and economics in the inter-war period: the Swedish comparison', *Bulletin of the Society for the Study of Labour History*, 20 (1970), pp. 8–10; and the contemporaneous comments of G. D. H. Cole and Hugh Gaitskell in M. Cole and C. Smith (eds), *Democratic Sweden* (London: Routledge, 1938), who examine trade and banking respectively.
45 Overy, *The Morbid Age*, p. 70.
46 Taylor, *English History*, p. 430.
47 Bassett, *Nineteen Thirty-One*, p. 350. Attlee was among those who supported the call for an Emergency Powers Act, which Stafford Cripps put forward at the 1933 Labour conference, to be implemented when Labour next came to power.
48 See M. Newman, *Harold Laski: A Political Biography* (London: Macmillan, 1993).
49 D. Caute, *The Fellow-Travellers: The Intellectual Friends of Communism* (London: Yale University Press, revised edition, 1988), p. 172. See also S. Samuels, 'The Left Book Club', *Journal of Contemporary History*, 1:2 (1966), pp. 65–86, p. 68; and J. Lewis, *The Left Book Club: An Historical Record* (London: Gollancz, 1970).

and deeply divided' by the events of August 1931, with many continuing to feel loyalty to MacDonald and his conception of the national interest – as the subsequent defection of Labour voters arguably illustrated.[50]

Part of the explanation for their behaviour in 1931 might be that the party managers were simultaneously heading off their own extremists, while providing the whole membership with something to believe in. It was the solid block of the unions, led by Bevin, which moved to take control of the party, especially in the wake of the general election defeat, not the socialist intellectuals. The need to convince the membership that the party had a future was undoubtedly acute in 1931 for these party power brokers. And it was Bevin who provided a clue as to why appeals to socialism were calculated to have this effect. Speaking at the Bristol TUC in September, Bevin took the platform after Arthur Pugh, MP, had opened the debate on economic and industrial reorganisation by referring to 'a great industrial revolution [that] is taking place before our eyes which transcends anything that occurred a century ago in its magnitude and its potentialities for good or ill of the workpeople'.[51] Bevin took up the theme, arguing that:

> cutting right across the world economy today was the new development in Russia.... That new economy involved planning and the attack on Russian planning did not arise because of Russian labour conditions, but because its planning was against the old world economy of scramble and individualism and profit.... The portent of that planning could not be overestimated ... lining up priests and parsons to denounce Russia did not work.[52]

The fact that the Labour-supporting *Daily Herald* could report 'tumultuous cheers' when Bevin said 'the old system is a washout' and the denigration of Russian planning was merely a capitalist lie suggests that he had chosen his words well. In invoking the Soviet Union he was seeking authority for socialism and arousing the emotions of his audience by referring to something that was salient for those present. For, as he told the International Transport Federation conference in Prague the following year, in Russia 'We are dealing with an actual living instance of superhuman effort to rebuild a state on socialistic lines.'[53]

Soviet socialism had the merit of actually existing and the left-wing cult of planning of the 1930s was very dependent on the perception that

---

50 Bassett, *Nineteen Thirty-One*, pp. 203, 333.
51 Quoted in the *Daily Herald*, 11 September 1931.
52 *Ibid.*
53 Quoted in A. Bullock, *The Life and Times of Ernest Bevin: Trade Union Leader* (Oxford: Heinemann, 1960), p. 503.

Soviet socialism was a success.[54] The advocates of social reform in Britain exploited the Soviet system to endorse their own position. The belief that somewhere in the world there was a country that was immune to capitalist crisis because it was building socialism is a crucial ingredient in the dominance of socialist rhetoric in the Labour Party from August 1931. Planning was now emphatically equated with socialism, although there continued to be non-socialist variants of it, as there had been before.[55] But socialism was not popular with the British electorate. Immediately after the general election of 1931 it looked as if Labour, to quote Francis Williams, would 'follow the Liberal Party into desuetude'.[56] There was little Labour could do except to call, as Herbert Morrison did in November, for a policy review 'to evolve concrete remedies … to educate the people in constructive socialism'.[57] By 1933 Bevin was already less confident that the stories of forced labour in the Soviet Union were merely right-wing propaganda. Labour began to follow Morrison's advice and under Hugh Dalton's leadership an economic programme was devised by 1937 that looked very much like the one implemented in 1945, while a new generation of party intellectuals wrestled with the theories of Keynes and Hayek.[58] It was not until the 1950s that 'Keynesianism' had been incorporated into Labour thinking as a core component of social democratic thinking. But there were always Labour socialists, even in the 1950s and 1960s, unable to free themselves from the conviction that socialist planning required a dominant state-owned sector of the economy and that whatever might be said about its primitive politics, the Soviet economy was proof of its efficacy.[59]

---

54 R. Samuel, 'The cult of planning', *New Socialist*, 34 January 1986.
55 D. Ritschel, *The Politics of Planning: The Debate on Economic Planning in Britain in the 1930s* (Oxford: Clarendon Press, 1997).
56 F. Williams, *Ernest Bevin: Portrait of a Great Englishman* (London: Hutchinson, 1952), p. 172.
57 *Daily Herald*, 2 November 1931.
58 E. Durbin, *New Jerusalems: The Labour Party and the Economics of Democratic Socialism* (London: Routledge and Kegan Paul, 1985).
59 See J. Callaghan, 'The British left and the unfinished revolution: perceptions of the Soviet Union in the 1950s', *Contemporary British History*, 15:3 (2001), pp. 63–83.

11

The right looks left? The young Tory response to MacDonald's second Labour government

RICHARD CARR

In Ronald Butt's analysis of *The Power of Parliament*, he argued that between 1929 and 1931 'parliamentary government appeared to be unstable government'.[1] Given Ramsay MacDonald's desire to blame Britain's contemporary malaise of rising unemployment and a declining world position on 'the [capitalist] system in which we live', this seems cogent enough.[2] Yet, as this chapter will show, dissent over the status quo was far from the sole preserve of the left. Quite aside from the calming, perhaps dulling, effects of MacDonald's own gradualist leadership, his Conservative predecessor as Prime Minister, Stanley Baldwin, was having much the same impact across the aisle. By analysing the internal dynamics of Conservatism through the 1920s and towards the formation of the National Government in 1931, what follows is intended to shed further light on the types of critique of democracy Butt and others highlighted (Tories were, after all, 42 per cent of the 1929 Parliament) and interrogate the relationship between thought and action within British Conservatism. To do so, our focus will be on young Conservative Members first elected to Parliament after 1918. While the idea of a rebellious and intellectually inquisitive group of youthful Tories may clash with popular notions of that party being rather backward looking, it is one we should begin to take seriously, for two main reasons.

Firstly, despite few making it to Cabinet rank before the mid-1930s, young men entered the inter-war Conservative back benches in numbers commensurate with neither our ingrained perceptions regarding the aged

---

1 R. Butt, *The Power of Parliament* (London: Constable, 1967), p. 116.
2 R. Skidelsky, *Politicians and the Slump: The Labour Government of 1929–1931* (London: Macmillan, 1967), p. 270.

structure of that party, nor the upper-class legend that *The Generation of 1914* had been annihilated on the battlefields of the Great War.[3] After the December 1918 election, 39 per cent of the Conservative parliamentary party had seen some form of uniformed service in the recent conflict, a figure rising to 48 per cent by 1924 and 52 per cent by 1929.[4] Far from an elderly Tory Party blindly acquiescing to Chancellor Philip Snowden's hopes for a traditional export-led recovery, then, a significant proportion of the Conservative caucus was unable to remember much of the days when Britannia dominated the free trade waves, letting alone wishing to go back to them. Such neophilia produced books like Walter Elliot's *Toryism and the Twentieth Century*, Harold Macmillan's *Plea for National Policy* and Edward Wood's claim (co-authored, rather oddly, with George Lloyd) that 1918 marked *The Great Opportunity* for British advancement.[5] The war had brought the state into play more than at any point in the recent past – from the 1916 Defence of the Realm Act's constraints on personal liberty to the McKenna Duties challenging Victorian notions about economic liberalism. To those just entering adult life, the notion of what a state could achieve was markedly different to similar points of reference but a few decades earlier.

Our second readjustment concerns the 1929–31 period more specifically. Oddly, given their different perspectives, academics of left and right have reached rather complementary conclusions. To be sure, Ross McKibbin disputed Robert Skidelsky's charge that economic alternatives to deflation were wilfully ignored by the Labour government.[6] Pointing to Scullin's failure in Australia and Roosevelt's rather mixed results across the Atlantic, McKibbin concluded that securing an economic recovery by deficit budgeting was unlikely at best – a view corroborated by W. R. Garside's analysis of Lloyd George's expansionist programme of 1929.[7] Despite such disagreements, most historians looking at the period concur that no

---

3   R. Wohl, *The Generation of 1914* (Cambridge, MA: Harvard University Press, 1979), *passim*.

4   R. Carr, *The Phoenix Generation at Westminster* (PhD thesis, University of East Anglia, 2010), *passim*.

5   W. Elliot, *Toryism and the Twentieth Century* (London: Philip Allan, 1927); H. Macmillan, *Reconstruction: A Plea for National Policy* (London: Macmillan, 1933); G. Lloyd and E. Wood, *The Great Opportunity* (London: John Murray, 1918).

6   R. McKibbin, *The Ideologies of Class: Social Relations in Britain, 1880–1950* (Oxford: Clarendon Press, 1990), p. 217; and Skidelsky, *Politicians and the Slump*, *passim*.

7   W. R. Garside, *British Unemployment 1919–1939: A Study in Public Policy* (Cambridge: Cambridge University Press, 1990), pp. 367–79.

Keynesian consensus existed sufficient to overthrow the existing political and economic orthodoxies.[8] While our analysis of young Tories does not dispute the broad accuracy of such a conclusion, it does offer a corrective regarding the extent to which British politicians accepted previous wisdoms. As Oliver Stanley remarked in the Commons in 1930, 'democracy is on trial and is waiting for somebody to do something'.[9] Given their rhetoric, such a charge should be analysed in terms of young Tories as much as anyone else. If they recognised the trial, action was a necessary corollary.

To achieve the re-evaluation of responsibility for contemporary woes suggested, we will sketch out the long-term background of dissent that existed among our cohort – certainly with Baldwin, but also the Westminster system more generally. While socially liberal Tory MPs of this era are sometimes described as 'the epitome of ... Baldwinite Conservative[s]', it is important to note that there existed a long period of dissatisfaction with his style of politics.[10] The British political structure, it will be noted, did not necessarily cater for a group of men whose principal formative reference was the war, and the expansionist – 'homes fit for heroes' – claims which followed. We will then turn to the rumblings of 1929–31. While contemporaneous squabbles on the political right have earned much attention – Churchill on India, Baldwin and the press barons – this should not blind us to the left–right debate that was also ongoing. The period 1929–31 marked a milestone in the struggle for the overall mastery of Conservatism. If the National Government was a victory for stability, it was also a rejection of the type of political adventurism espoused by many young Tories. In this vein we will lastly conclude with the fate of the great contemporary political adventurers – David Lloyd George and, most prominently, Oswald Mosley. If our first two sections outline an undercurrent of dissatisfaction, Mosley's later comment that 'the failure to secure a consensus in 1930 was a tragedy because nearly all the ablest men in British public life had ... foreseen the coming crisis' may not be simply the retrospective self-justification one might suspect.[11] Firstly, then, to the legacy of the war.

---

8 P. Williamson, *National Crisis and National Government: British Politics, the Economy and Empire, 1926–1932* (Cambridge: Cambridge University Press, 1992), pp. 17, 525. Recently, M. Worley, 'What was the New Party? Sir Oswald Mosley and associated responses to the "Crisis", 1931–1932', *History*, 92 (2007), pp. 39–63.
9 *The Times*, 22 July 1930.
10 J. Charmley, *A History of Conservative Politics 1900–1996* (London: Macmillan, 1996), p. 78.
11 Oswald Mosley, *My Life* (London: Nelson, 1968), p. 272.

Legacy of the war

'The politics of the thirties and forties would have been very different,' noted a Rab Butler too young to fight in the conflict, 'but for the sacrifices of the First World War. Those of us ... called to office would not have come to the front so early and with so little experience.'[12] Despite Bob Boothby's similar claim that the war 'wiped out a generation', unless German bullets were curiously selective in targeting only the most talented, this is difficult to substantiate.[13] Veterans, as we saw, streamed onto the Tory benches almost from the moment the guns stopped and while total loses may have been significant, they were not enough to annihilate a generation. What such comments do illustrate, however, is that the widespread cultural pessimism the war imbued – Graves and Sassoon through the written word, Lutyens in the Portland stone of the Cenotaph – seeped into political discourse. While Boothby and Butler had missed the conflict through their youth, those politicians too old to fight appeared even more chastened. When Neville Chamberlain visited Ypres – encountering numerous *ad hoc* cemeteries – he found 'the battlefields ... the most dreary sight imaginable'.[14] Likewise, as party leader, Baldwin would continually reference the national scars of conflict. Unveiling a 1926 war memorial in Harrow, he addressed the 'challenge of the dead' forwarded by authors such as Stephen Graham: 'I have got to give an answer and you will have to give an answer. The answer we can give will depend upon what superstructure we can build upon the foundations that have been cemented in their blood.'[15] Importantly, however, the conclusions men like Baldwin and Chamberlain were coming to about this superstructure were not necessarily shared by the young men.

Older Conservatives tended to view the war as either dysgenic or a harbinger of even more repugnant deeds of which humankind might be capable. Proclaiming the end of 'the mild and vague Liberalism of the early years of the twentieth century', Churchill believed 'we are entering a period when the struggle for self-preservation is going to present itself with great intenseness'. Denouncing 'the bland platitudes of an easy safe

---

12 R. A. Butler, *The Art of the Possible: The Memoirs of Lord Butler* (London: Hamilton, 1971), p. 8.
13 R. Boothby, *Recollections of a Rebel* (London: Hutchinson, 1978), p. 17.
14 R. C. Self (ed.), *The Neville Chamberlain Diary Letters* (Aldershot: Ashgate, 2000), vol. i, p. 333 (23 August 1919).
15 S. Graham, *The Challenge of the Dead* (London: Cassell, 1921); S. Baldwin, *Our Inheritance: Speeches and Addresses* (London: Hodder and Stoughton, 1928), p. 5.

triumphant age which has passed away', he added that 'England is now ... fighting for its life'.[16] If Churchill's belief in progress had been punctured by the war, Baldwin was similarly worried about the world around him. Constantly talking of the 'testing time for democracy', when 'skilful propaganda' could lead people to 'ends they would be the last to desire if they realised what those ends were', Baldwin kept the electorate in a state of fear through reference to 'extremists [who do not want] to have peace, but war'.[17] This was a discourse of pessimism and negativity, to which the 1929 Tory election slogan 'Safety First' constituted a fitting antidote.

By contrast, Tories of the younger generation, albeit occasionally naively, hypothesised a world where humankind could be reconciled by concerted governmental action. Though the 1929 electoral strategy was representative of both Baldwin's personal authority and a considerable body of Conservative opinion, it was nonetheless alien to the younger men within that party.[18] To be sure, up-and-coming MPs like Alfred Duff Cooper, Anthony Eden and Walter Elliot were careful to mind their language. They also shied away from openly dissenting from the party line: parliamentary debates on the 1926 General Strike and the subsequent Trade Disputes Act saw a remarkable degree of obedience from otherwise potentially troublesome young men.[19] Yet these were individuals with a profoundly different outlook to their leaders. Whereas the Neville Chamberlains had broadly taken from the war images of a destroyed Ypres, the younger men saw chance aplenty in the post-1918 world for some form of positive redemption, and one expressed in a more interventionist form of administration – previously a preserve of the political left.[20]

While Baldwin believed there to be 'little that a Government can do', figures such as Harold Macmillan were coming to very different conclusions.[21] Anthony Eden, who had written from the front to deride contemporary politicians as 'an unscrupulous set of narrow-minded, self satisfied crassly ignorant notaries', was similarly typical of a new type of

---

16 Churchill to Linlithgow, 7 May 1933, Chartwell Papers, Churchill Archives Centre, Churchill College, Cambridge, CHAR 2/193.
17 Baldwin, *Our Inheritance*, pp. 13, 30.
18 P. Williamson, '"Safety First": Baldwin, the Conservative Party, and the 1929 general election', *Historical Journal*, 25:2 (1982), pp. 385–409, 387, 390.
19 In the passage of the Trade Disputes Act, 181 veteran Tory MPs backed the party line, with just 22 abstentions – an 89/11 per cent split. The Tories received 386 votes for their position, equating to a 92 per cent turnout of their supporters.
20 C. Barnett, *The Lost Victory: British Dreams, British Realities 1945–1950* (Basingstoke: Macmillan, 1995) paints a negative impression of this trend.
21 S. Baldwin, *On England* (London: Philip Allan, 1927), p. 34.

post-war Tory.[22] Much has been written about the failure to bring about the promises of 1918, yet the very belief that such an undertaking was possible is equally important. To the 24-year-old Macmillan, 'scarred but not disfigured, and with all the quick mental and moral recovery of which youth is capable, life at the end of 1918 seemed to offer an attractive, not to say exciting, prospect'.[23] Though Britain's ensuing imperial and economic malaise rather dampened the spirit of the old guard, young veteran politicians remained full of vim, for they, as Mosley noted, were inclined to take expansionist rhetoric more seriously.[24]

Though Henry Page Croft had attempted to woo discontented Tories to his National Party in 1917–18, the 'khaki' election that followed the war was the real catalyst to reformist rhetoric. By July 1919 a group of Liberal and Conservative MPs had come together to form the New Members Coalition Group. The group expressed

> a desire among new members, who are not tied down by years of association with the old political shibboleths and who feel the urgency of the times demands political union…. They feel that the present Coalition Party, with its system of coupons, is not popular…. [S]ome evolution … of a really national and at the same time democratic party would be generally approved.[25]

Such talk, from men whom *The Times* felt 'it is worthy of note that the majority … were on active service until a few months ago', was conducted within an admittedly heady context. Soldiers mutinying, rail and coal strikes, and town halls being stormed by industrial protestors prompted Stephen Ward to dub the period potentially Britain's most revolutionary since the Chartist protests.[26] Within such an atmosphere, one might note, it was all too easy for Conservatives to show limited tactical dissent. Wood's cry that pre-war 'politicians had with certain, rare exceptions, appeared to have their attention fixed upon … preaching the party rather than the nation's gospel' could thus appear to be simply swimming with the tide.[27]

---

22 Anthony to Lady Eden, 23 December 1917, Avon Papers, University of Birmingham, AP 22/1/255.
23 H. Macmillan, *Winds of Change 1914–1939* (London: Macmillan, 1966), p. 105.
24 Mosley, *My Life*, p. 101.
25 *The Times*, 2 August 1919.
26 S. R. Ward, 'Intelligence surveillance of British ex-servicemen, 1918–1920', *Historical Journal*, 16 (1973), pp. 179–88.
27 Lloyd and Wood, *Great Opportunity*, p. 14.

The young Tory response

Yet one cannot be wholly cynical. As time passed, radical Tories did not cease their, occasionally slightly veiled, calls for change. Where Baldwin acted to quell strife, as during the General Strike, Macmillan could recognise 'his sympathy [and] understanding'.[28] Where ministers took concerted action, such as Chamberlain's house-building tenure as Minister of Health, they met with real approval.[29] Such praiseworthy examples were all too isolated, however. Thus, while public criticism of Conservative policy would surface only in the 1930s – once the economy further declined – the 1920s saw numerous tacit shots across the leadership's lethargic bow. Philip Williamson has been very adept in reinterpreting Baldwin, yet arguably there is room to push his theory a little further.[30] Though his reappraisal of the man as far from a bumbling incompetent was certainly a powerful corrective to received wisdoms,[31] it arguably glosses over some of the negative consequences of his lethargy. Rooting one's policies in common sense, limited scale and the preservation of individual freedom had undoubted advantages.[32] It also, as young Conservatives of the time argued, though they rarely invoked Baldwin's name, led to an incomplete harnessing of the increasing potential of state power.

As Conservative leaders occupied themselves with how best to sooth the people's ills – unemployment, poverty, housing – with conciliatory language, others were attempting to find the structures that would permanently solve such problems. Boothby, Macmillan, John Loder and Oliver Stanley perhaps said it best in their 1927 *Industry and the State*: 'that the Conservative Party stands in need of some definite industrial policy … cannot be disputed, for the present outlook can only be described as chaotic'.[33] Though their specific policies also marked a change from pre-1914 thought – calls for 'more widespread ownership' bore resemblance to Archibald Noel Skelton's similar desire for a 'property owning democracy' – it was in spirit that the great divergence from Baldwin was felt. When F. A. Hayek later spoke of the 'totalitarians in our midst' who would lead Britain along 'the road to serfdom', he was, in part, addressing

---

28 H. Macmillan, *The Past Masters: Politics and Politicians, 1906–1939* (London: Macmillan, 1975), p. 154.
29 *Ibid.*, p. 132. Also Eden in the *Yorkshire Post*, 26 January 1928.
30 Particularly P. Williamson, *Stanley Baldwin: Conservative Leadership and National Values* (Cambridge: Cambridge University Press, 1999).
31 Such as 'Cato', *Guilty Men* (London: Victor Gollancz, 1940); G. M. Young, *Stanley Baldwin* (London: Rupert Hart-Davis, 1952).
32 Baldwin, *Our Inheritance*, p. 10.
33 R. Boothby, H. Macmillan, J. de Vere Loder and O. Stanley, *Industry and the State: A Conservative View* (London: Macmillan, 1927), p. 6.

the inter-war young Conservative type.[34] Warning of a new 'common opposition to Liberalism' between left and right, he cited Harold Nicolson as evidence of a mind-set that 'had moved so far that only those whose memory goes back to the years before the last war know what a liberal world has been like'.[35] Nicolson was a reasonable example – young diplomat turned rebellious associate of Macmillan and Mosley – but Hayek could have chosen many others.

By 1927 Walter Elliot saw fit to praise the synthesis of producer and consumer interests seen in Mussolini's corporate state.[36] Dynamism was indeed to be admired. For, as Eden warned, 'Conservatism is not static. [T]he Conservative party in this generation ... should never overlook its progressiveness in essentials.'[37] A structure therefore had to be found to make the party fit for purpose. Industry needed to be heavily directed by the government – or, such men predicted quite independent of the later economic collapse, the consequence would be mass unemployment.[38] By 1929, for all his amiable air, Baldwin was manifestly not the man to deliver this. As Macmillan noted, 'among the young progressives, many felt that although we would always get a friendly word from him we would get no action'.[39] Leo Amery's Cabinet memorandum prior to the 1929 election was indicative of contemporary frustrations:

> No one expects us to compete with Lloyd George in extravagant schemes for borrowing hundreds of millions..., or with the Socialists in similar schemes plus a general policy of doles based on confiscatory taxation. But we are expected to do something, and something much bolder than can be done within the ultra-conservative financial limits which we have hitherto set ourselves.[40]

Most young Tories could not yet envisage solutions outside the traditional Conservative model, yet they were beginning to urge an expansion of that model's scope. With a sudden shock to the system – such as electoral defeat – theoretical opposition to lethargy had the potential to become something more concrete.

---

34 F. A. Hayek, *The Road to Serfdom* (London: Routledge, 2008 edition, first published 1944), pp. 186–206.
35 *Ibid.*, p. 12.
36 Elliot, *Toryism*, pp. 81–2.
37 *Yorkshire Post*, 9 April 1929.
38 See below, *The Times*, 17 December 1930.
39 Macmillan, *The Past Masters*, p. 114.
40 Amery memorandum, 18 March 1929, The National Archives, London, Cabinet Papers, CAB/24/202.

Rumblings on the right

The 1929 general election can be read two ways. Certainly by the high standards he had set himself in 1924 (47 per cent of the vote, 412 MPs), Baldwin lost catastrophically: a diminution in support of over 8 per cent nationally and over 150 MPs out of Parliament. Not only that but, having failed to offer any innovative scheme of public spending 'to appeal to the imagination of the public', many progressive members of the party – like Macmillan – even believed the defeat to be justified.[41] 'Safety First' was deemed 'feeble' by the deposed Member for Stockton, whose constituents 'very properly voted me out, and … I could not blame them'.[42] As Eden lamented, 'many of the younger men have fallen, and the Conservative party must be the poorer for the loss of the services of such men as Ellis, Lumley, Duff Cooper, Hudson and Macmillan'.[43] Yet the loss should not be understood in purely Conservative terms, for in 1929 Baldwin had achieved something quite remarkable.

Though he had lost power in the obvious sense that he had ceded office, 1929 was more ambiguous. Following the General Strike, save the odd measure from Chamberlain on local government, Baldwin's administration had achieved very little. On New Year's Day 1927, Eden had acknowledged that the notion of 'the present Parliament … persist[ing] for its full term is as certain as anything can be in politics'. This was indeed so. Yet Eden's electoral cry that Baldwin needed 'to go forward farther and faster in the direction of clearing slums and reconditioning them' was exactly what he had been demanding three years earlier in the pages of the *Saturday Review*.[44] Thus, even if young Tories could later see his administration as 'a government of reaction' and essentially 'sterile', Baldwin achieved a real feat in handing over the baton to MacDonald.[45] For in 1929, as Skidelsky notes, Lloyd George provided the real choice.[46] His 'Yellow Book' proposed expansionist schemes of road building and land reclamation that recalled the spirit of 1914: 'we mobilised for war', read the cover, 'let us mobilise for prosperity'.[47] Far better, then, if the Conservative government really had run out of steam, to hand over to Labour – who would attempt nothing too radical unless a sweeping majority allowed the

---

41 Macmillan, *The Past Masters*, p. 64.
42 Ibid.
43 *Yorkshire Post*, 8 June 1929.
44 Election leaflet, 1929, Avon Papers, AP/6/3/3; *Saturday Review*, 20 February 1926.
45 Boothby, *Recollections*, p. 50
46 Skidelsky, *Politicians and the Slump*, p. 67.
47 D. Lloyd George, *We Can Conquer Unemployment* (London: Cassell, 1929), pp. 10–17, 47.

complete overthrow of the capitalist order – than to allow a man of action potentially to rock the boat. This would be a recurring theme.

While Baldwin clearly wanted to win, 1929 was just about bearable. MacDonald's distrust of Lloyd George precluded the progressive majority being translated into coalition: when he and Baldwin met on the campaign trail, they had allegedly parted with the Scot saying 'well, whatever happens, we shall keep out the Welshman'.[48] This was but shorthand for progressives of all political creeds. Unlike 1945 or 1997, 1929 did not wipe out the Conservative Party. What it did accomplish, however, was the severe limitation of activist Conservatism. Those parachuted into Parliament in 1924 on the back of a sweeping Baldwinian majority were sent packing. Of the 50 Tory Great War veterans first elected in 1924, only 21 succeeded in 1929. The defeats could also be massive for such incumbents: Arthur Hope, armed with his Military Cross and Croix de Guerre, lost Nuneaton by over 12,000 votes; Christopher Brooke, with his DSO, surrendered Pontefract by over 7,000. Consequently, the Conservatives were denied a significant parliamentary caucus in the north and, when the economy tumbled, radical protest against Baldwin was less raucous than it might otherwise have been.

In 1929 Baldwin and MacDonald had mobilised over 16 million people to vote for a version of the status quo. Though McKibbin has claimed the Liberal vote in the 1920s to be primarily a form of Conservative protest – Lloyd George led a *Mittelstandspartei* in all but name – it is worthy of note that of the 8.1 per cent Baldwin lost between 1924 and 1929, 4 per cent went to MacDonald.[49] This trick was to be repeated in 1931, albeit carrying many young Tories back to Parliament. What the 1929 general election achieved was to squeeze the parameters of political acceptability, something which became abundantly clear almost immediately.

Labour took office pledging, rather strangely after five years out of power, to think over the nation's problems.[50] Criticism for this attitude was legion from the Independent Labour Party – James Maxton and John Wheatley both made similarly forthright parliamentary protests.[51] Yet among the Conservative elite there was indifference, and even sporadic praise. Churchill found Lord Privy Seal Jimmy Thomas – who had earlier outlined his plans for a very traditional export-led economic recovery – so sensible that he could find no major bones of contention.[52] The Tory press

---

48 'Cato', *Guilty Men*, p. 19.
49 McKibbin, *Ideologies*, pp. 261, 276.
50 *House of Commons Debates*, fifth series, 3 July 1929, 229, cols 64–5.
51 *Ibid.*, col. 164; Skidelsky, *Politicians and the Slump*, p. 106.
52 *House of Commons Debates*, fifth series, 3 July 1929, 229, col. 112.

was likewise almost effusive in its praise, for if Labour was in government merely to tinker, it was not the party of revolutionary Muscovites the right had feared.[53] To a significant proportion of young Conservatives, however, neither was Labour the solution to a crisis that was about to engulf the world financial system – the Wall Street Crash of 24 October 1929.

Twelve days later, a meeting took place at St James's Street, Westminster. In attendance were several young Tories, including Boothby, Macmillan, Elliot, and Charlie Baillie-Hamilton, Baldwin's former secretary.[54] All expressed doubts that the present system could halt rising unemployment, and the group debated the feasibility of a new party. Like Amery prior to the election, their concern was to 'find a policy which the mass of the Proletariat will be able to grasp at once as being helpful to the one great cause of their distress – unemployment'.[55] This is an important point: unlike the majority of their party, and even sections of Labour, they were not prepared to trade off employment levels for prosperity elsewhere. While Jimmy Thomas toed the 'Treasury' line in Cabinet, and gained the kudos of respectable Conservatism, these young men were looking to Keynes, Lloyd George and even Mosley as potential sources of radical inspiration. Though they took care to predicate any movement along the usual Tory totems of Empire and anti-Bolshevism, they believed that 'if indeed we obtain the assistance of the best Liberals and Socialists, which indeed all present desired, it was quite obvious that the new party must not begin as a species of offshoot of the old Conservative Party'.[56] Seemingly, given the difficulties they recognised, and Mosley would later face, in seceding from one of the major parties, they had elected to take the insurgent route for the moment.

The problem was that both Conservative leaders and Conservative opinion still conceptualised economics as a trade-off between free trade and protection. As has been well documented, Beaverbrook and Rothermere attempted to ginger Baldwin into an acceptance of imperial free trade over a two-year period, which culminated in the by-election victory at St George's and thereby a vindication of his leadership by March 1931. In actual fact, other than his loathing of press baron interference and the problems such a stance had brought him in 1923, Baldwin may well have come out for protection in a more forthright stance than he in fact did: certainly the 1932 Imperial Duties Act would bear such a stamp.

---

53 *Daily Telegraph* and *Daily Express*, 4 July 1929.
54 Memorandum, 5 November 1929, Beaverbrook Papers, Parliamentary Archives, Westminster, BBK/C/235.
55 *Ibid.*
56 Memorandum, Beaverbrook Papers, BBK/C/235.

Regardless, to young Conservatives such questions were ideologically neither here nor there. 'We have to re-think our political faith in the light of new conditions, and every problem requires a fresh analysis', wrote John Buchan.[57] 'They are both right, Free Traders and Protectionists', concurred Oliver Stanley, 'the arguments of both are incontrovertible, as indeed they are mutually irrelevant … the task of Conservatism to-day is not to bring back the old world, which has gone forever, but on its lessons to build anew'.[58] If the party's leaders were not prepared 'to build anew', rebellious Tories were arguably occupying something of a vacuum. Without the ability to set the debate, and lacking numbers in the depressed north after the electoral catastrophe, young Conservatism was somewhat stymied in its desire to take on Baldwin, let alone MacDonald.

While Labour wrestled with the dilemmas of what to do in the lag between capitalism's decline and the triumph of revolutionary socialism, so too were progressive Tories in a quandary. Increasing state power was seen, generally, as a good thing. Yet as Buchan, Elliot and Stanley noted in a letter to *The Times*, 'we have embarked on costly social services to an extent unknown elsewhere'.[59] They referred to the infamous 'abuses' of state benefit after Labour had removed the 'genuinely seeking work' clause from unemployment legislation in 1930.[60] As Henry Balfour proved, young Tories did not always succumb to contemporary baying for blood: 'there is a tendency … to say that the dole is abused and to try to build up through the popular penny Press an idea that there is an enormous amount of abuse. I am convinced there is not.'[61] Despite such level-headed stances, however, this was clearly a dilemma – for all that Labour fell from office in 1931 over a reluctance to cut spending, it was also quite problematic for youthful Tories to jettison their own penchant for a more interventionist form of government.

In 1930 Eden would urge his contemporaries to 'make a close study of the causes of the collapse of parliamentary government in Europe since the war. It has not been because these countries are temperamentally unfitted to work the parliamentary machine. It has been for a far simpler reason,

---

57 J. Buchan, 'Introduction', in D. Crisp (ed.), *The Rebirth of Conservatism* (London: Methuen, 1931), pp. ix–xi, at p. ix.
58 O. Stanley, 'The task of Conservatives', in Crisp (ed.), *The Rebirth of Conservatism*, pp. 197–203.
59 *The Times*, 17 December 1930.
60 Of the veteran Tories, 55 per cent voted in favour of a House of Lords amendment to reimpose the clause, compared with 52 per cent of the total party caucus. See Carr, *The Phoenix Generation*, appendix.
61 *House of Commons Debates*, fifth series, 1 December 1930, 245, col. 1882.

because Parliament has failed.'[62] Mosley was hardly unique in weighing the pros and cons of the totalitarian states. Boothby's meeting with Adolf Hitler began with him mocking the soon to be Chancellor: to Hitler's greeting of a raised arm and shout of 'Hitler', he performed the same action and exclaimed 'Boothby'. He departed, however, 'much impressed by [Hitler's] grasp of Keynesian economics'.[63] On a separate occasion, indeed, he also 'wonder[ed] whether Soviet Russia might not be the only country in the world where anything worth-while was being achieved'.[64] John Loder concurred, arguing for the necessity of putting 'Bolshevism in perspective'. While not ignoring its horrors, he believed it had been 'distorted in the western mind'.[65] Collectivism provided both 'hope' and 'lessons to be learned'.[66] These were profound statements from nominal Conservatives.

While glancing enviously abroad, matters at home threatened to come to a head. As unemployment rose above two million by the summer of 1930, and Labour continued to reject alternatives to instigate its drastic reduction, Baldwin's position was becoming increasingly untenable. Although, as Skidelsky notes, MacDonald's own lethargy made it improbable that Baldwin would lose any hypothetical election held after December 1929, he was also unlikely to secure the type of majority that would see the younger men returned to Parliament in the north.[67] Yet when the coup attempt came it was of a distinctly elderly nature – Lord Beaverbrook and Robert Horne conspiring for Baldwin's replacement with Neville Chamberlain or Lord Hailsham.[68] This was hardly the revolutionary change Britain needed, particularly when even Chamberlain regarded such a revolt as the work of heretics.[69]

Why Baldwin was not toppled is, however, a key point. Certainly without William Bridgeman's counsel, he would probably have resigned in March 1931. Importantly, as with the General Strike, he performed a very clever manoeuvre in claiming for himself the voice of progressive Conservatism while acting more ambiguously. Fully aware that even those wishing his downfall were unlikely to have anything to do with men like Churchill, Baldwin presented himself as the voice of the younger

---

62 *House of Commons Debates*, fifth series, 3 November 1930, 244, col. 614.
63 Boothby, *Recollections of a Rebel*, p. 110.
64 R. Boothby, *The New Economy* (London: Secker and Warburg, 1943), p. 20.
65 John de Vere Loder, *Bolshevism in Perspective* (London: Allen and Unwin, 1931), p. 213.
66 *Ibid.*, p. 228.
67 Skidelsky, *Politicians and the Slump*, p. 224.
68 R. C. Self (ed.), *The Neville Chamberlain Diary Letters* (Aldershot: Ashgate, 2002), vol. ii, p. 178 (6 April 1930).
69 *Ibid.*, p. 183 (17 May 1930).

generation.[70] Thus Butler, a bigger advocate of his, it must be said, than slightly older war veterans, could find 'it is sinister to think that as he services in the country [sic], his nearest – the Old Gang – are turning in on him'. Even as political allies unsuccessfully urged Baldwin to replace some of the deadwood in the Tory Business Committee with fresher faces, Butler could talk 'of his preference for younger men and his understanding of them'. This was no accident. For if young Tories remained suspicious of his inaction, eight years of calls for 'peace in our time, O Lord' gave Baldwin a national appeal that was almost hypnotic. His decision, by 1931, to re-adopt 'safeguarding' (the selected restriction of international trade) could also be read as a conversion to state intervention of sorts, and even if they were hardly uniformly convinced of its merits, the young Tories began to imbue their rhetoric with cries that Britain was becoming the 'dumping ground' of every major world manufacturer.[71] An old and, if the 1923 election was anything to go by, failed Tory agenda quietly slipped back into the mainstream. Meanwhile, young Tories, like Loder in Lewes or Duff Cooper in St George's, were rewarded for their silence with more amenable southern constituencies.

Attitudes to Mosley

Between 1929 and 1931, Britain was governed by individuals with whom a large and semi-influential body of men disagreed. Said cohort discussed, relatively openly, the possibility of alternatives. The palpable facts of rising unemployment and an arguable drought of new ideas from the status quo seemed to vindicate a revolutionary move: either the replacement of Baldwin with a more dynamic leader, or an alliance with progressive non-Conservative elements, of which Mosley and Lloyd George provided public examples. If Baldwin's convivial personality and the lack of credible Tory alternative stopped the former, the rejection of the latter is equally important. It is to that we now turn.

Clearly, there were reasons to dislike, and distrust, Oswald Mosley. Quite aside from Mosley's philandering, Eden found his economic schemes to be 'quackery'.[72] Writing of the January 1930 Memorandum,

---

70 Butler's account of the Baldwin 'retirement crisis', March 1931, R. A. Butler Papers, Trinity College Library, Cambridge, RAB C/4/29.
71 See Patrick Buchan-Hepburn's by-election campaign in East Toxteth, *The Times*, 25 January 1931.
72 *Yorkshire Post*, 31 May 1930. Amidst Mosley's quackery, Eden played a strange – and hitherto underexplored – role in quackery of another type: the push for Parliament to

which had received the backing of George Lansbury, Eden remarked that 'neither of them has the mental equipment or the knowledge of industry to be of any assistance to their chief. Their reported memorandum to the Cabinet has … little interest.'[73] Economics was never the future Prime Minister's strong suit and, as even Eden acknowledged, the debate over Mosley's resignation 'revealed how fluid are our party boundaries in these post-war years, and how little their limitations coincide with the economic views of those within them'.[74] Yet Eden aside, if Mosley's arrogance was possibly to be abhorred, his ideas were not dismissed so easily.

Speaking to Macmillan in July 1930, Nicolson famously found him at the end of his tether with 'the old party machines'. Hinting at a future Pitt-like ministry of young men, Macmillan believed 'the economic situation is so serious that it will lead to a breakdown of the whole party system'.[75] Throughout 1929–31, radical Conservatives were in constant contact, with Mosley not taking the leap into the New Party wilderness without an inkling he may have reasonable support from the right. Though it is well known that 17 Labour MPs signed the Mosley Memorandum of December 1930 – including Nye Bevan – his social schedule of the 1929–31 Parliament reads like a *Who's Who* of young talented Conservatives. In November 1930 he dined with Duff Cooper, Stanley, Macmillan, Bracken and Boothby. Later, Stanley, Macmillan and the future Conservative whip David Margesson came to stay at his house in Denham, while in May 1931 he attempted to woo John Moore-Brabazon to his cause.[76] Baldwin even began to talk of people hunting 'with packs other than their own'.[77]

One cannot dismiss the notion that while such men may have bravely served during the war, they essentially took the cowardly route out of the economic turmoil Britain found itself in. Boothby's letters to Mosley are illuminating on this point. Citing the example of Randolph Churchill, Boothby told Mosley he cared about his 'political future far more than about any single factor in public affairs'. He could 'conceive of no greater tragedy than that you should take a step which might wreck your chances, or at any rate postpone the opportunity of carrying through constructive work'. Yet he knew to his 'cost the limitations of the existing young

---

discuss sterilisation in July 1931. See B. W. Hart, *British, German and American Eugenicists in Transnational Context, c. 1900–1939* (PhD thesis, University of Cambridge, 2011), ch. 3.
73 *Yorkshire Post*, 15 February 1930.
74 *Yorkshire Post*, 31 May 1930.
75 N. Nicolson (ed.), *Harold Nicolson: Diaries and Letters 1930–39* (London: Collins, 1966), p. 51 (2 July 1930).
76 *Ibid.*, pp. 60, 68, 74 (29 November 1930, 15 February and 6 May 1931).
77 Boothby, *Recollections of a Rebel*, p. 82.

conservatives. They are charming and sympathetic at dinner. But there is not one of them who has the character or the courage to do anything big.'[78] Perhaps, it is true, Boothby should have looked in the mirror a little. Here was a man who believed the system of laissez-faire capitalism 'could no longer work', that Mosley 'was right and almost everyone else was wrong', and yet did not follow his instinct.[79] Boothby instead advised his friend 'to collar one or other of the [party] machines, and not ruin yourself by beating against them with a tool'.[80] Once Mosley had clearly decided in favour of a break with the old order, however, he was still a potentially attractive option.

Mosley's problem, as Boothby noted, was that 'our chaps won't play, and it's no use deluding yourself that they will'.[81] In a way, for all Mosley was in part a controlling megalomaniac, there was a sense in which power did not interest him. The assertion of absolute rationality, as his son noted, was more his driving motivation: people would either believe his case or they would not.[82] Thus it was with the Macmillans and Stanleys that one finds the greater degree of Machiavellianism. Walter Elliot would have proved most useful to Mosley in Scotland, 'but ha[d] spent the last twelve months consolidating his position in the Conservative party, won for himself a good deal of rank-and-file support' and 'won't give it up unless he's sure he's going to win'.[83] Stanley, as Cuthbert Headlam jealously lamented, had also been earmarked by Baldwin for an eventual rise.[84] The perceived key to personal success, as Boothby had singularly failed to do, was not to offend too many people.[85] Whether this was good for a nation seemingly requiring a new, dynamic form of leadership was an entirely different matter.

It would fall to Boothby, albeit crudely, to articulate the overriding question facing British Conservatism, and indeed British politics per se. Commenting on a Mosleyite opposition to the existing order, he remarked that people might well consider it akin to 'all the shits' jumping 'into the

---

78 Boothby to Mosley, 18 May 1930; Nicholas Mosley, *Rules of the Game/Beyond the Pale* (Elmwood Park, IL: Dalkey Archives Press, 1991), pp. 144–5.
79 Boothby, *The New Economy*, p. 45; Boothby, *Recollections of a Rebel*, p. 81.
80 Boothby to Mosley, undated, in N. Mosley, *Rules of the Game*, p. 152.
81 *Ibid.*
82 *Ibid.*, p. 181.
83 *Ibid.*, p. 151.
84 S. Ball (ed.), *Parliament and Politics in the Age of Baldwin and MacDonald: The Headlam Diaries 1923–1935* (Cambridge: Cambridge University Press, 1999), p. 261 (27 February 1931).
85 *Ibid.*, p. 288 (5 December 1933).

same basket'.[86] Yet this very interpretation could well be applied to the formation of the National Government in August 1931. Baldwin was an electoral failure, MacDonald and Snowden seen as traitors to their cause. Between 1929 and 1931 few could claim the moral high ground. Mosley has been portrayed as a man who failed to adhere to 'the rules of the game', yet the volume of criticism for the game itself renders such an assumption questionable. Macmillan's letter to *The Times* following Mosley's resignation is well known, but his 'hope [that] some of my friends will have the courage to support and applaud his protest' was intriguing.[87] Though producing a snippy repost from Butler, its sentiment essentially found favour with Oliver Stanley, who denounced 'the old gang' determined 'to play out to the end the old parliamentary game'.[88] Men like Mosley, Amery noted, contrasted sharply with the 'fluffyness' of the MacDonalds.[89] For all his bombast and fireworks, Mosley was making the speeches Amery 'would have like[d]' to have made.[90] Why, then, no formal alliance?[91]

Though the consensus behind Mosley was indeed wider than one might assume, it was unfortunate that the other pretender to the throne, Lloyd George, was an egomaniac of similar proportions. The two were advocating solutions that differed in detail rather than overall design, Keynes describing Mosley as a younger version of the former Prime Minister.[92] The Cambridge economist had indeed been wooed by both – contributing to *We Can Conquer Unemployment* in 1929, and 'finding it difficult to disagree' with either the Mosley Memorandum that forced Sir Oswald's resignation or the New Party manifesto a year later.[93] Short-term public works combined with a long-term restructuring of the powers of the state – verging on dictatorship – were integral to the plans of each. Yet, as Boothby later rued, Lloyd George was determined that potential progressives worship no other god than him. When Mosley sat down after his resignation speech, 'it was clear that he had the support not only of

---

86 N. Mosley, *Rules of the Game*, p. 152.
87 *The Times*, 27 May 1930.
88 *The Times*, 28 May 1930; *House of Commons Debates*, fifth series, 3 November 1930, 244, col. 84.
89 J. Barnes and D. Nicholson (eds), *The Leo Amery Diaries, Volume II: The Empire at Bay* (London: Hutchinson, 1988), p. 72 (18 June 1930).
90 *Ibid.*, p. 199 (8 September 1931).
91 S. Ball, 'Mosley and the Tories in 1930: the problem of generations', *Journal of Contemporary British History*, 23:4 (2009), pp. 445–59, makes some cogent points on this – there were many reasons to doubt Mosley, but the same was also true of Baldwin.
92 *The Nation*, undated but late 1930, Keynes Papers, King's College, Cambridge, A/30/231.
93 Keynes to Mosley, 2 February 1931, Keynes Papers, L/31/24.

the great majority of the Labour Party, but many other members'.[94] 'At that moment', Boothby continued, Mosley 'was the key figure in British politics'. Here, however, Lloyd George made a mistake – in Boothby's eyes – 'failing to appreciate the significance' of the moment, but arguably guarding his own position.[95] Instead of praising Mosley, he described his Memorandum as 'an injudicious mix of Marx and Rothermere'.[96] The moment passed, and Mosley gradually began to enter the wilderness. As he prepared to leave Parliament and take up arms – almost literally – against the National Government, similarly fierce critics of the *ancien régime* slipped quietly back into Westminster. By the summer of 1940 Mosley would be languishing in prison, while Macmillan and Duff Cooper occupied positions within a largely Conservative administration. Ten years earlier this could hardly have been predicted.

Conclusion

While Labour wrestled with the problems of office, then, young Conservatives were similarly perplexed. If failing to adjust to the war killed off the Liberal Party as a serious electoral force, as Michael Bentley argued, the Tory Party benefited from its uncertainties as much as they could not fathom its impact.[97] Youthful Tories appreciated that the state needed to enter the fray far more than their leaders would countenance. They also had much sympathy for the plight of the working man, alongside whom many had so recently fought. Yet where and when government needed to replace that traditional Tory bastion – industry – as the motor of economic dynamism were questions they failed to answer. The debate continued throughout the 1930s, with some, such as Macmillan, continually looking outside the party, and others, like Stanley, remaining unhappily within it.[98] The period 1929–31 was a microcosm of the type of questions Britain faced between the wars: if the MacDonalds could not provide a coherent answer, nor, it seems, could the young Tories.

---

94 Boothby, *Recollections of a Rebel*, p. 77.
95 *Ibid.*
96 *House of Commons Debates*, fifth series, 28 May 1930, 239, col. 1373.
97 M. Bentley, *The Liberal Mind 1914–1929* (Cambridge: Cambridge University Press, 1977), *passim*.
98 See Carr, *Phoenix Generation*, ch. 4.

12

Remembering 1931: an invention of tradition

DAVID HOWELL

The Labour Party conference of 1968 took place at the height of the Wilson government's unpopularity. Delegates met on a wet Blackpool Monday morning. Jennie Lee's opening speech from the chair was interrupted by miners protesting against pit closures. The principal debate on that first day saw the decisive rejection of the government's prices and incomes policy. Hugh Scanlon, recently elected President of the Amalgamated Engineering Union attacked the policy from the rostrum. Sat on the platform were members of Labour's National Executive Committee (NEC), including several ministers who were Oxford graduates – Wilson, Castle, Crossman and Benn. They did not include the Chancellor of the Exchequer, Roy Jenkins, who for many in the audience perhaps personified Scanlon's target when he said: 'If to perpetuate these things is the aim of the so-called intelligentsia of our party, then they are adding stimulus to the idea that an intellectual is one who has been educated above his intelligence.'[1] The official report then reads '(Applause)'. The comment had aroused a significant response.

One party member on the platform that late September afternoon emphatically did not qualify for Scanlon's indictment. Joe Gormley, the Lancashire miners' leader, would soon become the President of the National Union of Mineworkers. Years later he would reflect as follows in his autobiography *Battered Cherub*:

> The trouble was, as we have so often seen in the history of the Labour Party, the higher ranks were filled by people – they called themselves

---

1   Labour Party, *Report of the 67th Annual Conference* (London, 1968), p. 142.

intellectuals – who have little to do with the grass roots of the Movement. I'm talking about people from the middle classes, often from the professions. I do believe that they are essentially a different kind of Socialist from the man who has spent his working life wondering where the next butty or the next pair of shoes is coming from. They have never experienced that, and you cannot imagine experience. You have to experience, experience.[2]

Similarly, George Brown in characteristically bibulous mood exchanged pleasantries with Richard Crossman in 1955:

George Brown, warmed with wine, really revealed his trade union philosophy that culminates in the argument that 'It's our party not yours … just think what each of us was doing before the war. I was working for the party. And what was he doing? Writing!' The word 'Writing' was said with such exquisite loathing.
Brown claimed 'the trouble is … that there's a danger of their controlling the Party and we can't have that sort of nonsense'.[3]

Yet the party's leaders were successively Attlee, Gaitskell and Wilson, all of whom could qualify at least superficially for this anathema. They were accompanied in Cabinets and on the opposition front bench by many others. Thus, in Attlee's Cabinet the proletarian Bevin and Morrison (who were hardly comrades) were balanced by Dalton, Cripps and later Gaitskell.

While the roots of anti-intellectualism extended far back within the culture of the labour movement and indeed beyond, the party ethos within which these leaders and their diverse critics and allies operated was heavily shaped by the trauma of 1931 and its consequential folklore, with its approved memories and myths. These involved, cumulatively: the disintegration of the Labour Cabinet; the defections of three leading figures, two other Cabinet members plus a few other ministers and backbenchers; and the near electoral destruction of the Parliamentary Labour Party (PLP). No step necessitated the subsequent one, although some memories elided the process into a narrative of premeditated conspiracy. More fundamentally, the authorised memory included an insistence that the unions had saved the party and that henceforth middle-class socialists must demonstrate their reliability to a sceptical trade union jury.

As with nations, political parties must invent traditions, constructing usable pasts and at times of crisis and disillusion revising, and perhaps

---

2 Joe Gormley, *Battered Cherub* (London: Hamish Hamilton, 1982), p. 194.
3 Janet Morgan (ed.), *The Backbench Diaries of Richard Crossman* (London: Hamish Hamilton, 1981), p. 446 (7 July 1955).

innovating.[4] Labour's advent as a credible contender for office in the 1920s had produced authorised accounts of where it had come from and what it was. S. V. Bracher's 1924 *The Herald Book of Labour Members* celebrated the struggles of the pioneering generation, as did a growing crop of Labour autobiographies. These were complemented by Herbert Tracey's *The Book of the Labour Party*, published in 1925.[5] J. R. Clynes memorialised the Labour equivalent of the storming of the Winter Palace – its arrival in office in January 1924:

> As we stood waiting for his Majesty amid the gold and crimson magnificence of the Palace I could not help marvelling at the strange turn of Fortune's wheel which had brought MacDonald the starveling clerk, Thomas the engine driver, Henderson the foundry labourer and Clynes the mill-hand to this pinnacle beside the man whose forbears had been kings for so many splendid generations. We were making history.[6]

This romanticised recollection was characteristic of the genre. By the time it was published in 1937 the starveling clerk and the engine driver along with Snowden, once of the Inland Revenue, had defected.

MacDonald in the 1920s had star quality. His close election as chairman of the PLP in November 1922 meant in effect the creation of a leader who could personify the party in the Commons and above all in election campaigns. His style was flamboyant. The theatre of politics allowed him to present allegedly private feelings as public spectacle, as soliloquy intended to inspire popular emotion. One observer suggested that 'in the slums of the manufacturing town and in the hovels of the countryside he has become a legendary being – the personification of all that thousands of downtrodden men and women hope and dream and desire'.[7] Beatrice Webb might have characteristically labelled him 'a magnificent substitute for a leader',[8] yet whatever the political failures, the muttered criticisms of vanity, social climbing and remoteness by some disgruntled colleagues, his position within the party remained secure until August 1931. To some degree this reflected the development of institutional

---

4   Eric Hobsbawm and Terence Ranger, *The Invention of Tradition* (Cambridge: Cambridge University Press, 1983).
5   S. V. Bracher, *The Herald Book of Labour Members* (London: Labour Publishing, 1924); H. Tracey, *The Book of the Labour Party* (3 vols, London: Caxton, 1925).
6   J. R. Clynes, *Memoirs* (London: Hutchinson, 1937), vol. i, p. 345.
7   Egon Wertheimer, *Portrait of the Labour Party* (London: Putnam, 1929), p. 176.
8   Margaret Cole (ed.), *Beatrice Webb's Diaries 1924–1932* (London: Longmans, Green, 1956), p. 112 (2 August 1926).

practices within the post-war party. Under the vigilant stewardship of Arthur Henderson, customs and practices wrapped in an ethic of loyalty had made frontal assault virtually impossible. Critics could be regarded with a benign tolerance that could shift to effective marginalisation through a blend of manipulation and discipline. Protected by this power structure MacDonald could capitalise on two durable assets.

As the first Secretary of the Labour Representation Committee, he had been the party's principal architect, constructing usually with great patience the complex concordat between ethical socialists, who provided enthusiasm and serious purpose, and trade unionists, who contributed finance, organisation and pragmatic if sometimes sectional agendas. MacDonald had served his time, as he did once again after August 1914. His complex and often misrepresented attitude to British involvement in the war produced personal vilification and the serious risk of marginalisation in the party he had done so much to build. But progressives' disillusion with the Versailles settlement and the broader pacifistic ethos of the 1920s transformed potential martyrdom into political capital. MacDonald acquired a priceless political asset as the man who had paid heavily for his principles but whom events had proved right. MacDonald could be trusted. So could Philip Snowden, whose more austere personification of similar principles was widely respected.[9]

In contrast, Jimmy Thomas's trade union pedigree made him unique among those who sided with MacDonald in 1931. An active trade unionist from the 1890s, a trade union official from 1906, Member for Derby since 1910 and the senior official of the National Union of Railwaymen from 1916, he had refused to join the Lloyd George coalition in December 1916. His claim had been that he could make a better contribution to the war effort as a union official outside the government. His reputation had been built upon his skills as a negotiator, but by 1931 the plight of the railway industry was restricting the scope for his employment of these skills. During the first year of the 1929 government his responsibility for employment policies in the face of international depression diminished his status and led to his transfer to the Dominions Office in June 1930. At his new post he exuded enthusiasm for Empire and demonstrated his susceptibility to patriotic appeals.[10]

---

9 David Marquand, *Ramsay MacDonald* (London: Jonathan Cape, 1977), ch. 17; Snowden's appeal is well captured in Wertheimer, *Portrait of the Labour Party*, pp. 177–8.
10 For Thomas, see two articles by Andrew Thorpe: '"I am in the Cabinet": J. H. Thomas's decision to join the National Government in 1931', *Historical Research*, 64:155 (1991), pp. 389–402; 'J. H. Thomas and the rise of the Labour Party in Derby, 1880–1945', *Midland History*, 15 (1994), pp. 111–28. See also David Howell '"I loved my union and

John Sankey, the Lord Chancellor, on holiday in Llandrindod Wells in August 1931, was characteristically lugubrious: 'This has been one of the wettest and coldest Augusts in living memory.'[11] His senior colleagues were already facing a political crisis. A Cabinet committee of five was trying to construct a response to two intertwined crises – the majority recommendations of the May Committee on Public Expenditure and a financial crisis that threatened the maintenance of the gold standard. The May Committee's report had been published on 31 July. Its forecast budget deficit of £120 million for 1932–33 was accompanied by proposals for substantial cuts in public expenditure. Ministers were initially optimistic that measured discussion through the summer recess would produce a politically viable response by the start of the new parliamentary session that could attract support from enough Liberal MPs to secure a Commons majority. After all, for more than two years the minority government had navigated effectively between the competing pressures from financial authorities, Labour backbenchers, opposition parties and the Trades Union Congress (TUC). But the sterling crisis intensified and telescoped debate.

That Cabinet committee comprised MacDonald, Snowden, Willie Graham and two trade unionists, Thomas and Henderson. It met four times. No one queried the desirability of balancing the budget, but gradually confused disagreements developed over specific issues – the balance between tax increases and cuts, the acceptability of tariffs, and most fundamentally over the status of the exercise. Was this a provisional exploration of the options or were decisions being taken? Discussions between MacDonald, Snowden and representatives of the Conservative and Liberal Parties demonstrated that a parliamentary majority would be secured only on the basis of a programme of serious retrenchment.[12]

On 19 August the full Cabinet heard the committee's report. Tax increases could generate £89 million and expenditure cuts could save £78.5 million, of which £43.5 million would come from unemployment insurance. This last economy and the possibility of a revenue tariff proved significant points of difference in lengthy discussions. As yet, however, Cabinet disagreements seemed manageable. Opposition to cuts in unemployment benefit was expressed by a small minority, probably George Lansbury, Tom Johnston and Arthur Greenwood. On the following day

---

my country": Jimmy Thomas and the politics of railway trade unionism', *Twentieth Century British History*, 6:2 (1995), pp. 145–75.

11 John Sankey, Diary, 14 August 1931, Sankey Papers, Bodleian Library, Oxford, c285.

12 For the complexities of the discussions see Philip Williamson, *National Government and National Crisis: British Politics, the Economy and Empire, 1926–1932* (Cambridge: Cambridge University Press, 1992), ch. 9.

pressure from within the labour movement intensified decisively. Since the crisis had broken during the recess, most Labour MPs were away from London. Henderson in his capacity as Labour Party Secretary skilfully managed the scheduled monthly meeting of the National Executive. He made what one NEC member characterised as 'a quite moving statement' and other members agreed to leave responsibility for articulating the party's concerns with Henderson and Clynes, the two members who also sat in the Cabinet.[13] Similarly, 7 of the 12 members of the PLP Consultative Committee met and decided not to take a formal position.[14] However, the General Council of the TUC proved much less tractable. At a joint meeting of the General Council, the NEC and the five-member Cabinet committee, Bevin and Citrine responded critically to statements by MacDonald and Snowden. Subsequently, a General Council deputation met the Cabinet committee that evening and rejected the policy of retrenchment. MacDonald reflected that 'it was practically a declaration of war'.[15]

General Council opposition was the culmination of doubts about the ministers' priorities and their susceptibility to conservative influences that had their roots in the experience of the 1924 government and had intensified since June 1929. The TUC was developing its own economic policy, while Bevin's pugnacity was yoked to a confidence in addressing economic controversies that had grown from his work on the Macmillan Committee on Finance and Industry. More broadly, opposition was fuelled by an ethical sense that sacrifices should be proportionate to an ability to pay.

Some Cabinet ministers responded by attempting to construct an economic package that could maintain the government even if such a package could not satisfy the General Council. However, the latter's resistance had fortified existing Cabinet critics and had shifted the position of others. Henderson, always sensitive to the link between party and unions, offered the most significant opposition, based not on the substance of policy so much as on party management and in this context the symbolic power of particular choices. Such a choice came on the evening of 23 August. A proposal for a cut of 10 per cent in the level of

---

13 Labour Party, National Executive Committee minutes, 20 August 1931, Labour History Archive and Study Centre, People's History Museum, Manchester. The comment on Henderson came from Dalton. See his *Call Back Yesterday: Memoirs 1887–1931* (London: Muller, 1953), p. 269. This appeal followed the joint meeting with the General Council.
14 See Scott Lindsay to MacDonald, 20 August 1931, MacDonald Papers, The National Archives/Public Record Office, TNA/PRO, 3069/1314, but also the comments of Chuter Ede, a Consultative Committee member in the Commons: *House of Commons Debates*, fifth series, 8 September 1931, 256, cols 62–4.
15 Minutes of Joint Meeting, National Executive Committee minutes, 20 August 1931; MacDonald, Diary, 20–21 August 1931, MacDonald Papers, TNA/PRO, 3069.

unemployment benefit was carried only by a vote of 11 to 9. The division showed no clear demarcation. Both sides included trade unionists and ex-Liberals, party veterans and ambitious younger men. They doubtless took their positions with varying levels of confusion and enthusiasm.[16]

The effective end of the government left MacDonald in a quandary. He felt unable to lead Labour in opposition to policies that he had previously supported. Immediately following the vote on the 10 per cent cut, the King urged him to stay on as leader of a cross-party government. The matter was settled between the party leaders the following morning. MacDonald would head a National Government. It was stated that its life would be brief, and that it should be viewed not as a cross-party coalition but as a co-operation of individuals who happened to belong to different parties.[17]

Within the initial National Cabinet, the Labour contingent was four out of a membership of 10. MacDonald, Snowden and Thomas were joined by Sankey. The Lord Chancellor's reputation within the labour movement was built on his chairmanship of the Sankey Commission on the mining industry 12 years earlier. A largely non-partisan figure, he was close to MacDonald and was heavily involved in the Indian Round Table Conference. Another essentially non-partisan figure, Lord Amulree, retained his position at the Air Ministry but outside the Cabinet. Almost certainly Herbert Morrison considered staying with MacDonald but then worked hard to exorcise any suspicion that he had ever been tempted.

MacDonald was also supported by two more legal officers, Sir William Jowitt and Craigie Aitchison, and by two other junior ministers, Sir George Gillett, who had experience in the City, and Earl De La Warr. He eventually secured the support of nine backbenchers. They included his son, Malcolm, two former Liberal MPs, an unsuccessful Liberal candidate and two former Conservatives. All but one had first become Labour Members in 1929. Seven were graduates. Those who seriously considered going with MacDonald included John Oldfield, of Eton and Trinity College, Cambridge. Renegades and potential renegades could further bolster the image of a betrayal by unreliable intellectuals.[18]

---

16 Among trade unionists, Bondfield Shaw and Thomas supported the cut and Adamson, Clynes and Henderson opposed it. Wedgwood Benn and Lees Smith gave ex-Liberal support, and Addison opposed. Among the younger generation Morrison supported it while Alexander, Graham, Greenwood and Johnston all opposed it. The older socialists on balance favoured the cut – MacDonald, Passfield and Snowden, as against Lansbury. The balance was made up by the virtually non-partisan peers, Amulree and Sankey.

17 Marquand, *Ramsay MacDonald*, pp. 633–41; Williamson, *National Government and National Crisis*, pp. 333–43.

18 For initial expression of possible support see John Oldfield to MacDonald, 26 August 1931, MacDonald Papers, TNA/PRO, 3069/1315. His subsequent concerns were

Whether MacDonald could have acted more effectively to mobilise Labour support is debatable. He met many junior ministers shortly after the formation of the new government and apparently acknowledged that he could never lead the party again. Ponsonby noted that 'the great majority present were undoubtedly against him'. An early and aggressive response was chronicled by Dalton, whose diary recorded a 'counsel of war' in Henderson's room, where Bevin was in belligerent form. This reaction was rapidly formalised two days later, on 26 August, through a tripartite meeting of the NEC, the PLP Consultative Committee and the TUC General Council. A subsequent manifesto attacked not only the 10 per cent cut but also the whole programme of economies considered by the late Labour Cabinet.[19]

When Labour MPs and peers met on 28 August, the meeting also included members of the NEC and the General Council. Ramsay Mac-Donald, Snowden and Thomas stayed away but Sankey and Malcolm MacDonald both spoke and according to some accounts they were received with understanding. Yet Sankey's account suggests acrimony: 'Very hostile as all the Trade Unionists are there but I defended my position in a long speech.... Feeling bitter.... They have gone mad and talk about the class war.' Whatever the character of the exchanges, the emerging alliance of trade union leaders and some parliamentarians under the uneasy leadership of Henderson helped to ensure that defectors to MacDonald were few and unrepresentative of the wider party.[20]

Yet many backbenchers' initial sentiments were complex and confused. Three of the most senior party figures sat in a Cabinet alongside Conservatives and Liberals. MacDonald and Snowden had stood out against majority opinion in the PLP in 1914 and for many their stand had been vindicated. More broadly, for many backbenchers MacDonald had personified the rise of the Labour Party, a journey they had shared. Jack Lawson epitomised the self-improving, politically reliable culture of the Durham miners. A junior minister in the 1920s he would become a Labour elder statesman in 1945. (When US President Jimmy Carter visited the north-east of England during his presidency, James Callaghan gave him a copy of Lawson's autobiography, *A Man's Life*.) In 1931 Lawson wrote emotionally to MacDonald expressing his continuing respect and affection

---

expressed in his letter to Lucy Noel Buxton, 30 August 1931, Lucy Noel Buxton Papers, Norfolk County Record Office.
19 Ponsonby, Diary, 25 August 1931, typescript version in possession of Lord Ponsonby. The reference to the council of war is in Dalton, *Call Back Yesterday*, p. 273, and see also p. 274, 'The Trade Union leaders are full of fight'.
20 Sankey, Diary, 28 August 1931, Sankey Papers, c.285.

and hoping that the breach would be brief. Yet Lawson, sponsored by the Durham Miners Association, had no doubt about his political choice. The ethic of solidarity that had made the Durham miners such a firm backer of MacDonald's leadership now was turned against him.[21] Thomas, despite regrets at the highest level of the National Union of Railwaymen, was quickly disowned by the union that he had led for so long.[22] Complexities could be found also in the responses of local parties. Several made immediate declarations along the lines of the Manchester Borough Labour Party – 'the function of the Labour Party as of a Labour Government is to work in the interests of the working class'. In contrast, George Middleton, the Member for Carlisle, suggested considerable concern among party members about the treatment of MacDonald. In several cases the parting of the ways between local parties and pro-MacDonald MPs seems to have been free of acrimony. The high-profile cases of MacDonald at Seaham and Thomas at Derby both showed a minority opposed to instant condemnation. In Thomas's case this sympathy extended to the defection of four councillors and the backing of one branch of his union.[23]

The dominant expectation in the last week of August was that the National Government's life would be short. The introduction of emergency measures would stabilise the financial situation. Partisan alignments would be restored, in all probability as the prelude to a general election. The very different stabilisation of a National/Labour split was attributable in part to a well founded Tory belief that they could dominate a post-election Commons, but that the 'National' label could protect them from a partisan and damaging reputation for austerity. The pressure for an election was strengthened by the abandonment of the gold standard less than a month after the new government's formation, and the vigorously propagated insistence that fragile financial confidence was best protected by a heavy Labour defeat.

The alliance between influential sections of the PLP and leading figures on the General Council emphasised planning, public ownership and socialism. Henderson was often unhappy about the effective dismissal of much that the Labour government had done. His cautious response to the abandonment of the gold standard was disregarded by many in

---

21 Jack Lawson to Ramsay MacDonald, 1 September 1931, MacDonald Papers, TNA/PRO, 3069/1315.
22 See Howell, 'I loved my union and my country', pp. 172–3.
23 *Manchester Guardian*, 25 August 1931; For Carlisle, see Usher to Ramsay MacDonald, 23 September 1931, MacDonald Papers, TNA/PRO, 3069/1314; for Seaham and Derby, see references in David Howell, *MacDonald's Party: Labour Identities and Crisis 1922–1931* (Oxford: Oxford University Press, 2002), pp. 82–4.

the division lobby. There were rumours that he might join the National Government, thereby precipitating another split. In the fevered mood of September 1931 the future was hard to predict but the calling of an election for 27 October simplified the Labour position. The TUC–parliamentary alliance was firmly in control.[24]

From this vantage point 20 August became seen as a critical day, when senior ministers appeared to assuage the doubts of those within specifically party bodies but failed with the General Council. Relationships between the party and the unions were always subject to negotiation, not least because many involved could claim both political and industrial identities. The language of control and dominance was misleading. Between party and unions there were divisions of function, contrasting priorities, divergent and perhaps conflicting responsibilities. A post-1918 attempt at organisational unification between party and TUC institutions had foundered.[25] Yet what was remarkable throughout the 1920s was the degree to which party and unions worked together despite episodes such as the industrial conflict of 1926 that led some into critical exchanges.

One complicating factor was the changing social character of the PLP. The pre-1914 MPs had been almost totally working class in background and had largely reached Parliament through the trade unions. By the early 1920s recruitment was more socially diverse. MacDonald's strategy was to build a broadly based progressive party, aided by the fragmentation of the Liberals and by post-war disenchantment with older political options. One ex-Liberal recruit, Arthur Ponsonby, had been born in Windsor Castle, a former Tory, Hugh Dalton, was the son of a canon of Windsor. Noel Buxton, Liberal Member for North Norfolk before 1918, recovered the seat for Labour in 1922. Some local parties proved susceptible not just to the new entrants' supposed talents but to their obvious wealth. Birmingham's Labour organisation was generously funded by Oswald Mosley during the Labour chapter of his political odyssey. Derwent Hall Caine, a 1931 renegade, was a son of Hall Caine, the record-breaking novelist of the 1890s and author of the first million-copy best seller. Hall Caine provided political funding for both his sons (Ralph was Conservative Member for East Dorset) and exercised his literary skills with paternal impartiality in drafting their election addresses. Such episodes, although rarely as gross, generated mixed Labour emotions; deference jostled with resentment at patronage, real or imagined, and at the apparent ease with

---

24 Andrew Thorpe, *The British General Election of 1931* (Oxford: Clarendon Press, 1991), pp. 145–8; Williamson, *National Crisis and National Government*, pp. 427–33; see also the discussion in Howell, *MacDonald's Party*, p. 53 fn 106.

25 Howell, *MacDonald's Party*, ch. 5.

which positions within the party could be secured by the financially well heeled and socially well connected.[26]

For trade unionists, reliability was a cardinal virtue. By the late 1920s the consequences of fragmentation were all too apparent on the industrial side, in the decline in membership that had followed the General Strike. Institutionally the damage was expressed in the explicitly non-political mining unionism that had disempowered the official union in Nottinghamshire. George Spencer, the leader of the new union, was expelled from the PLP, despite MacDonald's qualified sympathy, and became a pre-1931 renegade.[27] 'Spencerism' became another subject for myths and authorised memories. Left-wing trade unionists, some of them communists, working through the Minority Movement, were condemned as Spencerites of the left. The anathema acquired enhanced credibility as communist trade unionists embraced the language if not always the practice of the sectarian New Line.

The insistence on solidarity was easily transferable to the political field. As the Independent Labour Party shifted to the left, its parliamentary group became a small radical section that often seemed a separate party in opposition to the 1929 government. To many trade unionists they seemed not the defenders of socialist principle but self-indulgent parasites who exploited the loyalty of back-bench trade unionist MPs. When Mosley and a handful of parliamentary supporters formed the New Party in February 1931 their departure could be cited as evidence that the rich and the flashy could not be trusted. Will Lawther, a Durham miners' Member with a radical past, made the point at a May Day rally: 'Some of us may have wanted to ginger up the Labour Party, but we have not adopted the questionable measures of Mosley. Every trade union member of the House of Commons has stood to a man and not deserted.'[28]

Such sentiments help to explain the events of the following August. Within the General Council, Bevin's forceful iconoclasm towards economic orthodoxy and Citrine's composed criticism, bolstered by the work of the TUC Research Department, offered a reasoned and credible response to ministerial proposals of economies. The economic arguments were complemented by differences over propriety and recognition, which in turn linked with controversies over the political identity of Labour. MacDonald's reaction to General Council criticism on 20 August was

---

26 For Derwent Hall Caine, see the entry in Keith Gildart and David Howell (eds), *Dictionary of Labour Biography* (Basingstoke: Palgrave Macmillan, 2005), vol. xii, pp. 119–23.
27 See George Spencer to MacDonald, 7 March 1927, and MacDonald's reply, 8 March 1927, MacDonald Papers, TNA/PRO, 3069/1172.
28 *Durham County Advertiser*, 8 May 1931.

scathing: 'The TUC undoubtedly voice the feeling of the mass of workers. They do not know and their minds are rigid and think of superficial appearances and so grasping at the shadow lose the bone.'[29] Such a denunciation was not unique for MacDonald. He had been at odds with several patriotic trade union leaders during the war and his ethical socialism could easily promote a view of trade unions as sectional and lacking a moral vision. Subsequently Lord Passfield (Sidney Webb) would be a prime exponent of the myth that the formation of a National Government had been a long-term objective of a corrupted MacDonald. But at the height of the crisis he described General Council members as pigs for refusing to accept cuts in unemployment benefit. An early draft of his post-mortem report on the Labour government not only indicted MacDonald but criticised the TUC leaders' behaviour since June 1929. They had demanded a privileged consultative status on legislation affecting trade union interests and had put forward their claims in an unacceptable manner. Where Webb saw aggressive independence and arrogance, General Council members saw a government that had forgotten the primary purpose of the Labour Party.[30]

By August 1931 the relationship had reached breaking point. The breakdown involved choices for those who were both politicians and trade unionists. Arthur Hayday was an officer of the highly respectable National Union of General and Municipal Workers (NUGMW). In 1931 he was also chairman of the TUC. Since 1918 he had been Labour Member for West Nottingham. He came from the east London politics of the Social Democratic Federation, the world of the NUGMW patriarch Will Thorne, and, like Thorne, he had taken a strongly patriotic line during the war. He could have been an exemplar for Joe Gormley. A journalist characterised him as demonstrating not the expertise of the study but the expertise of experience.[31] In the Commons he was a measured critic of the government's attempts to reform unemployment insurance. Even in the first days of the 1929 government he emphasised what would become his dominant identity. 'He was an industrialist before he was a politician. Were they going to leave it to the political intriguers who knew nothing about their movement? It was their industrial side that would have to bear

---

29 MacDonald, Diary, 21 August 1931, TNA/PRO, 3069.
30 See the handwritten papers relating to the crisis of August 1931 and the resignation of the Labour government. A note indicates that these were written in early September 1931, before an election had been determined upon. British Library of Political and Economic Science (BLPES), London, Passfield Papers, IV Section 26. For the 'pigs' reference, see Cole (ed.) *Beatrice Webb's Diaries*, p. 281 (22 August 1931).
31 *Yorkshire Post*, 30 June, 1930

the brunt of a storm.' As chair at the TUC in September 1931 he affirmed that 'courageous and determined action by the national bodies invested with authority in the labour and trade union movement has saved the working class from destruction'. A month later, as fraternal delegate to the Labour Party conference, he dismissed MacDonald and his supporters as 'political blacklegs'.[32]

Another member of Hayday's union could not move so easily between industrial and political identities. As Minister of Labour, Margaret Bondfield had aroused the anger of many trade union MPs, not least Hayday, for her susceptibility to establishment and populist scares about the abuse of unemployment benefit. On that last symbolic vote of the Cabinet she had supported the 10 per cent cut in benefit. When the National Government was formed the following day she wrote to MacDonald expressing her sympathy and admiration: 'May God give you the strength you need and the success you deserve in bringing the nation through this crisis.'[33] Three days later, on 27 August, she attended a meeting of her union executive together with Clynes, the Home Secretary and NUGMW President. Clynes was adept at manoeuvring through difficult situations without damaging his career. Originally sponsored in the Commons by the Independent Labour Party, he had disagreed with that party's opposition to war in 1914, but the exchanges had remained amicable. In 1918 he had been reluctant to break with the Lloyd George coalition but had followed the decision of his union. Defeated by MacDonald for the chairmanship of the PLP in November 1922, he had been a loyal lieutenant in all that followed. His opposition to the 10 per cent cut, however marginal he might have been to the Cabinet discussions, and his reputation for loyalty and conciliation meant that he faced no difficult questions.

Bondfield's case was different. Her time in the Cabinet had brought her into conflict with the TUC over issues of style and substance, despite her previous service on the General Council. In the 1920s she had worked hard to distance herself from her earlier feminist and suffrage campaigning, but her gender, allied to a puritanical outlook, ensured a lack of rapport

---

32 See discussion at TUC General Council on relations with Labour government, 26 June 1929, Modern Records Centre, University of Warwick, TUC Archive, MS 292 750 1/14; TUC, *Trades Union Congress Report* (London, 1931), p. 67; Labour Party, *Report of the 31st Annual Conference* (London, 1931), p. 201.

33 Bondfield's attempts to reform unemployment insurance in late 1929 provoked widespread criticism within the trade union group of MPs. See Will Thorne to MacDonald, 3 December 1929, MacDonald Papers, TNA/PRO, 3069/440. For Bondfield's immediate response to the formation of the National Government, see her letter to MacDonald, 24 August 1931, MacDonald Papers, TNA/PRO, 3069/1314.

in the masculine ethos of the TUC.[34] Her union executive asked her for an explanation of her support for the proposed cut in benefit. She was unapologetic: 'My attitude was having to choose between a moratorium and a cut. I voted for a cut as being of far less danger to the unemployed, coupled with an undertaking that the whole program of economy would call for equality of sacrifice.'[35] Within this loyal and discreet union the issue was not pushed any further. Had executive members known of her supportive letter to MacDonald, the tradition of discretion might have been severely tested. In fact, her response to the collapse of the government was even more complicated. On 25 August she had typed a memorandum that briefly chronicled the last days of the Labour government and explained her vote on the 10 per cent cut. She expected that the new government would have a brief life. Her characterisation of the split left her future open:

> Mr MacDonald, knowing the full consequences of his actions has decided to sacrifice himself to save the country from financial chaos; Mr Henderson has decided to sacrifice Mr MacDonald to save the Labour Party. When the House of Commons meets, we shall all of us have to make a decision as to our attitude to the measures to be brought before the House.[36]

She acknowledged that she must consult her union executive but remained clear that her role in Cabinet would constrain her actions in the voting lobby:

> If I accept the Party decision not to vote for any part of the programme contrary to the decision of the Party, I must claim my right to abstain from voting against those parts of the programme for which I gave my vote when I was a member of the Cabinet.[37]

Illness prevented her from participating in the often angry Commons debates and votes during September. Continuing doubts about her position led to her meeting with her divisional party executive in Wallsend.[38] Opinions were becoming polarised as an election seemed more likely. The complexities and ambiguities of individuals' earlier positions

---

34 For an example of a gendered stereotype, see Robert Skidelsky, *Politicians and the Slump: The Labour Government of 1929–1931* (London: Macmillan, 1967).
35 National Union of General and Municipal Workers Executive, 27 August 1931, Working Class Movement Library, Salford.
36 Bondfield, untitled typescript dated 25 August 1931, Bondfield Papers, Vassar College Archive, Poughkeepsie, New York, box 4.
37 *Ibid*. This line would be taken by National Labour ministers to undermine criticism by their former Cabinet colleagues.
38 Meeting with Wallsend Executive Committee, 25 September 1931, Bondfield Papers, box 4.

faded alongside the need to defend Labour against an onslaught from the National coalition. Following her defeat at Wallsend, Bondfield amended her August typescript. Her principal concern was that the National Government had held an all too successful election. The expectation of a brief emergency arrangement had been falsified. 'How wrong I was has been proved within a few weeks when MacDonald threw over the arrangement and headed a National Government. Henderson was right.'[39]

Bondfield's shifts were accompanied by one constant, as she made clear to her Wallsend activists. 'As an official of my organisation, if I could not carry out my Union's policy I should have to resign – I could do no other.'[40] This fixed point lies at the heart of the authorised version of 1931. If MacDonald, Snowden and Thomas were the villains, then there must be a hero. Arthur Henderson had been a Labour Member more or less continuously since 1903. He had been party Secretary since 1912 and a member of the Asquith and Lloyd George War Cabinets. In the first two Labour governments he was respectively Home Secretary and Foreign Secretary. His political record was complex. On the one side stood his residual Liberalism, his support of wartime conscription, his caution at the Home Office, his role as a machine politician and his dismay at the extent to which some of his parliamentary colleagues, urged on by Bevin, were ready to attack the 1931 renegades from the start. Yet twice, over the Stockholm Conference in 1917, and again in 1931, he had moved to where the labour movement's centre of gravity appeared to be. This could appear as the slavish following of majority sentiment or as a high-minded devotion to the movement regardless of personal inconvenience. Either way, his action in 1931 earned Henderson a place in Labour's pantheon. The final seal of approval was Mary Agnes Hamilton's idealised 1938 biography, which celebrated its subject's ordinariness as the time-served craftsman who personified the trade union presence among the party leadership.[41]

The approved history of 1931 presented a challenge to future aspirants to leadership. They had to demonstrate that they were exempt from the weaknesses and immune to the temptations that had allegedly produced the wreckage. By any standards Clem Attlee in the early 1920s had been a party intellectual, a critical sympathiser with guild socialism and the PLP's first Oxford graduate. Yet after 1931 he had few difficulties in appearing to be the antithesis of MacDonald. He had been shaped by Haileybury, Oxford and military service. Each had been an institution to which he

---

39 Handwritten amendments to typescript of 25 August 1931, p. 6, dated 11 November 1931.
40 Meeting with Wallsend Executive Committee, p. 15.
41 Mary Agnes Hamilton, *Arthur Henderson* (Oxford: Heinemann, 1938).

had given his loyalty. He applied the same ethic to the Labour Party. In the difficult 1931 Parliament he became once again the selfless and hardworking officer who encouraged the hesitant and unsure among the other ranks, as he had under a fire more deadly than anything produced by the National benches. His lack of star quality and respect for party procedures and protocols eventually earned him the respect of Bevin.

Hugh Dalton, another party intellectual, assiduously if often clumsily courted what he imagined to be trade union opinion. He harboured private (or, given Dalton's stentorian tactlessness, probably public) prejudices against some other intellectuals, not least Harold Laski. Herbert Morrison, in contrast, faced difficulties. Bevin's deep-seated hostility was distinctive but it fed on more widespread sentiments. Morrison's response to 1931 had been initially ambiguous; his conception of socialism and public service, as with MacDonald's, could make trade unions seem sectional and potentially antipathetic to socialist values. Sir Stafford Cripps was the most significant victim of the post-1931 settlement. A recent and talented entry to the party was bound to provoke trade union suspicion, and his wealth, complex shift to the left and sharp changes of policy fed the image of the rootless intellectual, provoking comparisons with Mosley.

The usable version of the past simplified what had been complex and ambiguous, but it also legitimised a viable alliance between trade unionists and middle- and upper-class progressives that could benefit from the discrediting of the established political elite in 1940. The Attlee government's achievements exorcised some memories of 1931, although financial crises in 1947 and 1949 stirred uneasy memories, not least since both crises came in August. The Cabinet divisions of April 1951 showed how images, taboos and myths remained embedded in party culture. *Tribune* compared Hugh Gaitskell's budget to Snowden's actions in 1931. When Dalton and Chuter Ede heard Bevan at an acrimonious PLP meeting they compared him to Mosley. Bevan had been one of Mosley's few supporters among Labour MPs following the latter's resignation from the MacDonald government.[42] In the subsequent years of left–right factionalism a praetorian guard of trade union leaders claimed to be holding the party together as in 1931.

The effectiveness of the post-1931 settlement owed much to the unity of sufficient trade union leaders on significant issues. The trade union left included a significant communist element and was limited in influence, an imbalance strengthened by the bipolarity of the early Cold War. From the late 1950s the tectonic plates began to shift. The party

---

42 Ben Pimlott (ed.), *The Political Diary of Hugh Dalton 1918–40, 1945–60* (London: Jonathan Cape, 1986), p. 534, for the *Tribune* article; entry for 20 April 1951, p. 539; for Mosley references, entry for 24 April 1951.

leadership could no longer rely on uncritical support from a majority of large unions. The first evidence came with Hugh Gaitskell's defeats in 1960 over Clause 4 and unilateralism. The seedbeds of change were complex, varying between unions. By 1966 these shifts were intensifying as more trade unionists responded critically to the Wilson government's policies on employment and incomes. The culmination was the battle over that government's attempt to reform trade union law, centred on the proposals in the ironically entitled White Paper *In Place of Strife*. In this Labour crisis, references to 1931 were commonplace. Wilson played the part of MacDonald, Callaghan that of Henderson and the implacable Snowden role was taken by Barbara Castle. The dynamics of the plot were in some senses very different: there was no urgent financial crisis; the action lasted months, not days; there was extensive participation, not the conclaves of the few. In one crucial respect, though, the outcome was the same. The TUC, in alliance with a section of the Cabinet and backed by many within the PLP, blocked proposals championed by the Prime Minister and some senior colleagues.[43] Wilson and Castle, however, did not leave the party. Some ministers remained for the crisis involving the International Monetary Fund in 1976, when Tony Benn circulated the Cabinet with the minutes of their predecessors' meetings 45 years earlier.[44]

Memories of the authorised legacy of 1931 faded with changing personnel. Thatcherism and the decline in trade unionism were the prelude to New Labour's determination to deny the party's past and to seek alternative legitimising traditions. Yet the current uneasy coalition of economic and social liberals committed to attacks on the poor and dispossessed justified in the name of necessity requires a response from Labour – the invention of another tradition that can legitimise an alliance between workers and progressive intellectuals. After all, the Cameron coalition is the heir to 1931.

---

43 Peter Jenkins, *The Battle of Downing Street* (London: Charles Knight, 1970).
44 Tony Benn, *Against the Tide: Diaries 1973–76* (London: Hutchinson, 1989), pp. 645–90.

13

Conclusion

CHRIS WRIGLEY

> Formed to maintain that gold standard which it declared to be the indispensable condition of national safety, within less than three weeks it abandoned that standard with the insolent explanation that industry would benefit by the change.
>
> (*Labour's Call to Action: The Nation's Opportunity*,
> 1931 Labour Party manifesto)

Central to any assessment of the second Labour government is its economic record. This record was castigated by Robert Skidelsky in his influential *Politicians and the Slump* (1967). His criticisms centred not so much on the financial crisis of 1931 but on the government's 'omissions over the previous two years'. As he saw it, the 'bold men' – David Lloyd George and Oswald Mosley – were 'driven to political suicide, while Britain, complacent and insular, came to the verge of disaster'. The Labour government 'rejected Conservative protection, the Liberal national development loan, the Keynesian and Mosleyite amalgams of both, preferring instead the advice of the least progressive sections of the "economic establishment"'. Instead, Skidelsky argued for 'a Ministry of Economic Affairs plus an expansionist Chancellor', with 'Bevin or Mosley in harness with Lloyd George at the Exchequer'.[1]

The limitations of the policies of the 'bold men' have been persuasively argued by several economic historians. For instance, while Lloyd George's proposals on unemployment were imaginative, if implemented they

---

1 Robert Skidelsky, *Politicians and the Slump: The Labour Government of 1929–1931* (London: Macmillan, 1967), pp. 386–8 and 390.

would have been highly unlikely to have 'conquered' the much higher levels of unemployment of 1930.² Robert Skidelsky in his biography of Mosley wrote of 'the futile attempt of trying to classify Mosley according to the conventional political categories of "Right" and "Left".³ In the present book Daniel Ritschel (chapter 4), nevertheless, does lucidly categorise Mosley's views and in so doing, like Skidelsky before him, offers an answer to A. J. P. Taylor's point, 'It is impossible to say where Mosley got his ideas from. Perhaps he devised them himself.'⁴ In Ritschel's case, he deflates some of the overblown claims and misconceptions concerning Mosley's proposals.

While Bevin, like Mosley, was attracted, at least for a while, to the possibilities of the Empire offering 'Greater Britain' markets, much as had been Sir Charles Dilke and Joseph Chamberlain 25–50 years earlier, Bevin's focus was on working people, especially trade unionists. Bevin was unlikely to work with Mosley, not least because of Labourist attitudes which are discussed by David Howell in chapter 12. As is discussed by Chris Wrigley in chapter 3, Bevin, Citrine and some other Transport and General Workers' Union figures were evolving, in a piecemeal way, alternative economic policies to those of Philip Snowden and James Ramsay MacDonald from 1927 onwards.⁵

As the economic crisis worsened through 1930 into 1931, the Labour government leadership retreated into economic orthodoxy. As is made clear by Robert Taylor in chapter 5, the Parliamentary Labour Party generally supported MacDonald and Snowden in their cautious approach. Arthur Henderson, much embroiled in foreign policy, was quiet, even timid, on economic policy. However, he was true to his trade union roots when it came to the crunch. Three decades earlier he had left Lib–Lab politics for the Labour Party out of loyalty to his union, the Friendly Society of Iron-Founders. It was always highly unlikely that he would go with MacDonald and Snowden, both disparagers of trade unionism, and break with the trade union movement. Henderson, as so often in his career, was in tune with the views of much of the membership of the Labour Party and trade union leadership.

---

2 See, for instance, W. R. Garside, *British Unemployment 1919–1939* (Cambridge: Cambridge University Press, 1990).
3 Robert Skidelsky, *Oswald Mosley* (London: Macmillan, 1975), pp. 17–21.
4 A. J. P. Taylor, *English History 1914–1945* (Oxford: Oxford University Press, 1965), p. 285, and quoted in Skidelsky, *Oswald Mosley*, p. 15. Like Skidelsky, Taylor was interested in Mosley, even dining with him (and being sneered at by Mosley afterwards).
5 As well as the chapter in this book by Wrigley, see also Skidelsky, *Oswald Mosley*, pp. 233–5.

The Labour Party was astounded that what had been deemed a road to ruin a few weeks before – the abandonment of the gold standard – was carried out within a few weeks by the National Government, with, on balance, good effects. In a pamphlet in late 1931, Ernest Bevin and G. D. H. Cole expressed grave concern that 'those in authority … sound as if they were still hankering after a return of the pound to the old parity'. They urged instead 'stabilization of the pound at a new and lower gold parity', thereby returning the advantage to exports and reducing 'permanently the real burden of War Debt and other fixed interest obligations'.[6]

Labour, after the terrible result of the 1931 general election, held a conviction that somehow the party had been robbed of its due. If Labour in 1924 had had an excuse for electoral disappointment in the Zinoviev letter, after 1931 the heavy defeat was ascribed to bankers and the 'treachery' of MacDonald and Snowden.[7] When reviewing the severe 1931 general election defeat, Citrine, on behalf of the Trades Union Congress (TUC), commented that 'they must examine the extent to which it had been possible for three men [J. H. Thomas being the third], whom they trusted most, to contribute to the disaster that had befallen. These three men had enabled propaganda to be used against the Movement which could not have existed without their assistance.' He concluded, 'The feeling of the General Council was emphatic that they did not wish these men to return.'[8] Given this view and Snowden's 'Bolshevism run mad' abuse of the party in the 1931 general election (chapter 10), it is curious that when the Labour Party in 1935 came publicly to reflect on the second Labour government, it dealt with the damaging claim of 1931 that 'the Labour Government was responsible for the financial crisis' simply by publishing Snowden's later observation:

> It is said that the crisis of 1931 and the great increase in unemployment was brought about by the extravagance of the Labour Government and in particular by the expenditure of the Government on Public Works. No statement could be more monstrously untrue.

---

6 Ernest Bevin and G. D. H. Cole, *The Crisis: What It Is, How It Arose, What To Do* (London: New Statesman and Nation, 1931), pp. 18 and 20.

7 On the bankers see in particular Philip Williamson, 'A "banker's ramp"? Financiers and the British political crisis of August 1931', *English Historical Review*, 49 (1984), pp. 770–806; and, more generally, Philip Williamson, *National Crisis and National Government: British Politics, the Economy and Empire, 1926–1932* (Cambridge: Cambridge University Press, 1992).

8 Minutes of the joint meeting of the General Council of the TUC, the National Executive Committee of the Labour Party and the Consultative Committee of the Parliamentary Labour Party, 10 November 1931, Bevin Papers, Churchill College Archive, Cambridge, BEVN 1/5.

Conclusion

To this was added Snowden's claim that the financial crisis 'was not due to anything inherently unsound in our financial position, but to the repercussions of general world conditions upon our commerce and our national Budget'. In this Snowden ignored the relative weakening of British finance, at least to the extent that it could not underpin the Austrian and German banks when they were in crisis.[9] Overall, the Labour Party's use in 1935 of Snowden's comments was intended to assist it evade renewed scrutiny and discussion of its economic policies and of the alternative policies aired by Mosley, Keynes, the Independent Labour Party, Bevin and others. This omission in 1935 has been remedied subsequently by historians, and this volume provides fresh reflections. The verdict on the second Labour government's economic record remains that it was very poor. However, the Mosley and Keynsian alternatives aired with much approval by Robert Skidelsky attract less support here. Bevin's views, although not always coherent, did evolve from the late 1920s and, combined with those of other economic thinkers, not least of J. M. Keynes and G. D. H. Cole, began to provide Labour with a different economic direction from the free trade finance of Snowden.

The Labour Party in 1935 preferred to move attention away from its economic record to other areas, asserting that, in view of 'the rapid development of the international crisis which plunged practically every country into economic, financial and industrial difficulties', 'the Labour Government's record of achievement was one of which the Labour Party has every reason to be proud'. Hence, it quickly moved on to 'Labour's work for world peace', unemployment measures, housing, education, industrial legislation and land and agriculture.[10] In several of these areas, Labour could point to reforms that had been achieved. For instance, in housing there was the 1930 Housing Act, which gave local authorities enhanced powers to clear slums and required them to prepare five-year plans for dealing with bad housing. The Housing Act also reinforced the 1924 Wheatley Act in housing provision in rural areas. Yet the 1930 Act was not as significant as the legislation of the first Labour government.

---

9 For the argument that the British were not as financially strong as before 1914, and so could not rescue the Austrian and German banks, while the US was not committed to such a role until after the Second World War, see C. P. Kindleberger, *The World in Depression* (London: Allen Lane, 1973). For a reassessment of German banking, see Hans-Joachim Voth, 'German banking and the impact of the First World War', in Chris Wrigley (ed.), *The First World War and the International Economy* (Cheltenham: Edward Elgar, 2000), pp. 165–85.

10 Labour Party, *Second Labour Government* (London, 1935), pp. 2–15 (quotations from p. 2).

Foreign policy under Arthur Henderson was a major area of success in 1929–31. Moreover, Henderson went on to be chosen by the Council of the League of Nations to be President of the Disarmament Conference. Labour's support for international arbitration suggested it was the heir to Gladstonian Liberalism and was the appropriate recipient of Nonconformist support. Also, concerns for peace coincided with concerns about unemployment, which, as Jonathan Davis shows in his fresh study of a major area of Labour's foreign policy (chapter 9), led to a successful rapprochement with the Soviet Union.

Like the authors of Labour Party's 1935 booklet, the contributors to this book find that the second Labour government was more fruitful in areas away from its main economic policies. This book provides two case studies of such domestic areas of policy, with discussions of consumer issues by Nicole Robertson (chapter 7) and of the land by Clare Griffiths (chapter 8). Land and agriculture were deemed issues areas worthy to be emphasised in the Labour Party's 1935 booklet, not least as the party hoped to recover seats in rural areas. Attlee's government in 1945 was to make considerable efforts to appeal to rural voters. However, consumer issues were not highlighted by the party in the 1935 booklet, though they were still pressed by the Co-operative Party and more generally by co-operators.

While some political contexts of the second Labour government have been explored in depth by scholars such as David Howell, Andrew Thorpe and Philip Williamson, there is still room for reassessments, as is demonstrated in this volume by the study of some Conservatives' attitudes by Richard Carr (chapter 11).

The second Labour government had many limitations similar to the first Labour government. Apart from being minority governments, they were led by MacDonald, Snowden, Henderson, Clynes and others of the first generation of Labour parliamentarians. Their almost Gladstonian economic views, sometimes combined with near millenarian views of 'socialism' (or very weak beliefs, in the case of Henderson and some other trade unionists), were threadbare by 1930. The second Labour government saw the end of one 'old Labour' with competing alternatives from Bevin and some trade unionists, the Independent Labour Party, other socialist thinkers and from Labour in local government. Some of these new policies were to be taken up by the majority government of 1945. Planning and a bigger public sector were coming in, while the remnants of the old Lib–Labism were fading.

Index

A Socialist Plan for Unemployment (1931) 110
Addison, Christopher 5, 90, 120, 137, 138, 141, 142, 144–6, 176
adulteration 123, 126
advertising 130
Agricultural Marketing Act (1931) 5, 120
agricultural policies 133–49, 224
Aitchison, C. M. 209
Alexander, A. V. 5, 124,142
Allen, Clifford 104, 105, 114
Allen, Sir Thomas 49, 50, 51
Allen, Vic 37
Alpass, J. H. 143
alternative vote 110
Amery, Leo 21, 192, 195, 201
Amulree, Lord 209
Anglo-Soviet trade 155–7, 165, 169
Anomalies Act (1931) 107, 111, 112
arable farming 133–49
Arcos Raid (1927) 154
Arnott, John 114
Attlee, Clement 2, 8, 9, 145, 182, 204, 217–18, 224
Australia 186
Austria 7, 175, 223

Baillie-Hamilton, Hon. C. W. 195
Baldwin, Stanley 2, 18–19, 21, 23, 32, 77, 86, 119, 120, 156, 185, 187–9, 191–3, 194–202
Balfour, Henry 196
Ball, Stuart 16, 32

Bank of England 6, 44, 46, 48–9
bank rate 46, 59, 66
bankers' ramp 9, 176, 222
Bassett, Reginald 9, 180, 182
Bayliss, Robert A. 121
BBC (British Broadcasting Corporation) 180
Beard, Jack 45
Beaverbrook, Lord 21, 45, 195, 197
Beer, S. H. 181
Benn, Tony 9, 203
Bentley, Michael 202
Betts, Frank 114
Bevan, Aneurin 68, 95, 199, 218
Bevin, Ernest 14, 38, 39–44, 46–54, 89, 94–5, 97, 172, 182–3, 204, 208, 213, 217, 218, 220, 221, 222, 223, 224
Birmingham 30, 212
Birmingham ILP conference (1930) 103
Black, Lawrence 132
Blair, Tony 10, 24
Blum, Leon 181
Board of Education 128–9
Board of National Investment 50
Board of Trade 121
Boer War (1899–1902) 2
Bondfield, Margaret 1, 94, 111, 215–17
Boothby, Robert 188, 191, 195, 199–200, 201–2
Bracher, S. V. 205
Bracken, Brendan 199
Bradbury, Lord 48
Bradford ILP conference (1932) 100, 101

Bradford Pioneer 114
Brailsford, H. N. 60, 70, 164, 165, 173
Bread Tax, The 145
Bridgeman, William 197
Bristol 30
Britain's Industrial Future 19, 32
British Empire 42, 44, 206
British Union of Fascists 56, 65
Brockway, Fenner 72, 73, 87–8, 89, 100, 103–4, 106–7, 110–13, 115, 158–9, 173
Brooke, Christopher 194
Brooke, Councillor (Bradford) 105
Brown, George 204
Brown, Gordon 13
Brown, Kenneth D. 117
Brown, W. J. 68, 86
Buchan, John 196
Buchanan, George 111, 113
Bullock, Alan 40
Burnett, John 126, 128
Burnley 177
Butler, R. A. B. 188, 198, 201
Butt, Ronald 185
Buxton, Noel 136–41, 147, 212

Callaghan, James 210, 219
Cambridge 134
Cameron, David 219
'Campbell case' (1924) 4, 21
capital levy 33, 50
Carlisle 211
Carlton, David 151, 157, 164, 169
Carr, Richard 15, 224
cartels 42, 67, 119
Carter, President Jimmy 210
Castle, Barbara 203, 219
Cecil, Lord Robert 157
census (1931) 24–36
Central Board of Control 60
Chamberlain, Joseph 42, 221
Chamberlain, Neville 21–2, 32–3, 188, 189, 193, 197
Chicago 47
Chicherin, Georgy 155
children 47
Churchill, Randolph 199
Churchill, Winston 4, 180, 187, 188–9, 194, 197
Citrine, Walter 38, 41, 44, 46, 50, 53, 54, 97, 172, 208, 213, 221, 222
City of London 30
Clarion 123
Clarke, Peter 51
Clegg, Hugh 37

Clinton, President Bill 10
Clydeside 104, 105, 171
Clynes, J. R. 1, 5, 91, 158–9, 179, 205, 208, 224
Coal Mines Bill (1929) 5, 6, 95, 109
coal mining 39, 47
Cohen, Gideon 101
Cole, G. D. H. 6, 50, 51, 52, 53, 60, 69, 72, 117, 121, 178–9, 222, 223
Cole, Margaret 52, 181
Collier, Lawrence 161
Colonial Development Advisory Committee 42
Committee on Finance and Industry 44
Committee on Food Standards (1931) 127
Committee on Production 60
Commonwealth 63, 73
Communist International 20, 116, 161, 163, 178
Communist Party of Great Britain 76, 106, 152, 170–2
company unionism 43
Conservative Central Office 21
Conservative Party 3, 14, 17–18, 21, 23, 24–36, 45, 88–9, 93, 95, 110–11, 123, 156, 167, 173, 180, 185–202, 211, 224
consumers 14, 50, 54, 61, 65, 66, 103, 117–32, 224
Consumers' Association 132
Consumers Council Bill (1931) 95, 120, 121–6, 132
contraception 35
Cook, A. J. 68
Cook, Chris 17
Cooper, Duff 112, 189, 193, 198, 199, 202
co-operative movement 11, 49, 123–4, 224
Co-operative Party 5, 124, 125–6, 224
Cornwall 36
corporate state 77, 79, 80, 82, 83–4
cotton textiles 47
Cowling, Maurice 18
Credit Anstatt bank 7, 175, 223
credit policy 44, 45, 58, 59, 62, 65, 66, 70, 75
Cripps, Sir Stafford 8, 204, 218
Cross, Colin 10
Crossman, Richard 203, 204
Cullen, Dr Carl Knight 116

Daily Express 21
Daily Herald 2, 155, 157, 167, 173, 175, 180, 183
Daily Mail 21
Dallas, George 135, 143

Index 227

Dalton, Hugh 23, 74, 88, 92, 157–9, 168, 204, 210, 212, 218
Davis, Jonathan 14, 224
De La Warr, Earl 209
Dear, Marcel 82
deflation 51, 58, 65, 66, 91, 171, 174, 186, 207
democratic control of industry 116, 119
Department of Health, Scotland 128
Derby 211
devaluation 49, 51, 54
Dilke, Sir Charles 42, 221
docks and harbours 39
Dollan, Patrick 108, 114–15
Dovgalevsky, Valeryan 159, 161, 162
Downs, Anthony 19
Dowse, R. E. 100
Dukes, Charles 95–6, 99
Duncan, Charles 94

East Anglia 135
East London 3
Economic Advisory Council 6, 51, 52, 142
Economic Consequences of Mr Churchill, The 48
Ede, J. Chuter 218
Eden, Anthony 189, 192, 193, 196–7, 198–9
education 76, 128
Education Bills 6
Edwards, Ebby 95
Eitigon and Company 160
Elliott, Walter 186, 189, 192, 195, 200
Ellis, R. G. 193
energy 76
engineering 165
excess capacity 38

Fabian Society 178
family allowances 76
farming 14, 27
fascism 51, 56, 64–5, 68, 75, 78, 80–2, 84
Fimmen, Edo 42
First World War 3, 51, 60, 98, 99, 119, 136, 170, 172, 176, 181, 188–92, 202, 215
Five-Power Naval Conference (1930) 5
Food and Drug Act (1938) 127
Food Council 119, 120, 121, 124–5
Fordism 70
France 181
Francis, Martin 122
free trade 14, 35, 45–6, 53, 133, 141, 143, 186, 195–6, 223
Freeden, Michael 83
Freeman, David 144

French, Michael 126, 127
furniture 129–30

Gaitskell, Hugh 203, 218
Gandhi, M. 6
Garside, W. R. 186
Geddes Axe 6
general election (1918) 17, 27, 171, 190
general election (1922) 3, 27
general election (1923) 3, 27
general election (1924) 18, 23, 33, 193, 194
general election (1929) 4, 13, 16, 20–1, 24–36, 140, 152, 156, 189, 193, 194
general election (1931) 7, 16, 54, 98, 101–2, 113, 180, 194, 212, 222
general election (1945) 18, 36, 194
general election (1935) 222–4
General Strike (1926) 3, 18, 38, 101, 171–2, 189, 191, 193, 197, 212, 213
General Treaty (with Soviet Union) (1924) 163
Generation of 1914, The 186
George V., King 7, 8, 161–2, 209
Germany 47, 136, 174, 175, 176, 223
Gillett, Sir G. M. 209
Gladstone, Herbert 172
Gladstonian Liberalism 224
gold standard 7, 38, 43, 44, 45, 46, 47, 48, 50, 51, 58, 66, 76, 177, 207, 211, 220, 222
Gormley, Joe 203–4, 214
Gosling, Harry 94
Gould, Harry 143–4
Graham, Stephen 188
Graham, William 5, 95, 120–1, 126, 207
Graves, Robert 188
Great Depression 13, 165, 168
Great Opportunity, The 186
Greater Britain, The 64–5
Greenwood, Arthur 5, 126–7, 207
Griffiths, Clare 14, 224
Growing Up Into Revolution 181
Gurney, Peter 126

Hailsham, Lord 197
Hall, Daniel 137
Hall Caine, Derwent 212
Hamilton, Mary Agnes 8, 92, 217
Harcourt-Smith, Simon 161
Hardie, James Keir 4
Harris Foundation 47
Hawtrey, Ralph 59
Hayday, Arthur 37, 93–4, 176, 214–15
Hayek, Friedrich 184, 191–2
Headlam, Cuthbert 200

Henderson, Arthur 1, 3, 4, 5, 7, 10, 38, 54, 91, 97, 151, 157–69, 170, 177, 179, 180, 182, 205, 207, 208, 210, 211–12, 216–17, 219, 221, 224
Hicks, George 40
Hilton, Matthew 121, 122, 125
hire purchase 129–30, 132
Hire Purchase Act (1938) 131, 132
Hire Purchase Bill (1930–31) 130
Hirst, Stanley 175
Hitler, Adolf 197
Hobson, J. A. 58, 67, 173, 175
Hodgson, R. M. 154
Hope, Arthur 194
Horne, Sir Robert 197
Horrabin, J. F. 111
housing 4, 30, 76, 110, 191, 193, 223
Housing Act (1930) 5, 223
Howe, Stephen 153
Howell, David 12, 15, 17, 19–20, 37, 70, 101, 221, 224
Hudson, R. S. 193
hunger marches 2, 8

ICI (Imperial Chemical Industries) 165
ILP *see* Independent Labour Party
IMF *see* International Monetary Fund
Imperial Duties Act (1932) 195
imperial issues 12, 74, 78, 173, 195
import controls 60
Independent Labour Party 14, 57–64, 65, 66, 68, 70, 72, 73, 75, 82–4, 89, 98, 100–16, 140, 170, 173, 174, 177–8, 194, 213, 215, 224
Independent Socialist Party 116
India 4, 6, 38, 110, 187, 209
Industrial Aspects of Socialism (1926) 60
Industrial Council (1911) 40
Industry and the State 191
inflation 61–2, 65, 66
International Federation of Trade Unions 41, 42
International Monetary Fund 9
International Transport Workers' Federation 42, 183
Irwin, Tom 103
Italy 51, 78, 80

Jabara Carley, Michael 156
Joad, C. E. M. 72
Johnston, Tom 1, 207
joint industrial councils 40
Jones, Tom 51
Jowett, Fred 104, 108, 110, 113, 114
Jowitt, Lord 209

Kamenev, Lev 154
Kerensky, Aleksandr 151
Keynes, J. M. 6, 46–51, 57, 66–8, 173, 182, 184, 195, 201, 223
Keynesian economics 6, 11, 14, 55, 64, 65–8, 74, 82, 173, 181, 187, 223
King's Lynn 144
Kirkwood, David 113
Kremlin 150–69

Labour and the Nation (1928) 5, 22, 105, 119
Labour Magazine 123
Labour Party 2, 3, 4, 7, 11, 12, 16, 18, 22, 24–36, 46, 54, 56, 58, 68, 70, 76, 103–16, 122–32, 145, 146, 148, 172, 179–80, 181, 182, 184, 196, 202, 203–19, 222–4
Labour Party in Perspective 182
Labour Representation Committee (1900–6) 3, 104, 206
Labour Research Department 119
Labour Woman 123
Labour's Call to Action (1931) 220
Labour's Appeal to the Nation (1929) 173, 174
land drainage 138
Land Utilisation Bill 148
Lansbury, George 1, 8, 10, 120, 173, 199, 207
Lansbury's Lido 2
Laski, Harold 8, 64, 182, 218
Lawrence, Susan 1, 98, 130, 175
Lawson, Jack 95, 97, 210–11
Lawther, Will 95, 213
Laybourn, Keith 10
Leach, William 114
League of Nations 5, 153, 157, 169, 223, 224
Lee, Jennie 85, 111
Leeds 30
Leeds Citizen 114
Left Book Club 182
Lenin, V. I. 154, 159, 171
Leventhal, Fred 10, 163
Liberal Industrial Inquiry 19
Liberal Party 3, 6, 19, 22, 23, 24–36, 45, 46, 51, 58, 62, 86, 89, 93, 141, 148, 172, 173, 207, 224
Linlithgow Committee (1922–23) 121
Litvinov, Maksim 155, 161
'living wage' 58, 59, 69, 70, 73, 84, 105
Lloyd George, David 19, 22, 27, 31, 46, 57, 86, 136, 147, 157, 171, 173, 186, 187, 192, 193, 194, 195, 198, 201, 220
Lloyd George coalition governments (1916–22) 18, 171, 190, 206, 215

Index

Loder, John 191, 197, 198
London 12
Lumley, L. R. 193
Lutyens, Sir Edwin 188

MacDonald, Gordon 97
MacDonald, James Ramsay 1, 2, 3–5, 6, 8–14, 34–5, 36, 37–8, 44, 51, 53, 54, 68, 77, 83–4, 85–99, 104–6, 113, 114, 115, 118, 136–9, 142, 146, 148, 152–9, 162, 164, 167–9, 172–83, 185, 193, 194, 196, 197, 201, 205, 207–19, 221, 222, 224
MacDonald, Malcolm 97, 209
MacDonald, Margaret 4
machine tools 165
MacKay, David 86
Macmillan, Harold 15, 186, 189–90, 191, 193, 195, 199, 201, 202
Macmillan, Lord 44, 48
Macmillan Committee 6, 45, 46–51, 66, 208
MacNeil Weir, Lachlan 9
malnutrition, 127–8, 129
Man, Hendrick de 82
Manchester 30, 171, 211
Manchester Guardian 68, 147
Margesson, David 199
Marquand, David 9, 10, 34
Marx, Karl 159, 202
Marxist Group 116
Maxton, James 68, 72, 89, 100, 104, 173
May Committee 7, 96, 112, 207
McGovern, John 113
McKenna, Reginald 47, 49, 59
McKenna Duties 186
McKibbin, Ross 11, 24, 83, 117, 186, 194
McKinlay, Alan 100
means test 2, 112
Meerut prisoners 110
Memoranduam of War Aims 171
Men Who Work Must Eat, The 120
mergers 43
Metropolitan-Vickers 165
Middlemas, R. K. 101
Middleton, George 211
Middleton, Jim 99, 113
Midlands 3
milk 127–9
Miller, Kenneth 158
miners 27, 35, 41, 47, 48, 171, 210–11
Miners' Federation of Great Britain (MFGB) 90, 95
minimum wage 105, 109, 119
Ministry of Agriculture 148

Ministry of Health 126–7
Ministry of Munitions 51
Minkin, Lewis 37
Minority Movement 213
Mond group of employers 41, 45
Mond–Turner talks 43–4, 53
Moore-Brabazon, John 199
Morel, E. D. 153
Morgan, Austen 9
Morgan, Kevin 10
Morrison, Herbert 16, 76, 89, 91–2, 176–7, 179, 184, 204, 209, 218
Mosley, Sir Oswald 1, 6, 14, 55–84, 92, 110, 187, 190, 192, 195, 198–202, 218, 220–1, 223
Mosley Manifesto 71, 73, 174
Mosley Memorandum 7, 62, 66, 72, 84, 110, 174, 198–9
Mowat, C. L. 174
Mussolini, Benito 82, 192
myths of 1931 8–9, 15, 36, 214

National Agricultural Party 147
National Confederation of Employers' Organisations 53
National Farmers' Union 134, 147
National Government (1931) 2, 7, 8, 16, 87, 96, 97, 98, 113, 127, 144, 177, 178, 180, 185, 202, 209, 211, 214, 222
National Health Insurance 110
National Industrial Commission 60
National Industrial Conference (1919) 40
National Investment Board 54, 80
National Labour Party 9
National Milk Publicity Council 129
National Minority Movement 171
National Party 190
National Planning Council 80
National Union of Agricultural Workers 135
National Union of General and Municipal Workers 90–1, 93, 95, 98, 214
National Union of Mineworkers 95
National Union of Railwaymen 206, 211
nationalisation 33, 49–50, 54, 67, 69, 71, 74, 148, 179
Nazi Party 175
New Economic Policy (NEP) 154
New Leader 70, 72, 102, 157, 173
New Party 64, 71, 75, 77, 78, 80–3, 111, 199, 201
NFU *see* National Farmers' Union
Nicolson, Harold 72, 192, 199
Noel-Baker, Philip 157, 167

Norfolk 135, 140
North Norfolk 27
Northern Ireland 30
Norway 166
Nuffield general election studies 36
NUGMW *see* National Union of General and Municipal Workers
NUM *see* National Union of Mineworkers
Nuneaton 194

old age pensions 76, 110, 119
Oldfield, John 209
Orders in Council 64
Orwell, George 181
Overy, Richard 175
Overy, Sir Esmond 163, 164–7, 168

Page Croft, Henry 190
Palestine 6
Parker's Piece 134–5, 136, 138, 149
Parliamentary History 16
Parliamentary Labour Party 14, 85–99, 103, 172, 204, 208, 210, 211, 221
Paton, John 113
Pelling, Henry 117
Perry, S. F. 124
Pethwick-Lawrence, F. W. 142, 178, 179–80
Phillips, Jim 126, 127
Phillips, Marion 111
Pimlott, Ben 18, 181
planning 59, 60, 71, 77, 224
planning councils 78
PLP *see* Parliamentary Labour Party
Plymouth 25
Poland 160
Ponsonby, Arthur 90, 153, 210
Pontefract 194
Portsmouth 25
Postgate, Raymond 8, 10
poverty 191
power 49, 50
Power of Parliament, The 185
Pravda 155, 156
Prayer Book controversy (1928) 19, 36
protection 19, 35, 52, 63, 140–3, 145, 173, 195–6, 198
Public Loans Board 109
public ownership 54, 67, 69, 70, 224
public works 59, 62–3, 65, 76, 110, 222
Pugh, Arthur 52, 183
Pugh, Martin 12
Pyatakov, Georgy 155, 160

quotas for wheat 140–4

railways 21, 40, 51
rationalisation 40, 43, 44, 46, 51, 53–4
Reconstruction: A Plea for National Policy 186
Remnant, Ernest 155, 161
Revolution by Reason (1925) 61, 69, 70, 75
Riddell, Neil 11, 37
Ritschel, Daniel 14, 221
Robertson, Nicole 14
Roosevelt, F. D. 181, 186
Rothermere, Lord 21, 195, 202
Rowe, E. A. 17
Royal Commission on Food Prices 120, 121
rural radicalism 27
Russian Orthodox Church 167, 168
Russian Revolution (October 1917) 151, 181, 205

Salter, Alfred 145
Sankey, Lord 5, 97, 207, 209
Sassoon, Siegfried 188
Saturday Review 193
Saville, John 173
Scanlon, Hugh 203
Schifferes, Steve 13
Schroeder, Gerhard 10
Scotland 140
Scott, Peter 129–30
Scottish Socialist Party 115
Scullin, James 186
Seeley, J. R. 42
Sexton, Sir James 94
Shaw, George Bernard 159
Shaw, Tom 140
Sheffield 3, 25, 171
Shepherd, John 10
shipbuilding 40
shop stewards' movement 171
Sinking Fund 50, 177
Skelton, Noel 191
Skidelsky, Robert 11, 55–6, 117, 186, 193, 220–1, 223
Smyth, James 100
Snell, Harry 87, 89–90, 91
Snowden, Philip 1, 5, 6, 8, 10, 35, 37–8, 44, 53, 54, 83–4, 91, 98, 99, 137, 141–3, 146, 148, 160, 164, 173, 178, 180, 181, 186, 201, 206, 207–10, 218, 219, 221, 222–3
'Socialism In Our Time' 89, 104, 105, 106, 110, 115, 116, 173
Socialist Labour Party 171
Socialist Plan for Unemployment, A (1931) 110

Index

Socialist Review 74, 75, 76
Society for Socialist Inquiry and Propaganda 52, 53
Sokolnikov, Grigory 163
South Africa 4, 38
South America 108
South Wales 171
South-East England 3
Soviet Union 5, 14, 51, 136, 150–69, 181, 183–4, 194
Spencer, George 213
Spring, Howard 9
SSIP *see* Society for Socialist Inquiry and Propaganda
Stalin, Josef 151, 154
Stanley, Oliver 187, 191, 196, 199, 200, 202
Sternhell, Zeev 80, 82
Stewart, W. W. 46
Strachey, John 68, 74–8, 80–2, 158, 159
sugar beet subsidy 145
Sweden 181
syndicalism 116, 171, 172, 178

Tanner, Duncan 10, 11, 24, 27, 83
tariffs 45, 50, 111, 133, 144, 173
Tawney, R. H. 5, 22, 52, 178
Taylor, A. J. P. 2, 180–1, 182, 221
Taylor, Robert 14, 221
Taylor, W. B. 135, 139–40, 143, 149
Tebbutt, Melanie 129
TGWU *see* Transport and General Workers' Union
The Bread Tax 145
The Economic Consequences of Mr Churchill 48
The Generation of 1914 186
The Great Opportunity 186
The Greater Britain 64–5
The Men Who Work Must Eat 120
The Power of Parliament 185
The Times 148, 196, 201
Thomas, J. H. 1, 5, 6, 8, 194,195, 205, 206, 207, 209, 210, 222
Thompson, Noel 75
Thorne, Will 214
Thorpe, Andrew 12, 14, 224
Tillett, Ben 44–5, 94
Times, The 148, 196, 201
Tivey, Leonard 125
Tomlinson, Jim 122
Toryism and the Twentieth Century 186
Toye, Richard 61
Tracey, Herbert 205
trade cycles 43

Trade Disputes Act (1927) 6, 34, 189
trade unions 11, 38, 48, 63, 90, 93–4, 105, 170–2, 177, 208–9, 210, 213, 218, 224
Trades Union Congress 7, 37, 40, 42, 44, 45, 50, 53, 54, 93, 94, 96, 108, 118, 124, 171, 176, 181, 207, 208–14, 222
transport 39, 49, 50, 76
Transport and General Workers' Union 38, 42, 44, 89, 94–5, 135, 142, 221
Treasury 6, 44, 45, 92
Tregidga, Gary 36
Trevelyan, C. P. 6, 90, 128
Tribune 218
Trotsky, Leon 154, 158–9, 162
tsarist debts 159
TUC *see* Trades Union Congress
Turner, Ben 40
Turner, John 17

Ukrainians 166
unadulterated food 123
undernourishment 127–8
unemployment 2, 5, 35, 38, 39, 45, 47, 50, 62, 88, 92, 94, 98, 99, 105, 107, 111, 117, 119, 137, 165, 171, 173, 174, 178, 182, 191, 192, 196, 197, 207–9, 214, 215
Unemployment Insurance Act (1930) 94, 96–7, 108, 109
Union of Democratic Control 3, 153
United States 2, 6, 13, 42, 43, 45, 47, 160–1, 176, 181, 186
university seats 30
Urbye, Andreas 166

Vickers, Rhiannon 153
Vienna 175

Wall Street Crash (1929) 2, 6, 13, 150, 195
Wallsend 216
Walton, S. 161
Wandsworth 25
war debt 222
Ward, Stephen 190
wartime controls 60
Washington Eight Hours Convention (International Labour Organisation) (1919) 119
We Can Conquer Unemployment 19, 173, 201
Webb, Beatrice 22, 178, 205
Webb, Sidney 3, 8, 22, 167, 170, 178, 181, 214
Wedgwood Benn, William 5
Weimar Republic 174, 175

Welsh, J. C. 92
Wertheimer, Egon 4, 153
Westminster St George's by-election (1931) 32
wheat 133, 135–45
Wheat Act (1932) 144–5
Wheatley, John 4, 88, 104, 108, 172, 194, 223
Where the ILP Stands (1930) 109
White Hart Hotel, Lewes 162
Whitely, William 95
Whitley Committees 40
Who Keeps Prices High 119
widows pensions 110
Wilkinson, Ellen 130–1
Williams, Andrew 153, 164, 167
Williams, Francis 184
Williamson, Philip 11–12, 17, 19, 54, 181, 191, 224
Wilson, Harold 203, 219

Winkler, Henry 153, 168
Wise, E. F. 73, 114, 145
Wohl, R. 186
women 20, 111–12, 122–3
Wood, Edward 186, 190
woollen textiles 40
Workers' Union 45
working-class housewife 122–3
World Disarmament Conference, Geneva 35
Worley, Matthew 12
Wrigley, Chris 10, 14, 221

Young, Allan 76, 81
Young Fabians 74
Young Plan 5

Zinoviev, Grigory 154
Zinoviev letter 21, 222